C0-AYM-589

AN IMMANUEL KANT READER

AN IMMANUEL KANT READER

Edited and Translated
with Commentary by

RAYMOND B. BLAKNEY

Harper & Brothers, Publishers New York

AN IMMANUEL KANT READER

Printed in the United States of America

FIRST EDITION

E-K

Library of Congress catalog card number: 60-7962

To John William Miller

ΣΟΦΙΑΣ ΕΡΑΣΤΗΣ

CONTENTS

PROSPECTUS

Here is a volume of selections from the four best-known works of Immanuel Kant. Mainly, the passages chosen for translation contain Kant's thoughts about the answers to two questions: *What do I know?* and *What ought I to do?* It took Josiah Royce to state Kant's problems so simply but the questions are authentic. They were urgent to Kant's generation when Europe was poised on the threshold of the age of ideologies. They are urgent today, made important by the contemplation of ideologies moving teeming populations in the direction of atomic war. Kant will not answer these questions for us but his struggle with them is a fair prospectus of what we may anticipate from our own efforts with them.

He died four years after the turn of the nineteenth century, after eighty fruitful years, during most of which he was a professor and lecturer at the university in Königsberg, Germany. Privately, his life was inconspicuous. His business was metaphysics. Few who saw him would have suspected that this teacher and writer of well-nigh unintelligible prose would have set all Europe by the ears before the nineteenth century was out. He gave form and substance to the issues that were to be the agenda of a century of intellectual discussion. Christians and Marxists alike got aid and comfort from reading or misreading what he wrote.

But this writing is a prospectus for this book and it is put where, normally, an introduction should be. Some comment, however, precedes each translated selection and all together, it should add up to an introduction. This arrangement is an attempt to beguile those who take up this book into reading the introduction imperceptibly, portion by portion. There is little of Kant's biography in it and small reference to his place in the apostolic succession of philosophers. The omission is deliberate. In an Immanuel Kant Reader extensive explanatory material would be a sidetrack, on which some people would stop indefinitely when they should pass on at once to the intended destination. Besides, there are many books about Kant; that there is one to meet each reader's need and to satisfy his taste for critical matter can be guaranteed in advance. Try reading an excellent little Pelican Book, *Kant*, by S. Körner. It is good criticism and good writing.

Is this translation trustworthy? That depends on one's judgment in such matters. It is my belief that good translation requires imagination and is creative writing. There are, of course, those who dissent from this view. Some people believe that responsible translation reproduces the original, as exactly as possible, idiom and all, in the vocabulary of the receiving language. For those who need this kind of service, I recommend Norman Kemp Smith, *Immanuel Kant's Critique of Pure Reason*; Peter G. Lucas, *Immanuel Kant: Prolegomena*; Thomas K. Abbott, *Fundamental Principles of the Metaphysic of Morals*; James Creed Meredith, *Immanuel Kant: The Critique of Judgment*. There are others but these are complete, immaculate, and of their kind, examples of honest workmanship. They are often less difficult to read than the original.

If the idea that good translation requires imagination is misleading, let it be said that no translator is ever absolved from the obligation to express his author's meaning accurately in the second language. In the case of Kant, who often made it hard for his compatriots to understand him, translation must generally be free, and for the more obdurate passages it must also be interpretative. It is unworthy of the craft to pass on opacity in the original text, word by word. Of course, in clearing up an apparently meaningless sentence, the translator may substitute his own thoughts for Kant's but if the translation is generally consistent, there will be a minimum of counterfeit in it.

Then there are semanticists, professional and amateur, to consider. Like Alice in Wonderland they require of all Humpty Dumpties that their communications should be intelligible. Others, like Alfred North Whitehead, aver that "the success of language in conveying information is vastly overrated, especially in learned circles." Both of these considerations apply to Kant. For example, a series of expressions, such as "mind," "understanding," "faculty of knowledge," "the power to think," "the function of judgment," etc., will be familiar to all readers of Kant in translation. They represent an equal number of expressions in German, on which Kant once commented as follows: "We have explained mind in many ways, as the spontaneity of knowledge, or as the ability to think, or the capacity to produce ideas or to make judgments. Under sufficiently strong illumination all these definitions amount to the same thing. We now describe mind as the power to regulate." (See p. 53.)

A strong case could be made for Kant's wish and ability to require of his words precise and constant meaning. His ideal in this respect would be found in modern symbolic logic where no words are used and the meaning of the symbols is precise and constant because they are purely formal and refer to nothing in particular. Kant also labored long and perhaps fondly over formal thoughts and words. When ordinary words are used, however, to analyze such intimate processes as knowing and morality, it is of no use to insist that their meaning should be either constant or precise. This would require that mind in man also should be constant and precise. Translation, therefore, calls for innovations. For example:

KANT'S WORD	*IS HERE TRANSLATED AS*	*INSTEAD OF*
synthetisch (1)	amplifying	synthetic
a priori	abstract and prior	*a priori*
Anschauung	awareness	intuition
Vermögen	facility	faculty
transzendentale	formal	transcendental
Mannigfaltige	field, as of sensation, phenomena, etc.	manifold
Synthesis (2)	organization	synthesis
pathologisch	psychological	pathological
Vernunft	reasoning (noun)	reason
Wille	willing (noun)	will

There are other innovations but these are fair samples. Generally they are required by the context or an explicit note by Kant. Speaking of "transcendental idealism," he says, "I too have sometimes called it *formal* idealism to distinguish it from the common material variety. . . . In many cases it seems advisable to use *formal* instead of *transcendental* to avoid misunderstanding." I am sure that readers who associate "transcendental" with Ralph Waldo Emerson will agree.

Moreover, Kant's own more imaginative and stimulating thoughts often lie buried under cairns of words from which they have to be liberated to be appreciated. Frequently the omission of repetitive passages or of redundant phrases exposes important thoughts that might otherwise go undetected. Not the least claim to be made for a book of selections is that the philosopher may be discovered in an abridgment sooner than in an unabridged presentation. To be sure, some of Kant's own monumental caution may be omitted by abridgment, when his groves of dependent and independent clauses are thinned out. If this is important, the reader is once again kindly referred to a complete translation.

A prospectus ought to answer another question, granted that the reader's interest extends this far: Is Immanuel Kant a profitable reading project today? This is the cue for the onset of the prospectus proper.

Kant's argument begins with the thought that space and time are contributed by mind, to make order in the world as we experience it possible. They are the forms into which sensations fit but, as Kant should be willing to say, this engaging hypothesis is one that can be neither proved nor disproved. Like Sir Isaac Newton, Kant considered space to be rectangular. That space had three dimensions was one of his favorite citations from contemporary thought. Two centuries later, Einstein's wholly mental conception of curved space, supported by observations of starlight bending around the sun, seemed to confirm Kant's idea that space is given by mind. On the other hand, it indicates at least a change of mind, and perhaps a contribution to mind from the rays of a star just behind the edge of the sun! Surely those rays reached earth before anyone was here to observe or understand them. Were *their* paths then contributions of mind?

We may accept Kant's doctrine that mind is an unexplained agent in man by which sensations are organized into "phenomena," and phenomena into knowledge. This is his most impressive achievement. He asserts, less convincingly but with a show of logic, that behind these phenomena there are "noumena," "things-themselves," about which nothing can be known because they are beyond experiencing. The real world then consists of phenomena, over which mind presides as the lawgiver. Is the world limited to perceived phenomena? No, indeed; the noumena are there also but they are purely formal matters and as far as we know, refer to nothing at all. They are boundary markers, so to speak; they are the "off-limits" signs, beyond which if mind goes, it inevitably falls among the thieves of illusion, is stripped of its identity, wounded, and left half-dead. The reader may find this difficult doctrine, but great with possibilities.

The distinction between pure and practical reasoning is also one of the more important stops on the highway of Kant's thought. Pure reasoning is what mind does when it is unoccupied with experience. It is formal and it also refers to nothing in particular. It is both abstract and prior. But is it? In Wonderland, Alice observed that the grin remained after the rest of the grinning Cheshire cat had vanished. Where else could this happen? Is the isolation of mind from sense conceivable? Or the isolation of sense from thought which gives it relevance? Does form ever come without substance? These questions reflect the possible absurdity of abstraction but not its uses.

Suppose, however, for the sake of the argument, that we agree to the notion of pure mind. What does it do? It makes its own laws, the laws by which it operates. It also applies its own pure ideas to "make sense" of the world of awareness. It also makes errors. Its structural defects make man prone to fallacies, contradictions of thought, and ultimate delusions. These ultimate delusions appear as beliefs that the existence of God and the nature of the universe can be demonstrated with mathematical certainty. As far as pure reasoning is concerned, God and the cosmos are off-limits, beyond the reach of human experience to which pure ideas apply. When one transgresses the boundaries of experience in thinking, illusions result. Kant's account of pure mind, the matter of *The Critique of Pure Reason,* ends on this negative note—to make room, as he said, for faith.

Then comes the second *Critique,* with the notion of "practical reasoning." Kant explains that this is pure reasoning used practically, as, for example, to make decisions. I should prefer to think of it as pure reason accommodated to facts, if there can be any facts apart from mind.* Still better, practical reasoning might be considered a correction of the absurdity of abstraction: it is a man's total, unresolved, and unanalyzed response to his problem; but I am not sure that Kant would agree to this. In any case, practical reasoning is required where "ought" enters a man's experience and creates a moral problem. It has no application to the world of nature. No one, says

* See the definition of practical reasoning, pp. 204 ff.

Kant, would ask what nature should be like any more than he would ask what properties a circle should have.

Kant's ethics fared badly as evolutionary theory developed in the nineteenth century. He delighted in the "moral law within" and in man's innate sense of duty, from which human freedom derived. His "moral imperative" is a modified version of the Golden Rule. It appeared from evolutionary theory, however, that there is nothing innate or God-given about moral laws. They are learned from the group into which a man is born.

Much has been said of the strictness of Königsberg where Kant was reared, with a view to explaining how he came so tediously to advocate duty for duty's sake, as the Prussians do, or to oppose duty to happiness, as the Scots were said to do. Kant would have replied to this by saying that an illustration mistaken as a proof is beneath the standard of performance required for philosophy, even when he, Kant, is the illustration. It is better to understand that the "moral law within" refers to the laws of personality, laws that may not be defied without pathological results, however gradual they may be. This is the meaning of duty. Kant's point is that moral law does not depend for its authority on a majority vote.

As far as religion is concerned, his discovery that theology is not substantiated by pure reasoning operating independently and that morality is the best argument for faith, measures the progress of a lifetime of profound religious concern. It could be shown without great difficulty that Jesus also was primarily a teacher of ethics; he too favored the "moral proof": it is purity of heart that entitles one to see God. Even this example, however, is no conclusive demonstration of the relative functions of theology and ethics. Kant's argument is set up in *The Metaphysics of Morals,* developed in *The Critique of Practical Reason,* and concluded at long last in the third critique, *The Critique of Judgment,* where the part purpose plays in the world is developed at length.

His complete works occupy between ten and fifteen volumes. During the preparation of this book I looked at an elegant, complete set of Kant sometime every day for several months and wondered at the patience the editing of those wordy books cost someone. But that wonder always deepens further at the thought of the temerity and tenacity of the man whose principal business in life it was to explore the intangible labyrinth of mind and to diagram the genesis of thought. Since then I have seen the ruins of the famed labyrinth where the Minotaur was said to have been confined; some authorities say now that it was never intended to confuse but merely to be a house fit for a king; it looked like a maze only to those who lived in huts and were informed by rumor. Kant set out to do something like that: to show not that mind is a labyrinth but the seat of whatever rational government the universe contains.

That does not make mind either simple or at once submissive to passing curiosity. There is a passage, for example, in James Stephens' whimsical novel *The Crock of Gold* which bears this out:

> A thought is a real thing and words are only its raiment, but a thought is as shy as a virgin; unless it is fittingly apparelled, we may not look on its shadowy nakedness: it will fly from us and only return again in the darkness crying in a thin, childish voice which we may not comprehend until, with aching minds, listening and divining, we at last fashion for it those symbols which are its protection and its banner.

Thus the poet. Now hear the philosopher.

RAYMOND B. BLAKNEY

Pierce College
Athens, Greece
January 1, 1960

Part One

THE CRITIQUE OF PURE REASON

1 METAPHYSICS IS MY FIELD (1781)

Metaphysics is mind-produce

Metaphysics, briefly, is an inquiry about reality. What is the world really like? What do all the facts and the experiences of men add up to? Metaphysics is the result of efforts to see what there is, and to see it all, critically, coherently, in the best possible perspective.

It is not surprising that those who create metaphysics should offer an endless variety of conclusions. Inquiries usually depend on the point of view and motives of those who ask questions and try to answer them. Nor is it really surprising that animus should creep into metaphysical debates. The only calm philosophy is dead philosophy. People, even professional thinkers, are often stirred to love, or anger, or resentment, or repentance by ideas. Philosophic thought worth the time and effort it takes is excited and exciting; the conclusions to which it leads can seem, in their own time and place, more important than life itself.

The debate in which Immanuel Kant became involved was exciting at times. Animus sometimes appeared even in his sober words. Learned war was part of the process by which the Enlightenment of the eighteenth century evolved and through which, also, metaphysics fell into disrepute, a disrepute from which only a giant could rescue it. Kant was the giant.

He found his life problem in the conflict. The Critique of Pure Reason *is one of the world's first-rate essays in metaphysics. In it he thought he had said the last word on the subject and that henceforth thinkers and investigators would merely fill in the details. This sounds presumptuous but Kant's explanation is humble enough. Metaphysics, he said, is only an introduction to the sciences. It deals in the principles by which knowledge becomes possible. It is an inventory of our intellectual possessions, systematically arranged.*

When a man's mind is ripe for speculative or creative thought, he needs metaphysics. It is also an antidote to the human longing to vault fences and go off into strange worlds.

It was Kant's first major effort. Its precise organization, which suggests the mind of a geometer, marshals a sufficient array of ideas and analyses to occupy the systematic thinkers of the nineteenth century and to warrant serious meditation in the "space age." It covers most of the topics ever discussed by metaphysicians but, as its title suggests, its primary field is the description of formal, abstract thought and the problem of knowledge. How does mind work over the data procured through sensation to produce knowledge? Kant's answer was not a compromise solution. It was the result of an original insight, a new viewpoint that made the aging metaphysical wars seem irrelevant.

We shall see that the major argument of The Critique of Pure Reason ends with the refutation of three conspicuous historic errors of thought or reasoning. It was undertaken, in the first place, to refute a constellation of errors by Kant's predecessors, errors which in effect denied the very possibility of thought as an expression of human competence. John Locke (1632-1704) insisted that there are no "innate ideas" and that there is nothing in mind that was not first in the senses. With this opinion, Bishop Berkeley (1685-1753) substantially agreed: "It is evident to anyone who takes a survey of the objects of knowledge, that they are either ideas actually imprinted on the sense; or else, such as are perceived . . . or, lastly, ideas formed by . . . compounding, dividing, or barely representing those originally perceived in the aforesaid ways." David Hume (1711-1776) also agreed. Ideas, he said, are images or copies of sense impressions, and mind functions simply in the associations of these ideas. As Dr. J. W. Miller has observed, these views provided and still provide a specious innocence for those who accept them. They make human error a failure of human mechanisms: "It is the distinction of Kant that he redefined the locus of error." Kant located error in thought in the reasoning mind,* which can be wrong be-

* See Kant's attack on illusion, pp. 81 ff.

cause it can be right. This is the distinctive human competence.

The following excerpt is from Kant's preface to the first edition of The Critique of Pure Reason.

There was a time when metaphysics was called the queen of the sciences, and if the will could be taken for the deed, the paramount importance of her subject matter would justify the honor. The present fashion is to disdain metaphysics and so, despised and forsaken, the matron wails like Hecuba: "But late on the pinnacle of fame, strong in my many sons, . . . now, exiled, penniless. . . ." (Ovid, *Metam.* xiii 508-10.)

Originally, under the sway of dogmatic philosophy, metaphysics was a despotic business; its legislation showed traces of an old barbarism; so it fell into the habit of internal wars and ended up in complete anarchy. Skeptics, also, who are really nomads of a kind and shun the settled ways of a country, periodically broke up metaphysics' civilization; but fortunately they were few in number and unable to prevent rebuilding the realm, even though it had to be rebuilt without any consistent plan. More recently, it has seemed as if all these controversies might end and the legitimacy of the claims for metaphysics might be settled for good, by virtue of a kind of *physiology of the human understanding* devised by the celebrated English philosopher John Locke.

It turned out that although he could trace the birth of the alleged queen to a vulgar origin in common experience, and so cast doubt on her pretensions, his genealogy was perjured. So, her claims secure, she proceeded to relapse into the former, moth-eaten dogmatism and contempt, from which she might have been saved. Now, after everything possible has been done for her, and as one might think, done in vain, the prevailing mood on metaphysics is one of weariness and complete indifference. In the sciences, this condition can be the mother of chaos and night, but at the same time, it can be the origin or prelude of a coming revolution and the clarification of a science that has become dark, confused, and unfruitful through misdirected zeal.

There is really no point in pretending to be indifferent to this kind of inquiry. Indifference to the subject matter of metaphysics is not compatible with being human. If they think at all, those who pretend to be indifferent soon go back to making the same metaphysical assertions they affected to despise, this, in spite of their attempt to disguise what they say by the use of popular expressions in place of academic language.

Indifference to metaphysics, nevertheless, is something that merits attention and reflection. It appears just now when the sciences are flourishing and affects those sciences most whose contribution to knowledge seems most indispensable, if it is available at all. It is clearly not due to frivolity but to the effect of mature judgment in our time. No one wants to be put off any longer with apparent knowledge. This indifference is an invitation to be re-engaged in the most difficult task of the mind: self-knowledge. It is a call to set up a court which can guarantee the just claims of mind and make an end of groundless pretenses, not by proclamation but by mind's own eternal and unchanging laws. This court is none other than critical evaluation of the mind's operations: the critique of pure reason.

By this I do not mean a critical evaluation of books and systems but of reasoning, the operation of the mind in pursuit of knowledge that is independent of experience. The court will therefore decide on the possibility or impossibility of metaphysics in general. It will determine its sources, its circumstances, and its limits solely on the basis of principle.

I have taken this road, the only one left, and I flatter myself that on it I have achieved the remedy for those errors which have hitherto divided the mind against itself, when it worked with matters not based on experience. I have not evaded the court's questions by pleading the incompetence of the human mind; I have rather classified all the questions according to principle. When I discovered a point at which mind was divided against itself, I resolved the problem involved so as wholly to satisfy mind. The answers to these questions have not turned out to be what dogmatic or visionary curiosity might suggest; for this kind of curiosity is to be satisfied only by the craft of magic, of which I understand nothing. This never was the point of view from which nature devised human minds. It is philosophy's function to root out the delusions from which misconceptions spring up, no matter what prized and cherished dreams may be destroyed in the process.

I have made completeness the first object in this work and I make bold to say that there cannot be a single metaphysical problem which is not solved here or for which the key, at least, has not been hung in a handy spot. Pure reasoning (the mind alone) is a perfect unity. It is so perfect that if its principle should prove inadequate to answer even one of the questions that arise from the nature of the mind, that principle would have to be discarded as unreliable for dealing with any other question.

As I say this, I think I see indignation mixed with contempt in the reader's face. These must seem like boastful and immodest claims on my part. They are, just the same, incomparably more moderate than the claims of an author of the most common of proofs, that the nature of the soul is simple or that the world necessarily had a first beginning. These authors pledge themselves to extend human knowledge beyond the possible bounds of human experience. I humbly acknowledge that this is outside my powers. Instead, my work is solely with the mind and its pure or abstract thoughts. I need not go very far to obtain full knowledge of these matters, since I encounter them in myself. Common logic provides an example of how all the simple mental acts can be enumerated completely and systematically. The subject of this inquiry is a related question: What can be accomplished through the mind alone when all the stuff and support of experience are removed?

2 KANT TAKES HIS CUE FROM HUME (1783)

The *Critique* needs a pilot plan

After the prodigious effort The Critique of Pure Reason *cost its author, he expected an immediate revolution in the learned world when it was published early in the summer of 1781. Time passed. There was neither a stir nor a whisper that could be traced to it. Sometime a year later, friends told him that those who tried to read it found his book obscure and hard to read. Sample essays in reading the* Critique, *either in German or a literal English translation, will convince almost anyone that those who objected to the* Critique *in its first year were justified.*

Even Kant himself came soon to understand the frustration of his readers. Rather than reorganize and rewrite the Critique *(which he probably never considered doing), he undertook to produce a short review of its main points, in what he called prolegomena or prefatory material. His choice of a title for his pilot project is typical of his honest, plodding genius: "Prolegomena to any future metaphysics that will be able to present itself as a science."*

His plan or sketch, he said, was "not for the use of pupils but for future teachers, to help them in discovering this science for the first time. My purpose is to convince all those who find it worthwhile that it is unavoidably necessary that they suspend whatever work they have in hand, forget all else that ever happened, and above all, that they raise the question 'whether such a thing as metaphysics is possible at all.' "

The Prolegomena *consists of about 150 ordinary pages. Its style is perhaps easier in some passages than that of the* Critique *and it does review the main issues of the now famous work. What follows is chosen from Kant's own preface to his* Prolegomena.

Since the essays of Locke and Leibniz were written, or better, since the beginning of metaphysics, as history records it, no event has been more decisive for this science than the attack of David Hume. He shed no light but he did strike a spark from which a light might be kindled in receptive tinder, if its glow were carefully tended.

Hume began with one important metaphysical idea. It was the supposed connection of cause and effect. He challenged the claim that this connection was conceived in the mind itself. He wanted to know how anyone could think anything so constituted that its mere existence necessarily called for the existence of something else; for this is what the notion of cause means. He proved conclusively that it is quite impossible to conceive the connection of cause and effect abstractly, solely by means of thought, because it involves the idea of necessity. We do not see that if one thing exists, another has to exist in consequence, and we do not know how an abstract idea of this relation could occur to anyone.

Hume concluded that the idea of cause constitutes a delusion which seems to be a human brain child but is just the bastard of imagination sired by experience. Thus, certain perceptions are joined together as the law of association provides. Then habit, which is a psychological necessity, is passed off as objective and as being discovered through insight. He then inferred that we cannot conceive a causal connection between events, even in general; for if we did, our ideas would be fictional, and knowledge, which is supposed to be abstract and necessary, would be nothing but common experience under a false label. This, plainly, means that there is not and cannot be such a thing as metaphysics.

However hasty and mistaken Hume's conclusion may be, it was at least based on investigation. This made it worthwhile for the bright people of the day to co-operate in finding a happier solution to the problem as he explained it. The outcome might well have been a complete reform of the science, but the unhappy genius of metaphysicians caused him not to be understood.

I frankly confess that many years ago it was the memory of David Hume that first interrupted my dogmatic slumber and gave new direction to my studies in the field of speculative philosophy.

I tried first to see if Hume's objection could be put in a general form. I soon found that the idea of a connection between cause and effect was by no means the only idea we conceive abstractly of relations between things. Metaphysics consists first and last of such ideas. I tried to count them and when I had succeeded as I wished, taking first one and then another, I went on to explain them. I was now certain that they are not derived from experience, as Hume has asserted, but that they spring from the mind alone. These explanations had seemed impossible to my smart predecessor and had not even occurred to anyone else, although everyone used such ideas without asking what the security behind them might be. This, I say, was the most difficult work ever undertaken on behalf of metaphysics. The worst of it was that no help at all could be had from metaphysics itself because the very possibility of metaphysics depends on this kind of explanation.

Having now succeeded in the solution of Hume's problem, not only in special cases but with a view to the whole reasoning function of mind, I could proceed safely, if slowly, to survey the field of pure reasoning, its boundaries as well as its contents, and I could do this working from general principles. This is exactly what metaphysics needs to build a system which is securely planned.

I am afraid, however, that working out Hume's problem to the uttermost (as in *The Critique of Pure Reason*) was bound to be received as the problem itself was when it was first proposed. It is misjudged because it is not understood; it is not understood because people will scan the pages of the book without thinking it through; and no one will make the effort required to read it, because the work is dry and obscure; it upsets familiar ideas and, finally, it is long-winded. Now I confess that I did not expect to hear philosophers complain about lack of popular style, entertainment, or agreeableness, when the very existence of a highly prized body of knowledge, indispensable to humanity, is at stake. This knowledge can be established only by the strictest rules of academic precision. Such a book as this may achieve popularity in time but not at first. There is an obscurity in it which is due to diffuseness of plan, by which one can easily lose sight of the main points of the study, and the complaint is just. I intend to correct it with these prolegomena.

Truly, it is not given to everyone to write so subtly and gracefully as did David Hume, or with the depth and elegance of Moses Mendelssohn. I flatter myself, nevertheless, that I could have made my exposition popular if I had wanted only to propose a plan and leave its execution to others, and if I had not cared so deeply for the welfare of the science over which I have worked so long. It required much discipline and no little self-denial to postpone the prospect of early favor for a later but more durable praise.

A mere sketch preceding *The Critique of Pure Reason* would be unintelligible, unreliable, and useless. It can, however, be all the more useful as a sequel to the main work. There it enables one to grasp the whole scheme and to examine in detail the main points of the science. It also permits improvement in the order of the *Critique* as it was first completed.

Here then is a sketch that comes after the completed work. It is based on the methods of logical analysis while the work itself was done in the style of factual writing. In this way it is possible to display the points and structural details of a very special process of knowledge, in all their natural combinations. If anyone finds this sketch, which I publish as *The Prolegomena to Any Future Metaphysics,* still obscure, he should consider that it is not necessary for everyone to study metaphysics. There are many people of great talent who do very well in basic and profound sciences allied more to observation, who do not succeed in research concerned wholly with abstract notions. In such a case one should turn his mental gifts to other objects.

3 METAPHYSICS CAN BE AS CERTAIN AS SCIENCE (1787)

"Copernican Hypothesis"

Four more years pass and in the preface to the second edition of The Critique of Pure Reason, *Kant exhibits confidence that metaphysics is ready for new strides ahead, comparable to those made by the physical sciences. He feels that this can be accomplished by what he chooses to call his "Copernican Hypothesis": things must conform to thought rather than thought to things.*

There is not much justification for calling this assertion Copernican. Whereas astronomers had once considered that the earth was stationary, and that the planets moved around it, Copernicus assumed that the sun was stationary and that we who observe are the ones who move. This assumption certainly brought spectacular success. Kant proposed an analogous reverse in point of view for metaphysics. He considered that making the basic laws of the human mind the interpreters of the world of things, rather than trying to adapt thoughts to fit the world as it appears, might also bring spectacular success to metaphysics. The following excerpt from the preface to the second edition of The Critique of Pure Reason *takes up this theme.*

From the earliest times to which the history of the human mind extends, among those wonderful people, the Greeks, mathematicians took the sure way of science. It must not be supposed that it was as easy to find the royal way for mathematics or to construct one, as it was for logic, in which the mind deals only with itself. I believe, rather, that a long time was spent in mathematics, just groping, particularly among the Egyptians. The revolution in mathematics came finally as the result of a happy thought of one man whose experiment indicated unmistakably the way that had to be taken. It was the way by which mathematicians could progress surely, everywhere and always.

The history of this transformation in the ways of thought, which was more important than the discovery of the way around the celebrated Cape of Good Hope, and the name of its lucky author, have not been preserved. There is a story, preserved by Diogenes Laertes, in which the supposed inventor of some of the lesser elements of geometric demonstration is named. It is now generally felt that his work was not necessary at all. The story shows, however, that the memory of the revolution brought about by the first hint of this new way of thought seemed so pre-eminent to the mathematicians that they could not let it be forgotten.

Whether it was Thales or another, a new light dawned with the first man who demonstrated the isosceles triangle. He found that he had not to study the figure he saw or even the bare idea of it and then read off its properties. He had rather to visualize by a construction what he had previously conceived in his own mind. Then, to know the truth with certainty, the truth that is prior to the event, he must not attribute anything to his figure except what followed logically from the idea of it.

It took much longer for physics to get onto the throughway of science. It is only about a century and a half since Bacon, by his ingenious proposals, incited the discovery of the scientific way and gave fresh vigor to those who were already on the track of it. The discovery of science also could be explained as the outcome of a quick revolution in the ways of thought. In this discussion I am referring to natural science only as it is based on experimental principles.

When Galileo rolled balls down an inclined plane, along with one whose weight he knew in advance; or Torricelli caused the air to bear the weight of a predetermined column of water; or more recently, when Stahl changed metals into oxides and back again to metals by withdrawing something and restoring it, a new light dawned on all students of nature. They learned that insight is possible only where nature's designs are produced by men's minds and that progress is made when one constrains nature to answer his questions according to fixed laws. Men must not toddle along in nursemaid-nature's harness. Accidental observations made without a prior plan never fall within a law, which they must do if there is to be understanding. Given his mental characteristics, according to which natural events line up in laws and rationally devised experiments, man goes to nature to be taught. He must not go in the character of a student who will accept anything the teacher says. He goes as an appointed judge who will compel the witness to answer the questions he puts to him.

Even physics owes the beneficial revolution in its rules to the thought that man must not attribute to nature what has to be learned. He must search nature for all those things that cannot be known merely by taking thought, and search by the rules his own mind provides. This is how the study of nature becomes a science, yielding certainty after so many centuries of blundering.

We come now to metaphysics, which is an isolated and speculative science of mind. It is above learning from experience and makes us our own teachers in matters of the mind. Metaphysics deals solely with ideas and not, like mathematics, with the application of ideas to things as they appear. Even though it is the oldest of the disciplines and would survive when all the rest have been dropped into the maw of an all-destroying barbarism, its fate still leaves much to be desired. It has not yet attained scientific certainty.

In metaphysics, thought is continually coming to a dead end, even when laws which common experience supports are under examination, purely as laws. Times without number it is necessary to go back to the fork because the road does not take us where we want to go. As for unanimity among the practitioners of metaphysics, there is so little of it that the discipline seems more like an arena, a ring constructed for those who like to exercise their skills in mock combat. At any rate, no contestant has yet succeeded in getting and holding a spot of his own. It appears, then, that to date, the procedure in metaphysics has just been to grope and worse than that, to grope among ideas.

How can it be explained that in this field, scientific certainty has not yet been found? Can it be impossible? If it is, why has nature visited our minds with a restless drive for certainty, as if this were the most important business of all? Not only that but there would be little reason ever to trust the powers of thought, if they fail in one of the most important projects of human curiosity, proffering illusions and giving at last betrayal. Perhaps it is only that up to now we have failed to read the road signs correctly. If we renew the search, may we hope to have better luck than has been the lot of those who preceded us?

It seems to me that the examples of mathematics and physics, having become what they are by sudden revolution, are remarkable enough to warrant attention to the essential element of their change, the change that proved so beneficial. It may be worth our while also to make the experiment of imitating them, to the degree the analogy between these two rational disciplines and metaphysics permits.

Hitherto it has been assumed that knowledge must conform to the things known; but on this basis all attempts to find out about the world of things by abstract thought, and thus to permit an extension of human knowledge, have come to nothing. Let us then experiment to see whether or not we do better with the problems of metaphysics if we assume that things to be known must conform in advance to our knowing process. This would appear to lead to what we want, namely, knowledge that tells us something about an object of thought before it becomes a part of our experience.

If my perception of an object has to conform to the object, I do not see how there could be any abstract knowledge of it; but if the objects of my perceptions conform to the laws by which I know them, it is easy to conceive of abstract knowledge, for all experience is a kind of knowledge involving the mind, the laws of which I must suppose were a part of me before I ever saw anything. Those laws get expressed in abstract terms but all my experience must agree with them.

This experiment succeeds as well as could be desired. It promises scientific certainty for the part of metaphysics that deals in abstract ideas, the corresponding objects of which may be checked off in experience. It involves a new way of thinking which enables us to explain perfectly how abstract knowledge, knowledge prior to experience, is possible. It also furnishes satisfactory proofs of the laws which form the mental framework of the natural world. Both of these achievements had been impossible heretofore.

4 THERE IS KNOWLEDGE FROM AND APART FROM EXPERIENCE

Logic supplies a language

Traditionally the kind of thought that goes into philosophy has required a thorough screening according to the rules of logic, the theory of thinking. One of the persistent lures to the study of logic through the ages has been the belief that if you know the laws of thought you know as much as anyone can know about what mind is.

Spinoza and Leibniz, who had vast respect for mind as reality in its own right and constructed their philosophies accordingly, were not only great logicians but they made notable contributions to the development of logic. In his younger days, still much impressed with these great men of intellect, Kant also produced in 1756 an essay on logic. He seems to have been satisfied with what he inherited in this field and felt that there was no need for further development of the subject. At any rate, his own contribution to logic as a separate discipline is generally considered negligible.

It is a little difficult to get back to the days before Kant and to understand the complacency with which human concerns were set off from each other. Science and philosophy came from different bins, so to speak. Mind was something apart from matter, and logic was separate from metaphysics. Certainly the way to begin with Kant is to see that with him the isolation of individual human concerns and functions was disavowed, even though the accidents of his language often betray this intention. The inner and outer worlds became twin aspects of one reality: mind was the world's lawgiver and the world realized mind. The Critique of Pure Reason studies this view.

It is an essay in formal logic because it studies mind at work. The logician's work is to think about thought in general. It therefore involves unconsidered thinking. No logician, thinking about thought in *general, can ever stop to consider his own thinking without resigning his profession, at least temporarily. Being a critic of thought in general, his work is not with live thinking. Live thinking cannot be studied except by setting up a third process of thought behind the second; but thought that can be analyzed has already been laid out on a white sheet and unwonted rigor and dignity have set in. Its relation to living mind is then an academic problem; at any rate it is ready to be an object of thought and therefore laboratory material for metaphysics. As Kant might say, the distinction between metaphysics and logic is formal rather than real.*

In logic the rules valid thinking obeys are also studied, along with the systematic and accidental errors in mind. In this work it soon appears that valid thought reflects the structure of the real world of which the logician, with his thoughts about thinking, is a real part. Logic needs to be checked against metaphysics.

Accordingly, the first Critique, *in broad outline, undertakes to reconcile the scientific version of the objective world with the personal realities of freedom, purpose, and the moral law. Kant is an insistent justifier of the scientific method and is equally insistent that the scientist, among others, must consider what he is doing, as much for the means as for the results. The justification of science is now familiar. What is less familiar is Kant's effort to fill in the details of Socrates' "know thyself" and to implement it. The following section consists of excerpts from Kant's own introduction to the* Critique.

There is no doubt that knowledge begins with experience. How else could mental powers be awakened to action, if not by the objects that excite our senses, in part arousing images and in part stimulating the mental activity by which the images are compared? Images must then be combined or separated and the raw material of sense impressions worked over into the knowledge of things called experience. In the order of time, life begins with experience; there is no knowledge before that.

But if knowledge begins with experience, it does not follow that all of it is derived from experience. It may well be that whatever knowledge we do get from experience is already a combination of impressions and mental activity, the sense impressions being merely the occasion. It may be that the mental additive cannot be distinguished from the basic stuff until long practice makes one alert to it and skilled to pick it out.

This then is a question that needs close study and for which no offhand answer will do: Is there knowledge apart from both experience and sense impressions? This kind of knowledge is called abstract and prior (*a priori*) in contrast to knowledge derived from experience, which is empirical (*a posteriori*).

The word "*a priori*" is not yet definite enough to indicate the full meaning of the question at hand. It is often said of knowledge derived from experience that it is abstract because it does not come immediately from experience, but from some general rule borrowed from experience. Of a man who undermines the foundations of his house, we might say that he might have known *a priori*, that is, abstractly and beforehand, that the house would fall. He need not have waited for the actual experience of seeing it go down. He could not, however, have known about the house falling, from abstract principles only. He needs first to learn that bodies are heavy and that they fall when supports are removed; this would have to be learned from experience.

In what follows, by *abstract* knowledge we do not mean knowledge independent of this or that experience but knowledge *utterly independent of all experience.* In contrast, there is empirical, or *a posteriori* knowledge which we get only through experience. Abstract knowledge is called *pure* when it contains no trace of experience. So, for example, the proposition, "Every change has its cause," is abstract but not pure because *change* is an idea drawn only from experience.

We need now a criterion by which to distinguish pure from empirical knowledge. Experience teaches one that an object is what it is, but not that it could not be otherwise. So, first, if a proposition cannot be conceived without thinking it *necessary,* it is *abstract.* Secondly, a judgment based on experience is never truly or strictly universal but only relatively so. But if a judgment is strictly *universal* and there is no possible exception to this, then it is not derived from experience and is valid, absolutely *abstract, pure.*

We need also to distinguish between two kinds of judgments, or statements: *analytic,* in which the predicate merely analyzes the subject; and *synthetic,* or *amplifying* in which the predicate adds something to the subject. If A is the subject of a statement and B is the predicate, there are two choices. If B is contained in A, the statement is analytic; if B is not contained in A but is related to it otherwise, the statement is synthetic, or amplifying.

For example, if I say, "All bodies are extended," this is an analytic statement of judgment. I need not go beyond the very idea of "body" to find the idea of "extension." On the other hand when I say, "All bodies are heavy," the predicate is quite different from what I think in the idea of "body" as such, and the addition of this kind of predicate to the subject makes the statement synthetic. Statements of experience always amplify the subject.

In abstract, amplifying judgments, no help can be had from experience. If I go beyond idea A and find idea B related to it, on what could such an amplification be based? Take, for example, the proposition: Everything that happens has a cause. In the idea of "something that happens," I can think of a time before the event and from it derive analytic judgments. But the idea of "cause" is something else; it does not fall within the idea of "something that happens." How then can I say something about this subject that is entirely unrelated to it? How do I know that cause belongs necessarily to that "something that happens," even when that something does not contain any notion of it? What is the unknown X on which one depends when he discovers a predicate B, foreign to A, which is, nevertheless, connected with it?

The unknown X cannot be experience because the principle just discussed adds a second conception (cause) to the first (existence), not only with wider generalization than experience can proffer but with an assertion of necessity. It is therefore wholly abstract and unrelated to experience. The whole aim of our speculative, abstract knowledge depends on synthetic, or amplifying propositions of this kind. Analytic judgments are of the highest importance and necessary, but only to clarify conception. This, in turn, is required for the secure and broader amplification by which something really new may be added to the matter of knowledge.

Examples from science. Mathematical judgments always amplify. One might think at first that $7 + 5 = 12$ is a straight analytic proposition. On closer inspection, it appears that the sum 7 + 5 contains nothing more than the combination of these two numbers. There is nothing to indicate what number embraces both. Arithmetical propositions always amplify.

Nor are geometric propositions analytic. That a straight line is the shortest distance between two points is an amplifying conception. Straightness has nothing to do with quantity, but only with quality. The idea of shortness is thus additive, and intuition is necessary at this point. Without it, amplification would be impossible.

The science of physics also contains principles which are abstract and amplifying. For example, there is the proposition that in all the changes of the physical world, the total quantity of matter remains unchanged. But in the idea of matter, I do not imagine its permanency. I think only of its presence in the space it fills. So I really have to go beyond the idea of matter itself and attribute something to it abstractly, something I never thought it involved. The proposition is thus not analytic but synthetic, or amplifying and yet it is abstractly conceived.

There must be amplifying and abstract knowledge in metaphysics too, even if metaphysics is regarded only as a pseudo science, necessary to human nature. It is not the duty of metaphysicians merely to dissect subjects and so, analytically, to illustrate abstract ideas. It is their duty to extend abstract knowledge and for this purpose they use principles which add to their ideas matter not originally contained in them. By means of abstract, amplifying judgments they may even go where experience cannot follow, as, for example, in the statement that "the world must have a beginning," and the like. So, metaphysics, at least by aim, consists of pure, amplifying propositions.

The characteristic problem then of pure reason is: How are abstract, amplifying judgments possible? That metaphysics has so far remained in the state of vacillating uncertainty and contradiction, is due to the fact that this problem was not recognized sooner, nor, perhaps, was the difference between analytic and amplifying judgment made clear.

From all this, the idea of a special science appears: *the criticism of pure reason.* An organized work on pure reason would contain a summary of those principles by which pure, abstract knowledge can be obtained. This, however, is asking much, and it is doubtful whether our present knowledge can be so extended and if it can be, in what areas. Let us therefore merely regard the criticism of pure reason as an introduction to a system of pure reason. Let this science be called a critique or critical evaluation and not a body of doctrine. Its function, as far as speculation is concerned, would be purely negative; the effort would not be to extend but to clarify our minds and to keep them from error. That alone would be great gain.

I call knowledge transcendental, or formal, when it concerns the way we know objects, rather than knowledge of the objects themselves; and then it should be as abstract as possible. A system of ideas of this kind would be called *formal philosophy* but this again is too much to undertake at this stage. It should contain a complete exposition of abstract knowledge, both analytic and amplifying. Formal philosophy thus conceived is a science for which the criticism of pure reason sets up a structured plan and guarantees the reliability of the pieces that make up the final structure.

In planning such a science as this, the chief thing to guard against is experience getting into it and making the abstract knowledge it deals with impure. Accordingly, even though the high principles and the basic ideas of morality are abstract, they still do not belong in formal philosophy. To be sure, they do not make the ideas of pleasure and pain, desire and taste, fundamental, since these are all the produce of experience. Nevertheless, such ideas are sure to get into a system of pure morality through notions of duty, either as hindrances to be overcome or as lures which must not be made into motives. Formal philosophy is wisdom-of-this-world about pure speculative reason; practical philosophy, on the other hand, which deals in motives, is related to feelings and belongs to knowledge born of experience. (See p. xv.)

5 MIND'S PRIMARY CONTRIBUTION TO KNOWLEDGE

Encounter at the border

In the introduction to The Transcendental Aesthetic, Kant tells about the primitive contribution of mind to knowledge. About the actual conditions under which mind encounters not-mind, he is not explicit. It is hard to imagine a border where the sensitive outer edge of pure impalpable mind is chafed by matter and tends to be divorced from matter and to seek an independent fortune. As we know it, short of death, mind is never wholly apart from matter, nor alien to it. This thought obscures the question how mind can affect not-mind, and vice versa. In any case, in the human brain, where the arena is narrowest, the distinction between the two is not clear.

Explicit description of what happens in this region would require the light of consciousness to be beamed on it in sharp focus. This is not quite as difficult as looking behind one's own eyes, but it is nearly so. Moreover, in the days of earliest infancy, we all lived even closer to matter than now; how embryo mind first reached out tentatively beyond its matrix must have passed quickly into oblivion. It is only surmised that then sensations of various kinds stimulated the nerves of infant eyes, ears, skin, tongue, and nose but were not identified with external objects. In time some of them did get connected with an object later to be known as "mother," and this was the primitive beginning of knowledge. The first identification, however, called for an installment of something distinctively human that could identify things.

The Scriptures introduce the Lord God as effecting the encounter: ". . . the Lord God . . . brought them unto Adam to see what he would call them: and whatsoever Adam called every living creature, that was the name thereof." The point is that naming, i.e., identification, is a human function that calls for a tertium quid. In the Scripture it is the Lord God. For Kant, it is mind. Of the relation *of mind, the form-giver, to not-mind, the form-taker, there is little more to be said than that*

> *These two come paired*
> *But distinct by their names.*
> *Of all things profound,*
> *Say that their pairing is deepest,*
> *The gate at the root of the world.*
> *(Lao Tzu)*

By the time Adam is able to identify an indefinite number of objects and call them all by name, the encounter in him between mind and not-mind has become habitual but it is not therefore better understood. Out of an infinite number of possibilities, mind or self is made aware of some portion of the world that is not-mind. How is that awareness effected? Let us say that the distance between an object and the brain is bridged by a wavelike stream of electromagnetic impulses. How then is the impression on the brain translated into awareness? How is awareness then shaped into identifiable phenomena that take a name? Just what is the nature of the encounter that takes place in the brain and yet is not of it? Kant has no explicit answers. Neither have I. Someday I may be able to identify the self in me to the extent that the questions about the essential creative encounter within may get explicit answers. Meanwhile we have to say that the translation of electromagnetic impulses into human meaning is a function of mind or God.

As for that shadowy region beyond the border where nothing is ever identified, the question has often been asked what that place is like, where consciousness never dawns and nothing is ever seen, heard, felt, tasted, or smelled. Is there such a region? Kant said there was, but his descriptions of it were limited to negations and it often appeared to be formal rather than actual, even to him. It recalls the Greek descriptions of Hades. *(See pp. 74 ff.)*

Of the varied processes by which things become known, there is one from which all thought stems. It is awareness (intuition), and it alone is direct or immediate. Ultimately all food for thought comes from the outside world through our awareness of it, but among humans this occurs only when mind is involved.

The property of mind by which external things are recognized may be called sensitivity. Objects appear to mind because of its sensitivity, and this is the only way awareness can occur. In functioning mind, then, awareness gives rise to thoughts and finally to concepts. Directly or indirectly, all thought goes back to awareness and so to sensitivity, because there is no other way to know external things. Sensation is the effect an object has on the sensitive mind. If awareness comes through sensation, it is said to be empirical; and the object so revealed, whatever it may be, is called "phenomenon," or simply "thing."

By matter, I mean the substance of a thing, to which sensations are traceable; by form, I refer to my awareness that the substance of something is arranged in a given order.

It is clear that sensations are not put in form by other sensations. The matter of which things are composed may be known through sensation but their form is provided by the mind, and form is therefore separate from sensation.

I call awareness (intuition) which does not participate in sensation, *pure* (that is, belonging only to mind). The pure form which sense impressions take on, the form or order in which the many elements of things are arranged by the mind, must be in mind beforehand. The pure form of sensitivity may be called pure awareness.

If, from your awareness of a body, you subtract the contribution of thought processes such as substance, forces, divisibility, etc., and then take away all that pertains to sensation, such as impenetrability, color, etc., there will still remain extension and form. These belong to pure awareness and exist only in mind, as forms for sense impressions, even if there were present no external objects or sensations from them.

Formal aesthetics is my name for the science that deals with the principles of mental sensitivity, which is prior to any sense experience. There must be such a science and it constitutes the first part of *the elements of form*, in contrast to the science that deals with the principles of pure thought, which should be called *formal logic*. In formal aesthetics, the contribution of the mind by ideas is first removed from sensitivity so that only empirical awareness remains.

Then all that pertains to sensation is taken away so that only pure awareness, the mere form of things, is left. This is the basic contribution of mind. In the course of this investigation two purely mental forms available for sense impressions will appear: space and time. These forms provide a theoretical basis for pure knowledge. They will now be considered in more detail.

6 THE SPECTACLES OF SPACE AND TIME

The world gets organized

The first practical consequence of Kant's "Copernican Theory" (see p. 11) now appears. The assumption is made that things to be known conform in advance to mind. It is made for purely practical reasons: to see if it will cure the impotence of metaphysics and gain for it the kind of respect that mathematics and the physical sciences have lately captured.

To begin with, things are arranged in space as mind provides. Space is a predicate, a visualization, an idea. It is infinite, it is one. It has all the earmarks of its origin in mind. Material things adjust to organization in space without a struggle. In fact, when they are first perceived they have already succumbed to mind's arrangement for them. It is all accomplished in advance. One can understand this only on the further assumption, already discussed, that mind and matter are not alien to each other; they are twin aspects of one reality.

Perhaps C. E. M. Joad's image may be useful: space and time are like spectacles, with the aid of which mind accomplishes its primary function, the organization of the world. In this case, however, it must be understood that mind is its own spectacle-maker. The image suggests that space and time are the basic conditions from which perceptions and conceptions of the world develop. The resulting knowledge is strictly subjective, i.e., space and time do not affect the world apart from mind if indeed, granting the "Copernican Theory," there can be any such world. The following excerpt comes from the section of the Critique *entitled* Formal Exposition of the Idea of Space.

There is a sense or sensitivity of mind, by which we reach out to things and see them located in external space. Within this space their form, size, and relative positions are or can be fixed.

There is an internal sense by which the mind is aware of itself or its internal states. This sense does not present the soul as an object to be observed. It is, however, a fixed function without which an awareness of internal states of mind would be impossible. Its operations pertain to the relationships of time. Time cannot appear as an external matter any more than space can appear to be something within.

What then are space and time? Are they real entities? Or if not, are they the delimitations of things or relations between things which exist whether anyone observes them or not? Or are they delimitations and relations which are inherent in one's awareness of the world and thus in the subjective character of the mind? If so, then without these properties of mind, predicates like space and time would never appear anywhere.

To understand this matter more clearly, let us first consider space.

1. Space is not an idea derived from experience of the external world. If my sensations are to be referred to things outside me, i.e., to things located at some point of space other than where I am, or if I am to be able to refer my sensations to differing objects located at several points, the idea of space must be present in advance. My conception of space therefore cannot be the product of experience or borrowed from the relations of things to each other. On the contrary, it is only by means of the idea of space that external experience becomes possible at all.

2. Space is the visualization which is necessary to the mind, and the basis of all external perceptions. One might imagine space with no objects to fill it, but it is impossible to imagine that there should be no space. Space is therefore a condition of the possibility of phenomena and not a form required by them. It is subjective, a visualization which precedes all external experience.

3. The demonstrable certainty of geometric propositions depends on the necessity of this mental visualization of space. If space were a conception gained empirically or borrowed from general external experience, the first principles of mathematical definition would be merely perceptions. They would be subject to all the accidents of perception and there would be no necessity that there should be only one straight line between two points. A theorem would be something to be learned in each case by experience. Whatever is derived from

experience possesses only relative generality, based on reasoning from observations. We should accordingly be able to say only that so far as anyone can see, there is no space having more than three dimensions.

4. Space is not a discursive or general idea of the relations between things. It is pure awareness or mental visualization. First of all, only one space is imaginable, and if many spaces are mentioned, they are all parts of the one space. They are not to be considered as leading up to the one all-embracing space, or the component parts from which an aggregate of space is formed.

Space is essentially one. The general idea of a multiplicity of spaces is the result of imposing limitations on space. Hence, it follows that the foundation of all ideas of space is a mental awareness, and it is thus not derived from experience. So geometrical principles, such as "The sum of two sides of a triangle is greater than the third," may never be derived from the general conception of sides and triangles but from an awareness or visualization which is purely mental and which is derived thence with demonstrable certainty.

5. Space is visualized as an infinite quantity. The general idea of space, which is to be found in a foot as well as a yard, would furnish no information about the quantity of the space involved if there were not infinity in the reach of awareness. Without this, no conception of relations in space could ever contain the principle of infinity.

Space is not in any sense a property of things or the relation between them. It is nothing but the form the appearances of things take to man's outer senses. It is the mental basis of sensitivity and makes possible one's awareness of the external world.

One may speak of space, extension, etc., only from the human point of view. Apart from one's awareness of the outer world, the idea of space means nothing at all. The space predicate is attributed to things only as they are sensed.

The rule that "things are juxtaposed in space" is valid within the limitation that "things" are taken only as objects of awareness. Add one condition and say that "things as they appear externally are juxtaposed in space," and the rule is universally valid.

This exposition therefore teaches the *reality* (objective validity) of space. Space is as real as anything else in the world. At the same time, it teaches the *ideality* of space, when things are viewed as only the mind can view them, as they are by themselves, apart from the activity of human sense. We also assert the reality of space as verifiable fact in human experience of the external world.

The *formal* idea of phenomena in space is a critical reminder that there is nothing of which one is aware that is a thing-itself (that is, something apart from man's perception of it). Space is not the form of things-themselves. The phenomena of which we are aware tell us nothing about things as they are apart from us, and in experience nobody ever asks about them as such.

7 GEOMETRY IS THE SCIENCE OF SPACE

Geometry may also be logic

Naturally, when Kant writes of geometry it is Euclid's geometry that he has in mind; it is the geometry of our own high school days, the geometry that happens best to suit man's everyday perceptions of things; and so it seemed to the great Sir Isaac Newton. Everyday perceptions do not require close scrutiny of Euclid's basic assumptions nor of the degree to which the demonstrations of Euclid depend on the illusions in a constructed or imagined figure. In our century, however, it has turned out that self-consistent geometries can be created almost at will and that some of them are more suited to a given set of facts about the world than Euclid's. The modern physicists are also saying that special kinds of space exist in the intimate parts of atoms and galaxies.

There are those who think today of geometry as logic and disdain the notion of a "science of space," as such. Bertrand Russell, for example, thinks that the best geometry has neither words nor figures. It is simply an analysis, in symbols only, of its axioms, and since it refers to nothing in particular, Russell feels secure in it. Kant was more venturesome, perhaps because he could not know, as Russell does, what geometry was to reveal within the next two centuries. His mathematical judgments amplified knowledge of the subject discussed. They were statements about something in particular, statements applicable to concrete things and to which the world of concrete things submitted. In this, Kant felt secure.

Geometry is a science in which the properties of space are organized abstractly and in advance. How, then, must space be visualized so that this kind of acquaintance with it may be possible? Visualization begins with awareness; an idea is not an adequate origin for a proposition that goes beyond it, as geometry illustrates. Geometric propositions are amplifying. The awareness is, however, prior; it is present in us before it is focused on any object. It is therefore a pure awareness and not empirical. On this basis geometric propositions are capable of being demonstrated with certainty, and with their demonstration goes the consciousness that they are necessary. For example: Space has only three dimensions. Propositions like this cannot be empirical, or judgments of experience, and they cannot be derived from any other such judgment.

How, then, can there be in one's mind an awareness of the outer world which precedes the objects themselves and from which the idea of these objects can be defined in advance? Obviously, this could not occur unless the idea originates in the mind of the observer. The formal nature of the mind is such that when it is affected by objects, it obtains immediate visualization or awareness of them, that is, of the form in which they are perceived. This is the only explanation that makes geometry intelligible as abstract, organized knowledge.

8 OBSERVATION MODIFIES THE OBSERVED

Time leads to self

Kant's treatment of time parallels that of space, even verbally, and need not be repeated. One difference is obvious. Space, says Kant, is three-dimensioned. Time is one-dimensioned. Our minds arrange events in a before-after order because we sense things as happening that way.

There is, however, a radical difference between the sense of time and that of space. The sense of space is felt to refer to the outer world. Sensations of space have a quality of externality about them. The time order belongs to an "inner sense." This observation leads Kant somewhat prophetically to consider the nature of this inner sense and to ask how one can be "inwardly aware" of one's self.

The presumption is that a person could not focus his attention on the inner sense that runs with time and reports it, without coming across the person with whom space and time originate and to whom therefore all phenomena pertain. Kant discusses elsewhere a pure ego, the ultimate subject of every predicate, who is an unknowable knower. For practical purposes, however, he uses an "empirical self," which can be observed because it is experienced as an object. He points to this empirical self from time to time with such phrases as "the unity of apperception," "the unity of self-consciousness," "self-awareness," etc. Not one of these phrases ever quite seems to get precise definition, except by some determined person who ponders well what Kant said and then decides what he meant. It is a weakness of the critical philosophy that the empirical self was not identified with the ultimate, pure knower.

Time is nothing but the form of inner sense, the awareness of ourselves and our inner states. Certainly it is something real. It is the form inner awareness takes and so, from the point of view of private experience, it has subjective reality. This means that I may visualize time and my place in it. It is also a way of visualizing myself as if I were an object to be studied. If I could see myself other than through the spectacles of sense, the conditions of a change in me from subject to object would yield knowledge that involves neither time nor change. Without the spectacles of sense the very idea of time would vanish. Time does not belong to objects but only to minds aware of it.

When anything is visualized through the senses it becomes a phenomenon. This means either that we give up the idea of an inner sense or that we treat our minds as objects, which is to say, as phenomena.

This is the difficulty: How can one be aware inwardly of one's self? That is, how can my mind, as the subject, to which time belongs, also be the object, to which time is denied? The question poses a difficulty common to every theory. Self-awareness is the simple visualization of the I, the ego, and if all the elements of self should appear spontaneously in the process, self-awareness would be like any other intellectual activity. But when the elements of mind gather in self-awareness, its content is changed, and accordingly self-awareness is affected too. The form self-awareness takes is determined by mind working by its own laws. So time, the visualized form of inner awareness, enters the process of combining the mind's elements. The result is not what it would have been if the combination had been spontaneous. Self-awareness is modified as the mind changes, according to its own needs.

If I say that external objects and even the soul are in space and time what they appear to be to our awareness, this does not mean that they are illusions. The principle that sensed objects are ideal does not lead to that thought. Quite to the contrary. When objective reality is attributed to space and time, the *forms* of perception, then and only then does illusion steal the show. If I attribute redness to the rose itself or extension to external objects, then illusion comes. If space and time are regarded as properties of things themselves, then two infinities, which are neither substances nor inherent in substances, exist. They also become the necessary conditions for the existence of everything else and would continue so even if things were all done away. Given this absurdity, Berkeley could not be blamed for putting all material bodies down as illusions. Indeed, if my own existence depends on the persistence of such a nonentity as time, then it too is illusion. But no one as yet has been guilty of this.

In natural theology God is considered as an object. He cannot be any object of which man is aware, nor can he be an object of sense awareness to himself. This is why, carefully, we avoid attributing to him any awareness that involves space and time. Knowledge to him, however, must be awareness rather than thought, for thought implies limitation.

What right have we to do this? May we make space and time the forms of things as they are apart from us? Can they be forms which would continue to exist as abstract conditions even after every actual thing had disappeared? If space and time are the conditions of *all* existence, they must be so for God too.

If we do not treat space and time as objective forms of things, then we must consider them the mental forms of our internal and external awareness, which is called sense awareness, because nothing comes from it as from an origin. It does not signal the existence of an object. As far as we may judge, only God's awareness could do that. Our awareness of an object depends always on its existence and the condition that the object stimulates us to visualize it.

Here, then, is one part of the solution of the general problem of the function of mind, namely, how are amplifying, prior judgments possible? We have now pure, prior awareness in space and time. Given these, we have shown how a proposition can go beyond the subject-idea to something which is discoverable in a corresponding awareness and which can be united with the original subject. These judgments, of course, reach only from the subject to the object and are valid only within possible experience.

9 LOGICAL THOUGHT MAKES AN ORDERLY WORLD

Thought also comes pure and empirical

In the Critique, after the Aesthetic comes the Formal Logic. What he did for sense awareness and mathematics in the Aesthetic, Kant undertakes to do for thought and physics in the Logic.

It is well to recall at the outset that the word "transcendental," or "formal," means that Kant is not concerned so much with what one thinks as with how one thinks it. In the Analytic, he tells us that things of sense appear as they do because our minds give order to them. Without mind there would be chaos in the world. Mind makes order out of the jumble of things because the mind has unity and order to give out.

The work to be accomplished in the Logic is to establish the abstract and prior elements of thought and to prove that by means of them abstract and objective knowledge of the physical world is possible. This is really a description of the function of mind in man and in the world as Kant saw it. It was a view that had to make its way against formidable contradiction: the order of things in space and time belongs in the external world and is learned by experience. Once again, it is Kant's point that abstract and prior amplifying judgments not only are possible but are the basis of the physical sciences.

The following passages are taken from the introduction to the Logic.

There are two sources of knowledge. There is mental sensitivity to the impressions made by things on one who is aware of them, and there is the power to recognize objects from past impressions. The first shows how objects are presented to us; the second, how we think of them. Awareness and ideas are the roots of all knowledge. Neither ideas without awareness nor awareness without ideas would result in knowledge. Both may be either pure or empirical. They are empirical when they contain sensation in the actual presence of an object. They are pure when sense is not involved. Pure awareness contains only the form of an object, and pure ideas contain only a form of thought. Pure awareness and pure ideas are abstract and prior; those containing sense experience are empirical.

Sensitivity makes mind impressible; intelligence moves mind to spontaneous expression. Man's nature being what it is, awareness always involves sense. It is the way we are affected by objects. As between the two, neither sensitivity nor intelligence is to be preferred. Without sensitivity, no object would ever be perceived; without thought, no object would ever be understood. *Thoughts without content are empty; awareness without ideas is blind.*

It is therefore just as necessary to put sense-content into ideas, that is, to supply to them an object of awareness, as it is to make sense awareness intelligible, that is, to organize it by ideas. Feeling and thinking are not interchangeable. *Mind sees nothing and the senses do not think.* Knowledge results only when the two are combined. The function of one must not be confused with the function of the other; there is every reason to keep the two separate. This is why we have separated the general science of sense, *aesthetics,* from the general science of mind, *logic.*

General logic is either pure or applied. In pure logic, consideration of the empirical conditions under which mind operates is omitted, i.e., the influence of the senses, the play of imagination, the laws of memory, the source of habit, desires, etc. So, too, the sources of prejudice are omitted, not to mention the supply of special kinds of knowledge. Special knowledge concerns mental operations only under special conditions, to know about which experience is required. General, pure logic is really just a set of rules of the mind.

In dealing with *formal aesthetic,* it appeared that there were pure and empirical awarenesses. Similarly, we may make a distinction between pure and empirical thinking. In this case, there could be a logic in which the content of knowledge is considered to some degree. It would include all the rules of pure thought and exclude all empirical knowledge. It would also set forth the origin of the knowledge of objects insofar as knowledge is not attributable to the objects themselves. In contrast, in general logic, the origin of knowledge is not studied but only its visualization, which may be abstract and prior, or empirical.

In expectation that there may be ideas which refer abstractly to objects, not as pure or sense awareness does, but by acts of pure thought, we offer a science which pertains to pure mentality. This science is to determine the origin, the extent, and the objective validity of abstract and prior knowledge and may be called *formal logic.* It deals in the laws of the mind as applied to objects abstractly. It differs from general logic, which refers without distinction to empirical and pure knowledge.

In formal logic, we isolate the mind and attend only to that part of thought which originates wholly in mind. The use of this pure knowledge presupposes that one is aware of the objects to which it can be applied. Without awareness, knowledge has no objects and remains, therefore, entirely empty.

One part of formal logic, therefore, sets forth the elements of pure knowledge and the principles without which no object can be conceived. This is *formal analytic.* It is also a logic of truth. No knowledge can contradict it without at once losing its total meaning and its bearing on any object, which would mean the loss of any relation to truth itself.

Because it is tempting to use this pure knowledge of understanding beyond the limits of experience, we run the risk of using its purely formal principles as sophistry. Since knowledge like this is meant only as a set of rules for the criticism of the practical use of mind, it is abuse to treat it as a general method of judgment or a basis for decision. Such use of pure reason would be dialectical (false).

The second part of formal logic will therefore be a critical study of this dialectic fake. It will be called *formal dialectic.* It will be a critical evaluation of the mind's operation in non-physical matters. It will expose the falsity of our intellectual pretensions and cut down our claims to discovery and expansion, until there remains only the critical evaluation which protects one against sophistical delusions.

10 THE BASIC, ABSTRACT, PRIOR PRINCIPLES OF THINKING

En route to the categories

By manifold, or field of impressions, Kant indicates a person's awareness of the world or any portion of it as it appears before mind takes charge. Thinking is what mind does, and thinking is organization. It is the process of connecting disjoined impressions, perceptions, memories, and imagined data. It proceeds, says Kant, under impulses from imagination, organizing this raw material under general, abstract and prior ideas. Mind's contribution is "organized unity." That is to say, when mind is through with it, the once raw material has acquired meaning and refers to some identifiable object. It is then knowledge.

Thinking is done in judgments, or statements. Judgment is therefore mind's front gate and through that gate one must go to find out how anything ever comes to be known. The first step in this adventure was taken in the Aesthetic: Mind contributes order to sense experience through its own abstract and prior ideas of space and time.

Similarly, in the endless number of judgments man must make, the material of these judgments must also be connected and organized under pure principles supplied by mind from its own resources. Kant finds that these principles are twelve in number, and they are organized under four major heads: quantity, quality, relation, modality. A very little examination will reveal that the three principles listed under each major head are closely related. Thinking, says Kant, is connecting, and this is what the twelve principles of logical judgment accomplish in part.

In a more general sense, Kant finds that there are twelve abstract, prior principles in mind which apply to anything one may be aware *of and which correspond, one to one, to the twelve principles of judgment. For these principles Kant borrows the name "category." In the broad sense, these categories are basic connectors, forms, or integrators. They belong to mind's basic structure. They are part of its permanent apparatus of thought.*

As for the number twelve, some critics feel that the category table is incomplete. The number, they say, is greater than twelve. Others say that the table is far too complete. However that may be, Kant's logic is really a fairly minor part of the critical philosophy. It is, nevertheless, a part of which Kant was proud.

By *analytic*, I do not mean an analysis of ideas, nor any philosophical dissection of their contents to make them more meaningful. A hitherto rare dissection of understanding mind itself is indicated. This is an operation within mind, designed to discover which ideas are both abstract and prior, examining them where they are born, by analyzing the pure use of mind. This is the real business of formal philosophy; the rest of it is just logical treatment of ideas. Pure ideas are traced to their origin in the idea-beds of mind where they germinate. They develop through experience until, at last, mind sets them free from the empirical conditions adhering to them.

Mind has thus far been explained negatively as the function of knowing apart from sense. Mind is not an instrument of awareness because there is no awareness except through sense. And excepting awareness, there is no avenue of knowledge but through ideas. Such knowledge as mind contributes must therefore be in terms of ideas, and discursive rather than perceptive. Awareness arises from stimulation of the senses, and ideas from spontaneous thought. Mind then can use ideas only for the purposes of judgment. An idea is never related directly to an object but always to some perception of it, perhaps to awareness, perhaps to another idea. Judgment is therefore secondhand knowledge of an object; it represents a perception of it.

In every judgment there is an idea which is valid for many applications, among which there is one in particular that is immediately connected with an object. For example, in the judgment "All bodies are divisible," the idea of divisibility has many applications; but in this case, it is applied to bodies and thus to some phenomenon in particular in which one might be interested. Objects are thus represented here via the idea of divisibility. Accordingly, all judgments are functions of the unity of mind's power to represent things.

Since every mental act may be reduced to a judgment, mind can be defined as man's function of judgment. Mind, as we have seen, is the thinking function, and thinking, in turn, is idea-begotten knowledge. Ideas are the predicates of possible judgments and so refer to perceptions of as yet unspecified objects. The idea of metal, for example, refers to anything metallic. It is an idea because it includes other representative notions and so may refer to other objects. This is how it becomes the predicate of a possible judgment. For example: A metallic object is a body. In this way the whole function of mind can be discovered if its unity can be expressed in judgments.

That this can be done is to be seen in what follows. Let us ignore the content of all judgments and concentrate wholly on their forms. It will then appear that thought in judgments can be classified under four heads, each of which includes three subheads, as in the following table:

Table of the Judgments

1.		
Judgment of Quantity		*Translator's Illustrations*
GENERAL	(Universal)	All men are mortal.
SPECIFIC	(Particular)	Some men are masons.
INDIVIDUAL	(Singular)	John is a mason.
2.		
Quality		
AFFIRMATIVE		Man is mortal.
NEGATIVE		The soul is not mortal.
INFINITE		The soul is immortal.
3.		
Relation		
DECISIVE	(Categorical)	God is just.
CONDITIONAL	(Hypothetical)	If God is just, he will punish sinners.
INDECISIVE	(Disjunctive)	God is either just or unjust.

4.

Modality

UNDECIDED	(Problematical)	If Mars is a planet, its age is the same as Earth's.
ASSERTIVE	(Assertory)	Mars is a planet.
CERTAIN	(Apodictic)	Mars's age must be the same as Earth's.

The mental function which unifies varied perceptions in a judgment also makes one aware of unity in the abstract organizations of perception. Generally this function is a pure idea or concept. Mind also introduces a formal element into perceptions through organized unity in one's awareness of things. For this reason these pure ideas apply abstractly and in advance to objects. This would be impossible in general logic.

Spontaneity of thought requires that those things of which one is aware should first be examined and then put together. This is the act of synthesis, or organization. To me, it means generally the arrangement or integration of perceptions into understandable knowledge. However raw and confused at first, or in need of analysis, knowledge is gathered and, in the process of organization, unified. This is where knowledge begins.

Later it will appear that organization is the effect of imagination,* which is a blind but indispensable function of mind. Without imagination there could be no knowledge, although one is rarely aware of it. It is then a function of mind to convert the organized material into ideas and so, for the first time, to produce knowledge properly so called.

General logic deals with the analysis of perceptions and their organization under ideas. Formal logic, then, deals with organization by ideas, not of perceptions but of the abstract organization of perceptions.

Objective knowledge begins with pure, or abstract awareness of the world of things. Then imagination organizes awareness, but even this step does not achieve knowledge. The third and final contribution comes from ideas in which things are visualized and which impart unity to their organization.

* See p. 60.

So, there are exactly as many pure ideas that abstractly and in advance refer to any object of which one might be aware, as there are logical functions listed in the table of judgments. Borrowing Aristotle's word, we call these basic ideas *categories*, meaning what Aristotle meant by the term, but applying the categories quite differently.

Table of the Categories

1.

Quantity:

One (Unity)
Many (Plurality)
All (Totality)

2.

Quality:

Reality
Negation
Limitation

3.

Relation:

Substance and attribute
Cause and effect
Community (reciprocity of active and passive)

4.

Modality:

Possibility-impossibility
Existence-nonexistence
Necessity-contingency

This, then, is a complete list of the original, pure, organizing ideas. It is only by means of these ideas that things of which one becomes aware can be comprehended or that one can *think* an object. The classification is systematic and is based on a principle used in common with the list of functions of judgment (which is the same as thought).

11 KNOWLEDGE IS VALIDATED

How do you know?

In the Analytic *the list of categories is conspicuous. It has the clarity of a diagram, but the choice of categories is less clear. What is arresting is Kant's explanation of how we know anything at all and his demonstration that there can be valid knowledge, first in mathematics and then of the physical world in general.*

Our minds organize sensations by means of space and time, which mind alone provides. The result in part is, Kant thought, a universally valid geometry, from which he concluded that space and time, as two basic principles of the mind, are also basic to the world. This he set forth in the Aesthetic.

The Analytic *generalizes on this. For knowledge of the world about us, our minds also provide twelve other pure ideas which organize thought. The categories are abstract and prior, and valid for the world of nature because the laws of the mind are also the laws of nature. Mind comes first and provides the means of assimilating the world to its own uses.*

The striking fact about the laws of nature is that they are necessary to everybody and are everywhere unexceptionable. This was a matter for envy to philosophers in Kant's day: mathematics and then physical science, rather than philosophy, displayed the essential unity of the world. Wherever one went, either in fact or imagination, geometry would be the same, physical laws the same, time sequences the same. It was Kant's discovery that this was so only because all minds work alike. Otherwise, for example, even the notion of translation from one language to another would be inconceivable. We, who number two and a half billions strong on the earth, do not live in many worlds but in one world, a world which derives its meaning from mind alone, mind which first was one.

If it were true, as many people believed, that nature teaches man and so forms his mind, we should live in as many different worlds as there are people. It would then be a hard conclusion to reach, for example, that all free movement in the universe is illustrated in the fall of a single pebble. The generalizations on which we depend can come about only as minds prescribe them. One pebble neither knows nor cares how another pebble moves. Here, then, are illustrative passages from the Analytic, *detailing special proof of the work claimed for categories. This special proof is in part explanation of the categories, in part authorization of them, and in part their deduction. Since it refers only to the way the categories work, Kant calls it* "transcendental," *i.e., formal deduction.*

Among the many strands from which the complicated web of human knowledge is woven there are some which are destined from the start to be used abstractly and to continue independent of experience. The claims made for these ideas generally require special demonstration (deduction). Their legitimacy is not established by a deduction based on experience, even though we do want to know how these ideas can refer to objects within one's experience, and yet be derived apart from it. The explanation of the way abstract and prior ideas refer to objects is to be called *formal deduction.* This is distinguished from *empirical deduction,* which shows how an idea is derived by reflection from experience. *Empirical deduction* applies not to the legitimacy of the use of the ideas but to the facts from which they arise.

Without doubt an investigation of the functioning of man's power to know, beginning with single perceptions and climbing to general ideas, is useful. We have to thank the celebrated John Locke for opening up this avenue. The deduction of pure ideas is not, however, to be achieved along these lines; it is to be worked out in another direction. Their future use, independent of experience, requires for them a very particular birth certificate, in which descent from experience is denied. Locke's attempted psychological derivation is not deduction at all, because it depends on matters of fact. It is rather an explanation of the possession of pure knowledge. It is clear, therefore, that only a formal deduction of pure ideas is usable and that empirical deductions will not do.

Our entire investigation of the formal deduction of pure ideas should be based on this principle: Pure ideas are the abstract and prior conditions of experience. They supply the objective ground of experience and are, accordingly, necessary. To know how they occur, the abstract and prior conditions necessary to experience must be discovered and kept separate from knowledge derived from experience. The categories are pure ideas which express the formal and objective conditions of experience with sufficient generality and which contain the pure thought involved in every experience. It is really a sufficient deduction of the categories and a justification of their objective validity to prove that no object is conceivable without them.

The famous John Locke, lacking these considerations and having come across pure ideas in the course of experience, proceeded to derive them from experience itself. Then, inconsistently, he went far beyond the bounds of experience in studies of knowledge. David Hume saw that to do this, ideas from pure origins are needed. He could not explain, however, how it was that ideas, disconnected in one's mind, came together in some object of thought. It never occurred to him that mind itself might be the author of the experience of its object.

So he, too, was led to derive pure ideas from experience, or habit, i.e., from a subjective necessity begotten of frequent associations of experiences. This finally came to be accepted as objective, but falsely so. Subsequently Hume explained, and quite consistently this time, that with ideas so derived and with their attendant principles, it is not possible to get beyond personal experience. The deduction of pure ideas from experience, as practiced by Locke and Hume, cannot be reconciled with the abstract and prior knowledge encountered in pure mathematics and natural science. It is therefore refuted by the facts.

The first of these men left the door wide open to fantasy. It is hard to keep reasoning within due bounds once it has had unlimited prestige. The second gave in entirely to skepticism because he believed he had found in the knowing process an illusion which generally passed as reasonable. We now turn to study whether or not reasoning can be steered between these two cliffs, its limits indicated, and still keep its proper field of function open.

If every perception or idea were isolated from every other, there could be no knowledge as we know it, because knowledge consists of perceptions and ideas conjoined and compared to each other. Since the senses cover a whole field of awareness, they need a synopsis corresponding to the organization that makes knowledge possible when mind spontaneously comprehends sense data. Spontaneity is the beginning of a threefold organization which is necessary to every kind of knowledge. It consists of (1) *comprehension*, in which awareness is made into perceptions by ideas; (2) imagination in the *recollection* of the various elements necessary to knowledge; (3) *recognition* of the resultant ideas. Thus we have three inner sources of knowledge which make understanding and its empirical product, experience, possible.

However ideas or images arise, whether from the influence of external things or inner causes, or abstractly, or empirically as phenomena, they belong to man's inner sense because they are simply modifications of mind. All knowledge is, accordingly, subject to the formal condition of inner sense, namely, time. Everything is arranged, connected, and related by time. This general remark is fundamental to all subsequent discussion.

Generally speaking, awareness means being aware of many things at once, and this could not be imagined if time were not marked in the mind by a succession of impressions. In any given instant each impression is an absolute unity by itself; so, in order to get unity in awareness (as the idea of space requires), it is first necessary to let the various elements of awareness run in succession through the mind and then pull them together. This is the act which I call the organization of apprehension, or understanding. It is applied directly to awareness, which actually is multiple and so requires organization if it is to be unified or comprehended by means of a single idea.

The synthesis, or organization of understanding must be carried out abstractly and in advance, since ideas which are not empirical are involved. The ideas of space and time would be impossible without it; the many elements of sense data must be organized before they appear. This is how the pure organization of understanding is accomplished.

Again, it is apparent that if I draw an imaginary line, or consider the time lapse from one noon to the next, or even think of a certain number, I must begin by getting a general idea of the aggregates or sets of perceptions involved. If I were to lose from thought the antecedent part of either of them, say the first part of the line, the first hours of the day, or the digits preceding my number, and if I were unable to reproduce the lost parts as I went on, then no general idea of either of these sets would be possible to me. Neither could I, in that case, have the foregoing thoughts of even the first and purest ideas of space and time.

The organization of understanding is inseparably connected with recollection. Since the former is the formal basis of all knowledge, both empirical and pure, the organization of recollection by imagination belongs to the formal activity of mind and is here to be called *formal imagination.*

Again, if I were not aware that what I now think is the same as what I was thinking a moment ago, recollection of a lost step in a series of perceptions would be useless. Each perception in its place would be new, and not part of the action that made the series. A series of experiences could never be complete because it would lack the unity which only consciousness can give it. When I count, if I forget how the series of numbers now in my thought has been added up, one by one, I can never understand how the final sum is produced. The sum is a concept which depends on my consciousness of the organized unity of the number series.

The very word "idea" could have been the occasion of these remarks; consciousness gathers up the items in a series or a field, one by one; then recollection pulls them all together in a single idea. The consciousness involved may be so weak that it is felt, not in the act or process of production but only in the final idea. Nevertheless, even though it is not very clear, consciousness must always be there. Without it, ideas and all knowledge of objects would be impossible.

At this point it is necessary to clarify what we mean by the phrase *perceived object*. We have said already that phenomena are nothing but sense perceptions and must not be regarded as objects otherwise. What, then, can one mean by objects which correspond to knowledge and yet are different from it? It is easy to see that an object can be thought of only as X, the unknown, because there is nothing in it that answers to what one knows of it.

We find, however, that in the relation of knowledge to objects, knowledge is controlled by its objects. An object prevents knowledge from being haphazard or arbitrary and, in certain ways, makes it abstract and prior. To point to a common object, the various elements of knowledge must be in agreement with each other, and knowledge will have been unified by the idea of its object.

It is clear that since we have to do only with the field of our perceptions, the object X, to which the field corresponds, is nothing by itself as far as we are concerned, because the object is not like our perception of it. The unity required by the object comes, therefore, from the formal unity of consciousness which appears in the organized field of perception. Only when unity has thus been effected can we say that we know an object.

There is a rule that abstractly and in advance makes both recollection of sense data and a unifying idea necessary. It says that as sense data are organized, unity of awareness grows too. According to this rule about awareness, as we are conscious that three straight lines have been combined or organized, a triangle, for example, will appear as an object. So unity regulates the field and limits it to the conditions in which the unity can be part of my conscious self. The idea that produces the unity is embedded in the consciousness of the object X, which I, in my predicates, think of as a triangle.

Knowledge requires ideas, however incomplete or dim they may be. If an idea is formal and general, it can serve as a rule. The idea of a *body* serves as a rule for knowledge of external phenomena and for unity in a field which is ordered by it. It can be a rule governing awareness, because it represents the necessary recollection of the many elements of a phenomenon; or it may represent the organized unity, in our consciousness, of those elements. The idea of a body, regarded as external, makes necessary the idea of extension and, also, impermeability, shape, etc.

Necessity is based on formal considerations: it originates in pure reasoning. The unity of consciousness is therefore formal because it is necessary to all other mental functions. The organization of awareness by the general idea of the object or objects experienced is also formal. Except on formal grounds, no object could ever get into one's awareness; for an object is only a *something* until it is organized with an idea.

This original formal condition is, of course, formal self-consciousness. Self-consciousness, otherwise, is a function of internal perceptions and is empirical and always changing. The stream of inner experience contains no fixed or abiding self and is usually called the *inner sense* or *empirical self-consciousness;* it does not, however, enable one to see one's self objectively. So there must be a consideration preceding *all* experience, which makes it possible and validates it by means of a formal assumption.

We cannot know anything, nor can there be integration or unity in what we do know, without knowing ourselves each to be *one*. This precedes all the data of awareness. No object could ever be perceived without reference to it. This pure, original, unchanging consciousness I now call *formal self-consciousness*, i.e., the formal self. That it deserves this name, will appear from the fact that even the purest objective unity, in the abstract and prior ideas of space and time, is possible only when one is aware of it. The numerical unity of self is therefore the abstract, prior condition of all thinking, as the field of space and time is the basis of sense awareness.

The formal self collects all the elements of a field of awareness into the idea of an object. It is thus said to be objective and should be distinguished from the subjective unity of consciousness. This is another form of the inner sense, another way of connecting the elements of a field which are empirically given. Whether I sense that the elements of a field of awareness are simultaneous or successive depends on the conditions. There is a self, an "I," which may be experienced as a result of the association of ideas, but it is phenomenal and contingent. By contrast, pure formal awareness in time of an actual field, is subject to the original self, or "I." This comes about by a necessary relation of the field to *I think*. Here is the abstract and prior basis of empirical organization. Here is the unity that is valid objectively. The empirical self, however, is not considered here because it is derived under special conditions from formal unity and has only subjective validity. One man associates the meaning of a word with one thing, another with another; thus the empirical self is not necessary or generally valid in actual cases.

The phenomena which coexist in one's experience are connected by a formal self. Indeed, connecting the many things of which one is aware would be impossible if one were not conscious of his own identity as the connector. The original and necessary self is also consciousness of another unity, equally necessary: the unity of phenomena organized by an idea. One could never conceive one's own identity among the many things perceived if one lost sight of his identity in his own actions. Here in the self, empirical perceptions also are organized by the formal unity of the self. In this way mental coherence becomes possible, abstractly and in advance, and accordingly it becomes possible more accurately to define ideas of objects generally: Perceptions have objects and in turn may be the objects of other perceptions. Phenomena are, however, immediate objects themselves, and awareness touches them immediately. Phenomena are not things-themselves, but perceptions which have their own objects. The object itself is not visible. It is not empirical. It may therefore be called "formal object X." (Cf. *noumenon*, pp. 75 ff.)

It is only the pure idea of a formal object that relates empirical ideas to objects. (In reality all we ever know about an object is that it is X, which means that it exists, unknown.) It is an idea that carries no definite image and so refers only to the unity found in things as we know them, if it has any object at all. It is simply the unity necessary to consciousness. It is therefore an organization of things by the function of mind, which unites them in one perception.

It is a unity that must be considered necessary, abstractly and in advance, because without it, knowledge would refer to nothing. So, relation to a formal object, that is, the objective reality of empirical knowledge, depends on a formal law. The law is that all phenomena which represent objects are governed by abstract and prior rules covering the organized unity of all objects. Objects are related in empirical awareness by these rules, and these rules alone. In experience they are subject to the conditions of self-consciousness just as much as in awareness they are subject to the formal conditions of space and time. This is how knowledge becomes possible at all.

It may seem absurd that nature should derive its order from man's conscious self or look to human minds for its laws. If we remember, however, that nature is not a thing-itself but a totality of phenomena, or a group of perceptions in mind, it will not be surprising that nature is known only by means of the root of all knowledge, the formal self. Without the unity derived from this self, a group of perceptions could not be the total object of experience, which we call nature. If the experience of nature were independent of the primary source of thought, it would not appear that nature's unity is abstract and prior, or necessary. If that were the case, I should not know even where to look for organizing laws or the general unity of nature. These matters would have to depend on natural phenomena, and would be empirical; and any unity so discovered would be coincidental. This would be very different from the broad and necessary connections indicated by the word "nature."

If it is desired to follow up the inward connections among perceptions to their point of convergence, where they are unified as experience requires, we must begin with pure self-consciousness. Awareness amounts to nothing until it merges into consciousness, directly or indirectly. If this did not happen there would be no knowledge. Among all the perceptions of a given moment, we are conscious, abstractly and in advance, of our own identity. This is how any perception becomes possible, and it is a firm principle which may be called the formal principle of unity in one's perception of a field of sense data.

This unity, however, presupposes or involves an organization which is as necessary to knowledge and as prior and abstract as the unity itself. Unification depends on pure imagination to organize a field of perceptions into knowledge. Such an organization is said to be formal if, ignoring differences of awareness, it effects only the necessary unification of the field. The unity involved is also formal when it refers only to the original unity of self and thus becomes prior and necessary. Formal and organizing imagination is thus the pure form of knowledge by means of which, abstractly and in advance, objects of experience become known.

Understanding is the self at work in imagination, unifying and organizing experience; pure understanding is the self at work when imagination effects a formal organization. Understanding, therefore, involves pure, abstract forms for knowledge, which carry the unity the imagination uses to organize the data or experience into phenomena. These forms are the categories; that is, they are the mind's pure conceptions, or ideas. This then is how man learns from experience: Mind focuses on objects of sense by its own necessity, via awareness and by means of an organizing imagination; then phenomena, the data of experience, conform to mind; by means of the categories, pure mind constitutes a formal and organizing principle of experience, and this shows how, necessarily, phenomena are related to mind.

First in experience is the phenomenon which becomes a perception when coupled with consciousness. Every phenomenon is a field of sense data which also includes occasional scattered perceptions. These must be connected by some other agent because sense cannot connect them. To that end, there is an active organizing power called *imagination*. When it operates with perceptions, I call its function *apprehension*. It makes over a field of awareness into an image, for which purpose it must first receive impressions, and this is what is meant by *apprehension*.

It should be clear that only apprehension can produce an image from impressions, or coherence among them. In addition, there must be subjective power to recall a perception with which the mind was once occupied and of which it has let go. A whole series of perceptions may thus be set up. This is the recollective function of the mind, and it is empirical only.

If perceptions, meeting at random, could reproduce each other, the result would be incoherence and an irregular clot of perception from which knowledge could never come. Recollection, therefore, must be regulated by imagination, which connects one perception with a second rather than a third. Recollection, regulated within mind or experience, is called *association* of perceptions.

There is an objectivity about unity in association, an objectivity that makes it impossible to apprehend phenomena at all except when unity of apprehension also is possible. If this were not so, coherence between phenomena and knowledge would be wholly accidental. Even if we still had the ability to associate perceptions, their associability would be uncertain or casual. In case this last were not true, some perceptions, perhaps our whole sense perception, might exist in the mind, separate in consciousness and unrelated to the self; but this is impossible.

Only by ascribing perceptions to my self—to the original self—can I say of perceptions that I am conscious of them. A law covering all phenomena depends on objective conditions which are abstract, and prior to the empirical laws of imagination. This law enables us to regard all phenomena alike as sense data, of themselves associable, and generally subject to the rules of permanent interconnection in recollection. I speak of this cause of association among phenomena as their *affinity*. It results from the unity of my self, which of necessity characterizes any knowledge that is mine. Accordingly, phenomena come to mind or are apprehended only in agreement with unity of self. This coming to mind would be impossible apart from the organized connections, the unity of phenomena, which is also necessarily objective.

The objective unity of the parts of consciousness within the primal self is necessary to perception. Whether they are close or remote, the affinity of phenomena, subject to law, is a consequence of the organizing power of imagination.

Imagination, therefore, is man's prior and necessary capacity to organize things, and this makes us call it *productive imagination*. If imagination effects only necessary unity in the organization of phenomena, it can be called formal. The foregoing may appear strange, but it must be clear by now that the affinity, the association of phenomena and their recollection according to law, which is to say the whole of human experience, is made possible by formal imagination. Without this, ideas of objects could never foregather in a single experience.

It is the permanent and unchanging "I" (pure apperception) that correlates perceptions when we become conscious of them. All consciousness belongs to one all-embracing pure apperception, "I," as sense awareness belongs to one pure inner awareness, namely, time. So that this "I" may function mentally, imagination is added and the organization effected by imagination, though of itself prior and necessary, is carried out in the senses. Phenomena are connected in a field of impressions only as they appear in awareness: for example, a triangle. When the field is once related to the "I," ideas of it fit into the mind, and imagination relates them to sense awareness.

Pure imagination is therefore a fundamental operation of the soul, and abstractly, in advance, all knowledge depends on it. It connects all that one is aware of with the unitary "I." It brings the two extremes of sense and mind together. Without it, the senses might report phenomena but not empirical knowledge, and so experience would be impossible. Real experience comes of apprehension, association, and recognition of phenomena and contains the ultimate and highest ideas, the ideas that formally unify experience and validate empirical knowledge objectively. These ideas constitute the basis on which a field of sense data is recognized. If they concern only the form of experience, they are, accordingly, categories. The whole formal unity of recognition by means of imagination depends on the categories, and in turn the whole empirical use of the categories (in recognition, recollection, association, and apprehension), even down to phenomena, depends on imagination. These four elements of knowing make it possible for a phenomenon to belong to our consciousness and so to ourselves.

It is we who bring order and regularity to phenomena and call the result "nature." These properties would not be discovered in nature if our own minds had not first put them there; for unity in nature means a prior, necessary, and certain connection of phenomena. How indeed could organized unity in nature be conceived in advance, if the original source of knowledge, the inner core of our minds, did not first contain it? What would there be to see if this mental condition of ours were not objectively valid, valid because it is the condition by which objects become part of experience?

We have explained mind in many ways: as the spontaneity of knowledge (in contrast to the receptivity of sense), or as the ability to think, or as the capacity to produce ideas or to make judgments. Under sufficiently strong illumination all these definitions amount to the same thing. We may now describe mind as the power to regulate. This is a more fruitful view and gets closer to the essence of the mind, which is always inspecting phenomena with a view to finding out rules. When they are objective, rules become laws and so are inherent in our knowledge of phenomena. Even though laws are sometimes learned by experience, such laws are only special cases of the higher ones, and the highest laws, to which all others are subject, originate in the mind, not in experience. It is from the highest laws that phenomena get their order and thus their eligibility to be experienced. Mind, therefore, is not merely power to make rules by comparing phenomena. It is itself nature's lawgiver. Without mind there could be no nature, no unity of the many, many phenomena, organized according to rules.

Phenomena as such cannot do without us; without us, they would exist only as sense experience. Nature as an object of knowledge by experience, with all that that involves, is possible only to the unitary self. This self is formal and the basis of the order which phenomena require if they are to pass into experience. The unitary self, working on a field of images, makes the rules, and the power to make them is called mind. Phenomena, therefore, necessarily depend, all in the same way, on mind to make them over into experience. From mind they derive the formal possibility of being experienced, just as intuitions depend on sense for their form.

To say that man's mind is the source of nature's laws, and so the origin of nature's formal unity, may sound exaggerated and absurd. The assertion is nonetheless correct and agreeable to our experience. Certainly empirical laws as such do not originate with pure reason, any more than the immeasurable world of things can be understood from sense awareness alone. Empirical laws are simply special cases of the pure laws of mind, pure laws which originally enable empirical laws. It is from these laws that things get their orderly character. In whatever form they may appear, things must agree with the mind's interpretation of sense data. Pure mind, therefore, appears in the categories as the law of the organized unity of phenomena, and in this way it makes formal experience possible.

This is all we have to accomplish in a formal deduction of the categories: to show that there is a relation between mind and sense which is intelligible, a relation which extends to the objects of experience and which finally makes pure ideas objectively valid by establishing their origin and truth.

If the objects of knowledge were things-themselves, that is, independent of our minds, we could not ever conceive them abstractly and in advance. Where, then, could we get any idea of one of them? If we took our ideas from objects (leaving out the question: How could we?), they would be empirical rather than pure. If we simply spin them out of ourselves, there would be no means of distinguishing them from any other ideas we might have, and we could not explain why anything should exist as we think of it, or why such internal ideas should not be totally empty.

On the other hand, since we have to do only with phenomena, it is not only possible but necessary that certain pure, prior conceptions should precede empirical knowledge. Being phenomena, they constitute internal objects only: there is no such thing as an external modification of sense. The idea that phenomena and objects alike, as they concern us, are internal, and constructions of and by ourselves, implies that they share a unity because they share a common conscious view. All formal knowledge by which, for example, a field of sense data is identified with an object, comes of this preconscious unity. The way a field of sense data is related to our consciousness precedes all knowledge of an object as the intellectual form of such knowledge, and so it constitutes a formal and pure knowledge of objects generally, within the thought process (categories).

The organization of the field by pure imagination, and the unity of ideas related to its first conscious view, also precedes empirical knowledge. This is how pure mental conceptions are possible abstractly and in advance and why, for experience, they are necessary. Knowledge never deals with anything but phenomena and the possibility of phenomena: their connection and unity, through the idea of an object, lies solely within us. This connection and unity must therefore precede all experience and give it form. Our deduction of the categories has been conducted on this basis because it is the only feasible way.

12 AN ART DEEP HIDDEN IN THE SOUL: SCHEMATISM

Imagination plays a crucial role

Long before it is complete, Kant's analysis of the knowing process acquires its quota of diverting questions suggested by his method. To be intelligible, the person, the nonphysical self, must be dissected into its component parts: the mind, the will, the emotions, the imagination, and the several mechanisms by which these departments are connected and function together. Are these segments and mechanisms, considered separately, real or imaginary? Does this kind of analysis destroy the problem to be solved? Or do these terms represent intellectual devices which are justified because a better understanding of the self at work emerges from their use?

There is an air, for example, about Kant's discovery of the categories, the pure intellectual predicates, general in form, that are applied only to possible objects of human experience, which suggests that, like a surgeon at work, he opened mind up and found these twelve pure ideas there. Actually, of course, he is not a surgeon but a logician at work with his "transcendental," or formal logic. It is logic that involves some kind of measurement or evaluation of intangible processes in persons which no surgeon could ever reach. So when he tells us that these categories are the tools by which the self projects its own character among the components of sense data, we may believe him, unless there is another way by which we see that order comes to human experience and so, as Kant says, into the world at large.

At this point, Kant's doctrine of the schemata appears. Mind and sense, as they are dissected out in the analysis of logic, appear to be discrete. How, then, can the categories be applied to sense data? His answer is: by means of a third entity in which both mind and sense have a share. Sense data belong to space and time, which are universal properties of mind; the categories also are, by defini-

tion, universal properties of mind, but restricted in application to possible objects of experience. At this point, productive imagination *plays a crucial role in the immediate problem; the common properties shared by categories and sense data are discovered, and the former are applied through productive imagination to the latter. In specific cases, the productive imagination takes appropriate forms, which Kant calls* schemata. *Causality, for example, appears in nature as uniform sequence, and this uniform sequence is its schema, i.e., the sense condition in which causality may be used.*

The knowing process, which is approximately instantaneous, can then be thought of as reassembled in a series of events. The first awareness of an object comes as a field of crude sense data to which mind applies the forms of space and time. Mind then organizes the field by means of its own pure properties, the categories. The application of the categories to sense data is made possible by the participation of both in the appropriate forms of imagination, the schemata. The schemata may very well be intellectual devices of formal logic, but they need not therefore be considered fictions. They are necessary to an intelligible account of the knowing process.

Formal philosophy is distinguished not only by the rules or the general conditions for rules which appear with pure ideas; it also indicates abstractly and in advance the cases to which these rules apply. It is thus superior to all other sciences except mathematics because it deals with ideas which refer in advance to their objects and which, because their high status makes it irrelevant, do not require subsequent validation. Its general function is to indicate the conditions under which objects correspond to ideas. Apart from such a correspondence, ideas would be nothing but logical forms without content. They could not be pure ideas.

Two chapters follow which will contain the formal doctrine of judgments. The first will deal with the sense conditions under which pure ideas may be used, that is to say, with the schematism, the patterns of pure mind. The second will deal with the amplifying judgments that can be derived from pure ideas under these sense conditions, which judgments undergird all knowledge. So the second chapter (Section 13) will treat the principles of pure mind.

The Schematism of Pure Mind. When an object is subsumed under an idea, there must be something about it which is homogeneous with the idea, or the idea must contain some element in common with it. So, empirically, the idea of a plate is homogeneous with the pure geometric idea of a circle, since the roundness of one is suggested by the other.

Pure ideas, however, are wholly unlike empirical, or sense awareness and are never found in it. How then can the latter be subsumed under the former? How can categories be applied to phenomena? Can causation, for example, be observed by the senses or contained in phenomena? It is this natural and important question that makes a formal doctrine of judgment necessary, to show how pure ideas apply to phenomena. In other sciences, where general ideas do not differ so much from specific ideas, and no investigation of the relation of one to the other is required, this is unnecessary.

Now it is clear that there must be a third something, homogeneous alike to categories and phenomena, which enables the application of one to the other. It must be pure, not at all empirical, part mental and part sensuous. Such is the formal schema, or pattern of mind.

In general, the concept of mind involves the pure, organized unity of a field of awareness. Time, the formal basis of inner sense and the bond of all images, contains a field of pure awareness. Formally, it is sufficiently homogeneous with the category that gives it unity so that it is general and is abstractly regulated. On the other hand, it is sufficiently homogeneous with phenomena so that time is a feature of every element in a field of sense data. Hence time indicates an application of categories to phenomena because it is a form, or schema of the mind's ideas. It mediates the subsuming of phenomena under categories.

After what has been proved in the deduction of the categories, I hope that no one will remain in doubt whether pure ideas are useful merely empirically or whether they also have formal uses. Are they conditions of experience and, so, do they refer only abstractly to phenomena? Or are they conditions of the existence of things in general and, so, do they extend to things-themselves, unrestricted by our senses? As we have seen, ideas are impossible or have no meaning without an object to which they, or elements within them, refer. So they cannot refer to things-themselves (without even asking how or whether such things could be known).

We also saw that objects can be known by us only when our senses are modified by them and, finally, that a pure, abstract idea contains, in addition to mental operations pertaining to the categories, an *architectonic of sense.* This is the general form through which the categories are applied to an object. It effects a formal arrangement of sense perception, through which the use of pure mind is restricted, and is called the mind's schema. The mental processes involved in such schemata become, then, the schematism or general forms of pure mind.

The schema itself is a product of imagination. Since, however, organization by imagination is not aimed at any special awareness but only at creating unity in sense perception, a *schema* must be distinguished from an *image.* Five points set in a row, thus . . . . . make an image of the number five. On the other hand, the printed figure 5 is a symbol of the general idea of five and constitutes its schema. If the number were 1,000, an image of 1,000 dots could hardly be checked for congruence with the general idea of 1,000. The figure 1,000, however, shares the nature of both the image and the pure idea, and so is an imaginative device for the application of the idea. This representation (by numbers, for example) of a general process of imagination, by which an idea is provided with a symbol, I call the schema of the idea.

The fact is that our pure sense ideas are not based on images of things but on schemata. No image would ever be adequate to the idea of a triangle. It could never attain the degree of generalization which would make it applicable to all triangles, whether right-, obtuse-, or acute-angled, but would be limited always to some portion of this range. The triangle schema exists only in thought and regulates the organization of pure spatial figures in imagination. Still less will an object of experience or its image ever be an adequate empirical idea, immediately related to the schema of imagination, like a rule or general idea governing awareness. The idea "dog" constitutes a rule by which my imagination might construct the outline of a four-footed animal; but it would be limited to no special shape, such as my experience, nor to some concrete image which I might call to mind or might specify, such as my pet dog, or a beagle.

The schematism of mind, applied to phenomena and their outlines, uses *an art deep hidden in the human soul.* It involves a technique which nature will hardly leave unguarded or open to human gaze. This is all we can say: An image is an empirical product of imagination* reproducing something remembered. The schema of a sense idea (such as space figures) is the product, the monogram of pure, abstract imagination, by which images first become possible. These images can be connected to the ideas to which they belong, but to which they are never wholly congruent, only by means of the schema. On the other hand, the schema of a pure idea never wholly fits an image. It is pure organization, regulated by the fact that unity comes of an idea, a categorical idea. It is a formal product of imagination, a product concerned with the control of inner sense by its own form, namely, time. It can be represented in many ways, but the ways must be related, as long as they are connected abstractly and in advance, to a pure idea and conform to the unitary self.

So that we may not further delay with dry and tedious analysis of the requirements of formal schema of pure ideas, let us explain them at once in connection with the categories and in that order.

To the external senses, the pure image of all magnitudes is space; for sensed objects generally, it is time. But the pure schema of magnitude as an idea is number, the result of the addition of successive homogeneous units. Generally, number is unity organized in a field of homogeneous awareness, unity due to the fact that I generate time as I apprehend what I am aware of.

The pure idea of reality is that in general it corresponds to sensation. The very idea of it indicates something that exists in time. So the idea of negation stands for nonexistence in time. The opposition of the two ideas arises from the distinction of a moment of time which is either occupied or empty. Since time is only the form of awareness of phenomena, what corresponds in phenomena to sensation is the formal matter of all objects, or things-themselves (that is, their reality or thinghood). Every sensation, however, has a degree or magnitude to which it can occupy a given time more or less (that is, it can occupy the internal sense) until it is reduced to nothing or to a negation. There is thus a relation, a connection, or better, a transition from reality to negation, which makes reality a representable quantity.

* See p. 40.

The schema of reality, as a quantity of something occupying time, is the continuous and uniform generation of realities in time, so that as time goes on, the degree of sensation may be diminished to nothing or increased from nothing to some given magnitude.

The schema of substance is the permanence of reality in time: it is a conception of reality as the substratum against which time is measured and which therefore remains when all else changes. Time does not pass; only changeable things pass away in time. So substance corresponds to unchanging and abiding time, and it is the unchanging and abiding substratum of phenomena. It is only in relation to substance that the coexistence and succession of phenomena in time can be determined.

The schema of the origin and cause of a thing is that reality from which the thing considered follows whenever it could occur. In the field of perception, it regulates succession.

The schema of community, or reciprocity, or the reciprocal causality of similar substances correlates the characteristics of one substance with those of another.

The schema of possibility organizes ideas with respect to time. For example, opposites cannot be simultaneously in a given thing but must occur one after the other. The schema is therefore a time regulator of the ideas of a given thing.

The schema of actuality is existence at a given time.

The schema of necessity is the existence of an object for all time.

One sees from all this that the schema of each category involves a particular time control. The schema of size is the generation of time, and its organization, by successive observations of an object. The schema of quality is the organization of sense, or perception by means of the idea of time; it is the occupation of time. The schema of relation permanently connects perceptions by the rules governing time. Finally the schema of modality and its categories is time itself, time correlated with the way an object fits time. The schema of relation permanently connects perceptions by the rules governing time. The schemata are thus abstract and regulated determinants of time. The regulations involved refer in the order of the categories to the time series, the content of time, the order of time, and lastly to the comprehension of time as it refers to objects.

This indicates that what the mind's schematism accomplishes is unity in the inner field of awareness and therefore, indirectly, unity of self. Unity of self is an active function related to the inner sense. The schemata of pure ideas are therefore the true and only means by which these ideas get related to objects and so gain significance. In the end, the categories are of empirical use. By them phenomena are organized and thus rendered experiencable.

13 SYSTEM OF THE PRINCIPLES OF PURE MIND

The mind has its own inviolable rules

Mind is the world's first lawgiver: it therefore has rules which describe its own character and predict the possibilities of knowledge. These rules, or principles can be deduced from the way the mind presides over sense data by means of the schemata. In Sections I and II of the chapter which follows in 13, two introductory and familiar principles are mentioned. The first is analytic: No judgment may contradict itself; *the second pertains to amplifying judgments:* An experience must fit into the self's unity or be rejected. *For example,* one may not assert that *"the sea is boiling hot" or that "pigs have wings"* without very special justification, *such as a sense of humor.*

There follows then the "systematic presentation of the organizing principles of mind." The system followed is, as before, the system of categories. Corresponding to the four major classes of categories, quantity, quality, relation, and modality, Kant lays out four sets of principles by which mind operates its categories. The first two he calls mathematical because they are the basis of the general applicability of mathematics to the real world: (1) Awareness involves space and time and can be measured. (2) What sensation reports involves intensity and is measured by degree.

Much more important are his dynamic principles, corresponding to relation and modality, which he calls successively analogies of experience and postulates of experience. "Analogy" is a term Kant borrowed from mathematics, and certainly Newton's famed three laws of motion are analogous to Kant's "analogies." The first analogy means that there is in nature a real but undefined analogue of the experience of time as permanence or duration, which may be called "substance." The second analogy means that experience of time as succession has its objective analogue: For every event of nature there is a prior event which is its cause. The third analogy is that my experience of time as simultaneity has its analogue in the reciprocity of things in nature.

The first two of these analogies should be understood as general principles defining (1) the basis of objective experience, and (2) the basis of causal inquiry. The third analogy is regulative and is supplementary to the first two. It has no independent necessity of its own. All three involve the "inner sense" of time and are designed to lock it securely to the world of external experience without specifying what is "out there."

In Section IV, we come to the postulates of experience, *which correspond to the fourth class of categories, namely, those of modality. These postulates define* possibility, existence, *and* necessity. *Anything is possible if the idea of it meets the formal conditions of experience. Anything is actual if sensation reports it. If it is* actual *and* universal, *it is* necessary. *These rough approximations to Kant's exceedingly careful but not-too-clear statements are sufficient to indicate the main point of the postulates of experience: What is the relation of my inner life to my experience of what is not-I? Briefly, these postulates say that inner and outer reality are equally certain and that they are correlative. It is as certain that what is not-I exists as that I exist myself.*

It now becomes our work to set forth systematically the judgments the mind produces abstractly and in advance. The categories furnish natural and secure guidance to this end, for it is the relation of the categories to experience that constitutes the mind's pure knowledge. Their relation to sense in general will exhibit the complete system of the formal principles of the employment of the mind.

Section I. *The Highest Principle of Analytic Judgments.* Whatever we may know or however we know it, the universal and only negative condition applied to judgments is that no judgment may be self-contradictory; for if it were, it would come to nothing, whatever it referred to. The proposition, then, that no subject can have a contradictory predicate is called the principle of contradiction. It is a general and negative criterion of all truth, and since this present inquiry is concerned chiefly with amplifying knowledge, we must be careful never to offend against this principle even though we may not expect from it any disclosure of the truth.

Section II. *The Highest Principle of Amplifying Judgments.* General logic has nothing to do with solving the problem of amplifying judgments. It hasn't even a name for it. In formal logic, however, it is the most important task of all, and really the only one when abstract, amplifying judgments are discussed.

If knowledge is to have objective reality, that is, if it is to refer to an object, the object must be actual, and the idea of it must be referable to experience through schema. It is therefore the possibility of being experienced which gives objective reality to abstract knowledge. Experience depends on the organized unity of phenomena, on an organization of the perception of an object by ideas. Without this, knowledge would be nothing but a rhapsody of perceptions which would never fit into any context regulated by coherent consciousness.

The highest principle of amplifying judgment is that an object, as it is experience, should be subject to the conditions necessary to organized unity in the field of awareness. The formal and prior condition for organized awareness is the activity of imagination, based on the formal unity of self. When this is applied generally to possible empirical knowledge, prior and abstract amplifying judgments become possible in the light of the foregoing principle. We then say that accordingly, the conditions under which experience is possible are identical with the conditions under which it is possible to experience objects, and so there may be objective validity in an abstract and prior amplifying judgment.

Section III. *A Systematic Presentation of the Organizing Principles of Mind.* That there should be any principle here at all is solely due to mind itself, which not only is the authority regulating all occurrences but also is itself the source of the principles which require that every object, to be known, must be regulated. These principles are necessary because, without them, appearances or phenomena would never tell us anything about the objects to which they correspond.

There can be no real danger that we shall mistake empirical principles for mental principles, or the reverse. Such confusion is easily prevented. The logical necessity evident in purely mental operations is absent from empirical judgments, however widely they may be applied. There are pure, abstract principles in mathematics which I shall omit since they are derived not from pure ideas but from pure awareness. I include, however, those on which the possibility and objective validity of mathematics are based. They proceed from ideas to awareness rather than from awareness to ideas. Their use in organization is either mathematical or dynamic. Their application is concerned in part with awareness and in part with the existence of phenomena.

The abstract conditions of awareness are absolutely necessary to experience; of themselves, the conditions for the existence of an object of awareness are only accidental. Principles used in mathematics will therefore be unconditionally necessary, i.e., apodictic. Those used dynamically will be to some degree abstractly necessary, as they are used empirically in thinking of experience, but only mediately or indirectly. Despite their general certainty in dealing with experience, they do not exhibit the immediate evidence of necessity found in mathematical principles. We shall, however, be better able to judge this matter at the end of this system of principles.

The table of categories is a natural guide to a table of these principles, since the principles are really rules for the objective use of the categories. All principles of pure mind are therefore: (1) Axioms of awareness; or (2) Anticipations of perception; or (3) Analogies from experience; or (4) Postulates of empirical thought in general. I have named them more with an eye to their application than their content, and I proceed to discuss them in order.

1. *Axioms of awareness:* of which the principle is that *awareness involves extension.* In other words, phenomena are of all magnitudes and are sizable. As we are aware of them in space and time, they must become apparent through the same kind of organization of sense data as that which results in space and time.

By the words *magnitude* or *size,* I refer to my awareness of the parts of something preceding and making possible the appearance of the whole of it. I cannot imagine a line, however small, without drawing it—in thought—and generating all its parts in order from a given point. Only in this way can the initial awareness of a line be obtained. It is the same with even the smallest period of time. Here, I think of the advance from one moment to another and find a given period of time generated from its parts. Since the pure awareness of any phenomenon is either space or time, it is quantitative or sizable and can be known only through the successive organization of part with part in apprehension. Geometry, for example, is based on this kind of successive organization of its figures.

This is a formal principle of the mathematics of phenomena and greatly extends our abstract knowledge. It alone makes pure mathematics, with its complete precision, applicable to the objects of experience. As we have seen, empirical awareness is possible only by means of pure awareness of space and time. What, therefore, geometry has to say about pure awareness is valid for empirical awareness.

2. *Anticipations of perception:* of which the principle is that *reality in the sensed object is intensive, that is, a matter of degree.*

Perception is empirical consciousness, containing sensation. Phenomena are the objects of perception and not pure or formal awareness alone, like space and time. They contain, therefore, besides the awareness of the matter of an object, the reality of sensation, which is subjective and which refers to the object. There is, then, a possible step-by-step transition from empirical to pure consciousness, in which the reality of sensation finally vanishes and only pure, formal consciousness of awareness organized in space and time remains. This indicates therefore a converse process by which a sensation may increase from its beginning in pure awareness, when it is nothing, to any desired degree. Since, then, sensation is not objective and does not contain awareness of either space or time, its magnitude is not extensive but intensive.

The knowledge which enables one to know and determine abstractly and in advance what is to be learned by experience may be called *anticipation*. Sensation cannot be anticipated. If, however, there is something in each sensation, and in sensation in general, which *can* be known in advance, this also will clearly deserve the name *anticipation*. It may be surprising that anything in the experience of sensation can be predicted, when the content of a sensation can be discovered only in the experience itself. Yet this is actually so.

To one trained by formal studies to carefulness, anticipation of sensation must seem strange. The assertion that by taking thought in advance an organizing principle can be anticipated, giving the degrees of reality in phenomena, awakens doubts and difficulties. It is a question not unworthy of study: how abstract statements can be made about the organization of phenomena, when the statements anticipate purely empirical events which are of the nature of sensation.

The quality of sensation, for example, in color, taste, etc., is solely empirical and cannot be predicted abstractly or in advance. But the idea of the reality of the objects to which sensations correspond means that they actually exist, and it indicates generally that the relevant empirical consciousness has been put in order. In inner sense, empirical consciousness can be raised from zero to any desired pitch, so that an extended quantity of awareness, such as an illuminated surface, may excite as much sensation as the aggregate of many other quantities, such as smaller illuminated surfaces. An extended quantity of awareness may therefore be treated abstractly and represented as the totality of sensation experienced at any given moment. In ordered awareness it may increase, for example, from zero to a given degree.

Thus, although the nature of sensation is known only after the event, the result of its property of gradual growth can be anticipated. It is noteworthy that in quantitative things generally, only one quality can be predicted abstractly, the quality of continuity. Of qualities in general, nothing can be known abstractly except that they are intensive, that is, that they vary in degree. Everything else must be left to experience.

3. *Analogies in experience:* of which the principle is that *connected or organized perceptions make experience.*

Experience is empirical knowledge, that is, knowledge which defines an object by perception. It is an organized field of perceptions, of which a person is or may be conscious. In experience, however, perceptions come together haphazardly. No necessity requires that their interconnections take any particular pattern, or specifies their continued existence in space and time. But the relation of objects in a field of perceptions is arranged in experience, not as it may be reconstructed after a time, but in the order of the objects' occurrence in time. This can come about only through the time idea, which organizes the perceptions in a field abstractly and in advance. It carries necessity with it, and perceptions are thus organized into experience.

Time appears as duration, succession, and coexistence. Consequently there will be three rules for the time relations of phenomena. These rules precede experience and make it possible. They are not concerned with phenomena themselves but only with the existence of the phenomena and their interrelations. So these rules are neither axioms, nor anticipations, nor constitutive principles but *analogies* which regulate perceptions so that unified experience may result from them. Their significance and validity appears in the empirical work of mind.

A. The First Analogy: *The Principle of Permanence of Substance* is that in all phenomenal changes, substance endures and is permanent; the total quantity of it is neither increased nor diminished.

As one sees the field of phenomena, it is a succession of things and is, therefore, always changing. On the face of it, one cannot tell whether its various events occur simultaneously or in sequence. For this purpose, something fundamental is required, something that stays there, something permanent, something of which change and coexistence are only the modes of its being in time. So, simultaneity and succession are time relations, which are possible only in that permanent substratum which is the enduring correlate of all being and appearance, of all change and its concomitants. It is the substratum of the time experience. There is no time without it.

Time is not self-evident; so the permanence in phenomena is the substratum by which time is defined and, accordingly, the basis of organized unity in perception or experience. All that is, and all change, are to be regarded as states of the enduring substratum. As for phenomena, substance is their substratum, and change pertains to the defining conditions of their substance. The unity of experience would never be possible if new substances could begin to exist; for in that case we should lack the means, the identity of the substratum, against which to establish time's unity. This permanence is really only the way we take to represent to ourselves the existence of things as they appear.

B. The Second Analogy: *The Principle of Time Sequences* is that changes all occur according to the law connecting cause and effect.

A field of phenomena, or appearances is apprehended successively. The parts are perceived one after the other, but whether they follow one another in the object itself calls for further reflection. For example, the apprehension of a house standing before me, as a field of appearance, is a succession. The question then arises whether the house itself, considered as a field of appearance, is a sequence, and this, no one admits. What is apprehended in succession now appears as an image while the phenomenon as I see it, though only a sum of images, is regarded as the object for which the image stands. An object is distinguished from every other form of apprehension by a rule which requires that its field be organized in a special way. In all phenomena or appearances, the object is the element which meets this condition.

Let us study a field of perception containing an event, of which the preceding state is percept A, and the succeeding state, percept B. It is observed that B can only follow A; A cannot follows B, but only precede it. For example, I see a ship moving downstream. My perception of its position downstream follows my perception of its position upstream, and it is impossible that I should have first seen her downstream and then up. The order in which the perceptions succeed each other in my apprehension is fixed, and apprehension is bound to it.

In the previous example of a house, my perceptions could begin with the roof and end with the basement; or begin below and end above; or I could take in the field of awareness from right to left or left to right. In this case, there was no fixed order specifying where I must begin, to cover the field empirically. But in the perception of something in the process of happening, there is always a rule which determines the order of percepts. In this case, the subjective succession of apprehension must be derived from the objective succession of phenomena. Otherwise the order of apprehension is indeterminate, and one phenomenon is not distinguished from another.

The objective succession will follow the order in the field of phenomena, so that conforming to the rule, the apprehension of an event follows the apprehension of the preceding event. Only thus may I assert, not only of my apprehension but of a phenomenon, that it involves a succession and that I cannot arrange my apprehension except in the order of this succession.

Let us say that nothing precedes a certain event; there is nothing from which that event necessarily follows. In that case any perception of succession would be wholly a matter of apprehension, that is, subjective. We should then have only a play of images related to no object at all. The experience of an event, then, always presupposes that something preceded it from which, by rule, it follows. Without a rule that prescribes the necessity, I could not say of any one object that it is the consequence of another. Mere succession in my mind does not justify me in assuming a succession of objects. We have to show, then, that not even in experience do we attribute succession to objects and distinguish that succession from the subjective succession of our minds, unless there is a rule which requires us to follow the actual order of perceptions as they occur rather than any other order.

In the organization of phenomena, the images of a field are always successive. There is order in imagination by which the present, to the extent it has come to be, refers to a preceding state, as a correlate of the present event. Here the preceding state, even if undetermined, still governs the present event as its consequence and connects the present with itself in the time series. It is, therefore, an indispensible law of experience that phenomena of times past determine those in succeeding times and that what happens in the later times may occur only as the rules for past phenomena require them to occur. It is only in phenomena that the continuous succession of time may be perceived.

In other words, the relation of cause to effect is the condition of objective validity in empirical judgments, which is to say, it makes experience possible. The principle of the causal relation in the sequence of phenomena is therefore also valid for objects of experience and is the basis on which all experience is possible. Thus, as time is, for the senses, the abstract condition for continuous progress from what is, to what follows, so mind, operating through the unified self, is the abstract condition for determining the position of phenomena in time, placing it in the series of causes and effects. Inevitably the causes lead to the effects and so render empirical knowledge of the time relations universally and objectively valid.

C. The Third Analogy: *The Principle of Coexistence* is that substances, as far as they can be observed to be coexistent (simultaneous) in space, are completely reciprocal.

If, in a field of substances seen as phenomena, each could be completely isolated so that none acted on others or received any influence in return, I would say that their coexistence would not be perceptible and that the existence of one would not by any means imply the existence of any other. There must, therefore, be something other than the mere existence of A and B by which A determines B's position in time, and B determines A's. Only thus can these substances appear as coexistent.

When one substance is the cause of another, the first affects the position of the second in time. Each substance, therefore, contains the cause of certain effects in other substances and, at the same time, the effects of causes located in those other substances. This means that substances must be dynamically interrelated if their coexistence is to be experienced. Now, as for the objects of experience, anything without which these objects could not be experienced is necessary. It is therefore necessary that all substances of coexisting phenomena should participate in a community of reciprocal interaction.

4. The general *Postulates of Experience* are: (1) Anything is *possible* if the idea of it meets the formal conditions of experience. (2) Anything is *actual* if sensation reports it. (3) Anything is necessary if it is actual and universal.

The categories of modality do not enlarge the ideas to which they are attached as predicates. They express only their relation to mind. On this account, the principles of modality, which are the postulates of experience, are only explanations of the ideas of possibility, actuality, and necessity as applied to experience. They concern possible experience and its organized unity, in which alone the objects of knowledge appear.

The postulate of the possibility of things requires that ideas of them should agree with the formal conditions for experience. This general form of objective experience contains all the organization required for knowledge of an object. An idea would be empty and objectless if its organization did not stem from experience. Either it is derived from experience and is an empirical idea or it is abstract, a pure idea, upon which experience formally depends. In this case, it still comes from experience since its object is encountered only in experience. If an idea abstracts a form of experience, it has objective reality: it applies to possible things. As for reality, it refuses concrete conception apart from experience. For reality involves sensation, which is the material of experience. It does not touch the forms of relations with which one may play in fancy.

The postulate of the actuality of things does not require immediate perception of the sensation by which one is conscious of the object whose existence is to be known, but a connection of the object with some perception, as defined by the analogies of experience. A *mere idea of a thing is not the mark of its existence*. For even though the idea is complete, existence has nothing to do with completeness but only with the question whether the perception of the thing could precede the idea. The idea is merely possible if it precedes perception. The perception which provides content to the idea is the sole mark of actuality. A thing may be known abstractly to exist, prior to perception, if it involves certain perceptions as provided by the *analogies* of experience.

The third postulate concerns the material necessity of existence and not merely the logical and formal necessity which connects ideas. The necessity of existence does not appear from ideas but only from perceived things, as the universal laws of experience provide. Now, no actual thing is known to be necessary from the conditions determining other things, except the existence of the effects of given causes as the causal law provides. Therefore we know, not that things themselves are necessary, but the existence of their states, and this is known only as the causal law provides, from other states which are perceived. The criterion of necessity is in the law of possible experience, the law that whatever happens is determined abstractly and in advance through its cause in the field of phenomena. Only those effects in nature whose causes are specified are known to be necessary. The sign of necessity extends only to the limits of the field of experience.

The proposition that nothing happens through blind chance is an abstract law of nature. So is the proposition that in nature no necessity is blind but is always conditioned and therefore intelligible.

14 PHENOMENA AND NOUMENA

Mind has boundaries

Mind in me, says Kant, has the property of being sensitive to the world around me, and accordingly, I am aware of an infinite variety of sense data coming to me from my environment. As I get it, fresh from the world, this sense data is a chaos. I organize it so that individual objects appear and "it makes sense," and from it, ultimately, I gain knowledge of the world. I do this through mind-furniture, which I call categories. They are original with mind and native to it. I do not acquire them by or through experience: they are not partly but purely mental. They are architectonics, through which experience is organized.

The categories work by virtue of imagination, which is a function of mind and which selects the spots at which appropriate categories are applied to sense data. For this process there are of course rules, which are part of the fine-structure of mind and which govern the specific application of categories. These rules I call schemata. So my life and my world take order, and from it knowledge comes and phenomena appear. The phenomena are my percepts or experiences of objects in the world about me. There is, therefore, ample room for my domain to expand. The world contains an infinity of objects which are possible phenomena but which have not yet rung my doorbell.

But does the world contain, in addition, real objects which are not possible items of experience, entities which may not be phenomena? I assert that it does, although I cannot tell positively what they are. Negatively, I can say that an object-itself, apart from my awareness, experience, or knowledge, must be something. Reality is not exhausted by my mind. So, I call that something a noumenon, or thing-itself, in contradistinction to a phenomenon, which is al-

ready my experience. In this negative sense it marks the boundary beyond which mind does not go because experience cannot follow.

Of course, mind has objects like God or the $\sqrt{-1}$, *which are not even possible phenomena and which yet are by no means fantasies. As objects of mind, they are entitled to be called noumena. May these in any way be objects of experience? Not unless we assume a special intellectual perception, and this we may not do. Phenomena are experience but noumena are not. Of noumena, one can only say that they can be thought without contradiction. This result will form the basis for an examination of metaphysics for illusions.*

We have now explored the land of pure reasoning and carefully surveyed every part of it. We have measured its extent and put everything in its right place. It is an island, by nature enclosed within unchangeable limits. It is the land of truth (enchanting name!), surrounded by a wide and stormy ocean, the native home of illusion, where cloud banks and icebergs falsely prophesy new lands and incessantly deceive adventurous seafarers with empty hopes, engaging them in romantic pursuits which they can neither abandon nor fulfill. Before we venture on this sea, we ought to glance at the map of the island and consider whether or not to be satisfied with it, lest there be no other territory on which to settle. We should know what title we have to it, by which we may be secure against opposing claims.

We have seen that the produce of mind is not borrowed from experience but is for use only in experience. The mind's principles may be either abstract and constitutive, like mathematical principles, or merely regulative, like dynamic principles. In either case they contain nothing but the pure schema of possible experience. Unity comes into experience from the organizing unity of mind, which the mind confers on self-consciousness via imagination; and phenomena, as the data of possible experience, must fit into that unity abstractly and in advance. These rules of mind not only are true but also are the source of all truth, the reason for the agreement of our knowledge with objects. They contain the basis on which experience is possible, that is, experience viewed as the sum of one's knowledge of objects. We are not, however, satisfied with an exposition merely of what is true;

we want also to know what mankind otherwise wants to know. This long, critical inquiry would hardly seem worthwhile if at the end of it, we have learned only what would have gone on anyway in everyday mental operations.

Even if our minds do work satisfactorily without such an inquiry as this, the inquiry has one advantage. The mind that is in us is unable to determine for itself the limits of its own uses. That is why the deep inquiry we have set up is required. If we cannot decide whether certain questions lie within our mental horizon, we must be prepared for getting lost among the delusions that result from overstepping our limitations.

If we can know certainly whether the mind can use its principles only within experience and never purely formally, this knowledge will have important consequences. The formal use of an idea is its application to things in general and to entities for which we have no sense data; the empirical use of an idea is its application to phenomena, or to objects of possible experience. It is evident that only the latter application is practicable. For example, consider the ideas of mathematics, first as pure awareness: space has three dimensions; there can be but one straight line between two points; etc. Although these principles are generated abstractly in the mind, they would mean nothing if their meaning could not be demonstrated in phenomena. It is therefore required that a pure idea be made sensible, that is, that one should or can be aware of an object corresponding to it. Otherwise, the idea, we say, would make no sense, i.e., it would be meaningless.

The mathematician meets this need by the construction of a figure which is, to the senses, a phenomenon, even though abstractly produced. In the same science, the idea of size finds its meaning and support in number, whether by fingers, or abacus beads, or in strokes and points on the printed page. The idea is always abstractly conceived, as are the amplifying principles and formulas derived from them; but finally, their use and their relation to their indicated objects appear only in experience, even though they contain the formal conditions of the possibility of that experience.

That this is the case with all the categories and the principles spun out of them, appears as follows. We cannot really define the categories, or make the possibility of their objects intelligible, without descending at once to the conditions of sense and the forms of phenomena, to which, as their only objects, the categories must be limited. If this condition is removed, all meaning, all relation to an object disappears, and no example will make the meaning of such an idea comprehensible.

The idea of size is not explainable except by saying that it is the definition of a thing achieved by the thought of how many times a unit goes into it. This how-many-times is based on successive repetition and therefore on the organization in time of something homogeneous. In contradistinction to negation, reality can be explained only if time is considered as all-encompassing and either full or empty. If permanence (everlasting existence) is left out, nothing remains of the idea of substance except the logical presentation of a subject, a subject which I try to realize by imagining one that can never be a predicate. If time is omitted from the idea of cause, the time required by rule for something to follow from something else, there would be nothing left in the pure category but the conclusion that something follows from something else. As for the idea of community, if the definitions of possibility, actuality, and necessity involve only pure thought, there is no explanation of them that is not obviously tautological. The magic which substitutes the logical possibility of an idea—the idea is not self-contradictory—for the formal possibility of things—there is an object which corresponds to the idea—deceives and satisfies only the uninstructed.

So the *Formal Analytic* has this important result, that abstractly and in advance, mind can anticipate only the general form of a possible experience, and since only phenomena can be objects of experience, the mind cannot go beyond the limits of sensibility within which objects are perceived.

A basic illusion, which is hard to evade, is met at this point. In their origin, the categories are not based on sense, as are the *forms of awareness*, space and time, and they seem, therefore, to permit application beyond all objects of sense. On their part, once again, they are nothing but *forms of thought*. At the same time, if we call certain objects *appearances, sensed entities or phenomena*, we distinguish our awareness of them from what they are in their own nature. In so doing, the objects-themselves are placed in opposition to the sensed entities, even though awareness does not show the opposition. Or we may oppose other possibilities, objects of mind but not of sense, to sensed entities. All these objects which are not sensed we may call *intelligible entities* (*noumena*). The question then is: have the mind's pure ideas any meaning for noumena, so that they may be a means of knowing them?

At the outset, however, an ambiguity appears which could give rise to serious misunderstanding. When an object in a certain relationship is called a phenomenon, the mind simultaneously forms an idea of the object-itself and, therefore, conceives that it can produce ideas of such objects. And since mind yields no ideas other than categories, the supposition that the object-itself is thought of through these pure ideas arises. So one may be led to treat this wholly indeterminate idea of an intelligible entity, of something generally outside sense, as if it were a determinate idea of an entity which can be known in some special way.

If *noumenon* means something which is not an object of sense and so is abstracted from awareness, this is the negative sense of the term. If, however, it means an object of nonsensible awareness, we presuppose a special kind of awareness, which is purely mental, not part of our equipment, and of which we cannot imagine even the possibility. This would be *noumenon* in the positive sense of the word.

The doctrine of sense perception is thus a doctrine of the noumenon in the negative sense. It is a doctrine of things to be considered apart from normal human awareness, things or entities which are not phenomena but things-themselves. At the same time, for entities considered apart from normal awareness, the categories are of no use. They have meaning only within the awareness which is unified in space and time.

The possibility of a thing can never be proved from the fact that an idea of it is not self-contradictory; it can be proved only when the idea is supported by a corresponding field of awareness. If, then, the categories are applied to objects which are not phenomena, it is necessary to postulate an awareness other than sense awareness. The object would then be a noumenon in the positive sense of the word. Since this kind of awareness, i.e., intellectual awareness, is not part of our minds, the use of the categories cannot be extended beyond the objects of experience. There may indeed be intelligible entities corresponding to sense entities. There may be intelligible entities unrelated to our senses, but if so, the ideas of our minds, being merely forms of sense awareness, would not apply to them. Noumenon must therefore be understood only in the negative sense.

Withdraw thought (the categories) from experience, and no knowledge of any object remains; for awareness by itself involves no thought and does not refer to any object. But if awareness is withdrawn, the forms of thought remain, that is, the means of defining an object as a field of possible awareness are still there. So the categories outreach awareness, since by them objects in general are thought without reference to the special way they are perceived. They do not, however, govern a wider field of objects. This would be impossible unless another kind of awareness were presupposed, and there is no justification for this.

The division of objects into phenomena and noumena, and the world into a world of the senses and a world of mind, is not admissible in the positive sense, even though the division of ideas as sensible and mental is legitimate. For we cannot conceive a mind which knows objects, not discursively or through categories, but by a nonsensible awareness. What mind acquires through the idea of noumenon is a negative extension. It is not then limited by sense but rather, it limits sense by applying the term "noumena" to things-themselves, which are not phenomena. It also limits itself, since noumena are not to be known by means of categories. They can be thought of only as unknown somethings.

If, then, we say that the senses present objects as they appear, and the mind, objects as they are, the statement about mind is to be taken in the empirical rather than in the formal sense. It means that objects must be presented as objects of experience, as completely related phenomena, and not as things apart from experience and sense, objects of pure mind. With all formal and extraordinary knowledge classifiable under the categories, the objects of pure mind will always remain unknown. Understanding and sense define objects only when used together. When they are separate, we have awareness without ideas, or ideas without awareness. Neither, alone, can be applied to any determinate object.

15 THE ATTACK ON ILLUSION

"Something there is that doesn't love a wall"

In reading The Critique of Pure Reason thus far, it has been convenient to substitute "mind" for "reason" because generally, by reason, Kant has meant the whole knowing process. Now, midway in his essay, in The Transcendental Dialectic, Kant temporarily makes reason one among other functions of mind. It is a confusing switch but one to which readers of Kant should be accustomed. Reason now is the high court of mind and issues all-inclusive, organizing, and unifying ideas which do transgress the rules of knowledge. There are three such ideas: God, soul, and universe, and to describe them Kant introduces a new term: transcendent. Reason's three ideas are not "transcendental," i.e., formal; neither are they "knowledge" or principles of experience.

If, however, a man looks up and off and out-beyond, and is not content within the limits of experience, and lets his reason begin freely to operate, these three ideas are normal results and they are transcendent. That is to say, they are the result of mind not staying within the bounds of experience but claiming autonomy whenever it is occupied with reasoning. For this is the nature of man's mind, that it will not stay within any formal bounds as long as knowledge is conditioned, partial, or relational. Man, being conditioned, partial, and a creature of relations, cannot be satisfied short of reaching the top of the highest peak, where reality is met as unconditioned, whole, and unrelated. This belief is the mainspring not only of Kant's philosophy; it had been the mainspring of German philosophy ever since it was first offered in German, by Meister Eckhart (ca. 1300).

True to his critical philosophy, however, Kant says that reason's three ideas are "regulative." They are boundary markers, so to speak, indicating the limits of human knowledge. They are illegitimate *only when they are represented as being what they are not: items of knowledge supported by experience; and because they are misrepresented with all the subtlety with which a man can beguile himself, a special science is required to study reason (as Kant now means it) and its produce. This science is dialectic, "the logic of illusion," a critical evaluation of mind's operation in nonphysical matters. (See supra Section 9, the closing paragraph.)*

We have already called dialectic a logic of illusion. This does not mean that it is a doctrine of probability, for probability is truth known merely on insufficient grounds. There is still less reason to regard appearance and illusion as identical. For neither truth nor appearance are in the object, but in the judgment by which one thinks of it. The senses do not judge, and so they do not err. Truth and error, and the illusion which leads to error, come with judgments, i.e., in the relations of objects to minds.

It is not our work at present to deal with empirical illusion (for example, optical illusion) which occurs even in the use of otherwise correct rules of the mind, and through which, under the influence of imagination, our minds go wrong. We are here concerned rather with formal illusion, which works by principles not intended for application to experience, in which there is at least a criterion of correctness. Formal illusion, despite the warnings by criticism, leads one away, beyond the empirical use of categories, to entertain the delusion that one really has extended the reach of mind beyond warranted limits.

Principles applicable only within possible experience are here called *immanent*; those which tend to transgress these limits are *transcendent*. *Transcendental* (*formal*) and *transcendent* are not interchangeable words. The principles of pure mind, as explained above, are applicable only empirically and not beyond the limits of experience. A principle, then, which removes these limits and requires their actual transgression is to be called *transcendent*.

Logical illusion, in which forms of reasoning are imitated (the illusions of formal fallacies or paralogisms), results solely from lack of attention to the rules of logic. Logical illusion disappears at once when one's attention is called to it. Formal illusion, on the contrary, does not end when it is discovered nor when formal criticism exposes its emptiness. (Take, for example, the illusion in the proposition that the world must have had a beginning in time.) The reason for this is that mind, considered subjectively, has ground rules and maxims governing its use, which rules have the appearance of objectivity. So it happens that the subjective necessity of certain connections of ideas may be taken for an objective necessity which defines things-themselves. This is an illusion which can no more be forestalled than the sea can be prevented from appearing to be higher at the far horizon than at the shore, because it is seen through higher rays of light, or than the moon can be prevented by an astronomer from appearing to be larger when it rises, even though he is not deceived thereby.

It is enough, therefore, if in *formal dialectic* the illusions of formal judgment are discovered and its deceptions forbidden. There is, however, no end to formal illusions, as there can be to logical illusions. For we have here to deal with something natural and unavoidable, something based on subjective principles which pass for objective principles. So there is also a natural and unavoidable *dialectic* of pure reason, not one in which a blunderer gets entangled because he is ignorant, or which a sophist might devise to deceive an intelligent person. It is a dialectic inseparably attached to human thinking, which does not cease to play tricks even when it is exposed, or to refrain from backing the mind into momentary error, out of which it must be lifted again and again.

Mind may be regarded as the unifier of phenomena by rules. Reason is then the unifier of the mind's rules by principles. Reason is never applied immediately to experience or to objects but only to mind itself so that, abstractly and in advance, by means of its own ideas, it imparts unity to the mind's many kinds of knowledge. Reason's unity is different from the unity given by mind.

This, then, is the question we must answer for the present in a preliminary way: Can reason be isolated from mind and therefore constitute an independent source of ideas and judgments, through which they are applied to objects? Or is reason simply a subordinate function of mind which imparts logical form to given knowledge, and arranges either mental perceptions among themselves or subordinate rules under higher ones? The fact is that reason requires that a variety of rules shall be unified in principle so that there may be thorough-going harmony in mind, just as mind, in turn, subjects the variety of awarenesses to ideas, and so organizes them. But reason's principle prescribes no law for objects, nor does it contain the basis for knowing or defining objects. It is simply a subjective law of housekeeping, applied to the mind's stores and intended to reduce its ideas to the smallest possible number by comparing them. It does not allow us to demand such uniformity of objects as would be mentally comfortable, or to extend our minds, or to attribute objectivity to one's personal rules. In a word, the question is whether reason itself, pure reason, contains abstract, amplifying principles and rules and, if so, what they are.

In the first place, the reasoning of syllogisms is not used to subject awareness to rules, as the mind does with its categories. It works on ideas and judgments. In the second place, in its logical use, reason seeks the general condition of its judgment (the conclusion), and the syllogism itself is nothing but a judgment made under a general rule, the major premise. But since reason must seek, as long as may be, the condition of a condition, by means of a prosyllogism, and so is subject again and again to experiment, it is easy to see that the peculiar function of reason in logic is to discover in an unconditioned final term, something which completes the unity of conditioned knowledge.*

This logical rule, however, cannot become a principle of pure reason except on the assumption that, given one condition, the whole series of conditions follows, one term subordinate to the next, and that the series as a whole is unconditioned.

The principles which are derived from this supreme principle of pure reason will, however, be transcendent. It will be impossible to make any adequate empirical use of them. The supreme principle will therefore be different from the mind's principles, the use of which is wholly immanent, since their only theme is the possibility of experience. Take the principle of the series of conditions extending up to the unconditioned final term (either in the organization of phenomena or the general thought of things). Is it objectively applicable? What consequences follow from it for the empirical use of mind? Or is there no such objectively valid mental principle? Is it only a logical precept which requires elevation to ever-higher conditions, until perfection is near and the highest mental unity possible to man

* For discussion of the series alluded to in this passage, see pp. 122 ff.

enters knowledge? We have to find out, I say, whether this requirement of reason, through a misunderstanding, has been treated as if it were a formal principle of pure reasoning or whether we have been too quick to postulate such unlimited perfection to the series of conditions of objects. In this case, what other misunderstandings and delusions have crept into syllogisms whose premise is derived from pure reason? These questions provide the work of formal dialectic which we shall develop from its sources deep in the human mind. The dialectic will be divided into two parts. The first is about transcendent ideas of pure reason. The second is about transcendent and dialectical syllogisms.

The mention of reason's ideas at once suggests something not confined to experience, because it concerns knowledge of which experience is only a part. All experience pertains to it, yet none is commensurate with it. Reason's ideas serve for comprehension; the mind's ideas merely help perception. If an idea contains something unconditioned, it can never be an object of experience even though all experience pertains to it. The idea of the unconditioned final term of a series of phenomena is something to which inference from experience leads and by which the usefulness of ideas may be estimated, but it is not itself a part of organized experience. Thus, as the mind's pure ideas have been called *categories,* reason's ideas are now given a new name, *transcendent ideas,* a name which has now to be explained and justified.

Plato used the word "idea" to mean something not borrowed from sense but far surpassing those pure ideas of mind with which Aristotle was concerned. Plato found nothing in experience to correspond to it. To him, ideas were archetypes of things-themselves and not merely keys to possible experience, as were the categories. To his mind, they issued from the Supreme Reason, thence to be shared by human reason. Since, however, human reason is now no longer pristine, man has to labor in his philosophy at the recollection of bygone ideas which have long since grown dim. Plato was well aware that the mind's need soars above the mere spelling out of organized unity among phenomena, so that taken together, phenomena can be read as experience. He knew that reason is naturally elevated to knowledge far beyond the possibility of experienced objects. Such knowledge has, nevertheless, its own reality and is not just lucubration.

Plato's *Republic* is supposedly a striking example of dreamlike perfection which has its place only in the brain of an idle thinker. Brucker thought it comic that a philosopher should maintain that a prince could rule well only if he participated in the ideas. It would be better, however, to go back over Plato's thoughts, and where that great man left us helpless, to set the matter in its true light through fresh efforts, rather than to put his work away as useless, on the sorry and ruinous excuse that it is impracticable. Nothing can be more harmful or unworthy of a philosopher than a vulgar appeal to alleged contrary experience.

Even though this perfect state may never come to pass, the idea which sets up a maximum as an archetype, to move the legal organization of mankind nearer to perfection, is still right. For no one may or should try to determine how far mankind can go, or to say what gulf remains to be crossed before the goal is realized. Freedom empowers men to pass beyond any specified limit.

It is not only in morals that human reason shows real causality. Ideas also are operative causes of actions or objects. Plato correctly sees clear proof of nature originating from ideas. Plants, animals, the ordered regularity of the world and presumably, therefore, of all nature, show clearly that ideas made it all possible. No single creature, under the conditions in which it exists, meets the perfection in the idea of its kind. Neither does any human being measure up to the idea of humanity, the archetype of his character, which he carries in his soul. These ideas are nevertheless completely defined in the Supreme Mind as the individual, unchangeable, and original causes of things; but only when all of them are gathered up together in one world, is the result wholly adequate to the idea.

Aside from Plato's hyperbole, the philosopher's spiritual movement up from reflection on the physical world as a copy to the architectonic arrangement of it by purposes, i.e., by ideas, deserves attention and imitation. The peculiar worth of his ideas appears, however, in the fields of morality, legislation, and religion. In these fields man has experience of goodness, an experience which is possible only because of ideas, however incomplete their empirical expression may be. When its worth is not recognized, someone has judged Plato's teaching by the empirical rules his own ideas invalidate. As for nature, experience presents the rules and is the source of truth, but in moral laws, sadly, experience is the mother of illusion. It is therefore most reprehensible to limit a person's scope or to deduce laws prescribing *what ought to be done* from consideration of *what is being done*.

In what follows, I shall speak of "absolute" validity in contrast to "comparative" validity, or validity in a special sense. The latter is validity restricted by conditions; the former is validity without restriction.

Reason, formally conceived, is aimed solely at the absolute totality of organized conditions and will not stop short of absolutely unconditioned reality. Pure reason leaves to the mind everything immediately related to awareness or its organization by imagination. Of the mind's ideas, reason retains for its own exclusive uses only the idea of the absolute whole and is intended to carry the unity organized by the categories, even up to the utterly unconditioned ultimate. This may be called the reasoned unity of phenomena, as the unity expressed by the categories is mental unity. Thus reason uses the mind, not because it contains the basis of possible experience . . . but solely to direct it to a unity of which the mind itself has no idea, with a view to gathering all mental activity bearing on objects into an absolute whole. The objective use of the ideas of pure reason is therefore transcendent, while the use of the mind's pure ideas is always immanent, since they are applied only to possible experience, as their nature requires.

By "idea" I understand now a conception, necessary to reason, for which there can be no corresponding object in sense experience. Thus reason's pure ideas which are now being considered are formal, and from their point of view, all experience is defined by the absolute totality of conditions. These ideas are not arbitrarily invented but are by-products of reason that play a necessary part in the uses of mind. Finally, they are transcendent and go beyond the bounds of experience; there can never be any object adequate to a formal idea. Since, then, an idea is a conception of a maximum, no concrete instance of it can ever be given. Thus, the word "idea" tells much about its objects, the objects of pure mind; but it says little or nothing about the mind which is its subject, or about mind's reality as an idea based on experience. Since this is impracticable, the idea might as well not exist. This is why they say of a conception like this: *It's only an idea!*

So we might as well say that the absolute totality of all phenomena is only an idea; and because it cannot be projected as an image, it must remain an insoluble problem. Since, however, in the practical use of mind, our concern is only to apply the rules, concrete, if partial, instances of an idea of practical reason can actually be cited. Indeed, this is the indispensable condition of the mind's practical use. The concrete instance is limited and faulty, but it is unrestricted and therefore it is influenced by the idea of absolute perfection. Thus, practical ideas are fruitful and indispensable to mental action. Pure reason works causally in ideas . . . and we must not say of wisdom that *it is only an idea.* On the contrary, it is the idea of the necessary unity of all possible aims, and it serves as the original and least restrictive of rules in practice.

If it must be said of the formal ideas of reason that they are only ideas, that need not mean that they are superfluous or trifling. Even if they define no object, unnoticed they serve at the base of the mind as a canon of its extension and self-consistent use. Mind gets no more knowledge by means of this canon than it would get unaided, but it is better and further led. . . .

Pure ideas generally deal with organized unity of perceptions; formal ideas, on the other hand, deal with the unconditional organized unity of the totality of conditions. It follows that there are three classes of formal ideas containing in order: (1) the absolute unity of the thinking subject, (2) the absolute unity of the series of conditions of phenomena, and (3) the absolute unity of the condition of objects of thought generally.

The thinking subject is the object of psychology; the sum total of all phenomena is the object of cosmology; and the *thing* carrying the highest condition of possibility of all that can be thought, the Being of all beings, is the object of theology. Thus pure reason offers the idea of a formal doctrine of the soul, of a formal science of the world-whole, and finally, of formal knowledge of God. Mind itself could not even plan one of these sciences, let alone construct it with impeccable logic by the best logical use of reason, in syllogisms designed to enable passing from phenomenon to phenomenon, to the limit of ordered experience. They are pure and genuine products, or problems of pure reason.

The study of metaphysics has really only three proper objects: the ideas of God, freedom, and immortality. They are thus arranged so that the second idea, when added to the first, leads to the third as a necessary conclusion. Any other matters dealt with serve only for the attainment and realization of these three ideas. They are not needed for purposes of natural science but only to transcend nature. Insight into them would make theology and morals—and these two combined in religion, that is, the highest ends of human existence—dependent altogether on speculative reasoning. In a systematic layout of the ideas, the amplifying order cited above might be most suitable in the investigation which must precede it, but the analytical reverse of this arrangement is more to our purpose. Thus we shall move from the immediate experience of psychology and cosmology to theology.

16 REASON ALONE CANNOT EXTEND KNOWLEDGE

"The world may be known without leaving the house"

So Lao Tzu used to say and so, too, prophets and philosophers have said after him, especially those to whom mind has seemed the world's principal wonder and delight. The great rationalists Descartes, Leibniz, and Spinoza, in the century just prior to Kant, were among these. They sought the key to reality's infinite store in mind, God's or man's, but in mind. Mind itself, just by functioning, could discover its own mystery without experiment, or observation, or any reference otherwise. This was the origin of the learned but speculative "doctrine of the soul," or rationalist psychology, as Kant knew it.

To us who have lived in a century when only evidence that is both experimental and public can give learning credibility, the rationalist psychology of the seventeenth century may seem incredible, at least in the terms in which it was couched. But it had its point then, and it still has a point to make, as readers of Kierkegaard, Sartre, Heidegger, and Mounier, among others, will testify. There is so very much about persons that experimental psychology must miss because it is not equipped to evoke it.

Kant begins his formal attack on the illusions of reasoning with a critical examination of rationalist psychology. He reduces its basic reasoning to a syllogism, that is, to three bare statements logically connected. A syllogism is really an oversimplification of whatever it discusses. Nothing about our souls or psyches is ever reducible to a major and minor premise and a conclusion. Of course, Kant's attack also is rationalistic and therefore liable to the basic errors of mind. The syllogism is, nevertheless, a brilliant instrument for making a point, and legitimate to the extent the point is well taken. Kant's point, within limits, is well taken.

Stripped down, the allegedly fallacious syllogism of the rational *psychologists would run like this, with apologies to Kant: (1) A subject is substance; (2) A thinking being is a subject (of "I think," for example); (3) Therefore a thinking being (I, you, he) is substance (as any object is). In this word diagram, the fallacy comes of using subject and substance in two senses each. In the major premise (1), substance is a category, applicable only to objects of experience and never to pure beings. In the conclusion (3), substance is used in the sense of the substance of any object. In the major premise, subject is the purely logical subject of categorical judgment. In the minor premise (2), the subject is the self-consciousness in "I think." Both premises are analytic, or explanatory statements; the conclusion is an amplifying judgment, in which an idea not mentioned in either premise is introduced. This of course gives the illusion that reasoning brings forth new knowledge.*

Having disposed thus of the idea that soul is substance, the other three ideas concerned in the paralogisms are also seen as illusions. Since the soul is not substance, it cannot be a simple substance, or numerically identical in time, or related to other possible objects in space. It would be far better, Kant points out, to start with the category of modality rather than that of substance and find that because I think, I am a subject, a simple subject and identical in all thought.

It is inconceivable that a formal idea should have an object, even though the idea is required by the laws of mind. The formality of these ideas appears from the syllogisms by which they are derived. The premises of these syllogisms have no basis in experience. In them, reasoning moves from the unknown to the unconceived, to which process reality is attributed because of an inevitable illusion. The syllogisms are fakes, but neither fictitious nor accidental. They derive from the very nature of mind itself.

There are three kinds of syllogisms of illusion, i.e., of dialectic, and three ideas which result from them. In the first kind, which I call a *paralogism,* the reasoning moves from a formal subject with no predicate to the idea of the absolute unity of this subject, even though the thought process is without substance. This illusory inference I call a *formal paralogism.*

The second kind of false syllogism concerns the formal idea of the absolute whole of the series of conditions which defines or determines a given phenomenon. My idea of the organized, unconditioned unity of the series is always self-contradictory. From this I conclude that there must be, and is, another and opposite unity, although I have no idea what it is. I shall call the predicament of reasoning in this illusory inference the *antinomy of pure reason.* (see Section 17.)

The third kind of false syllogism is illustrated in this: From all the conditions required by objects of thought, I infer the organized and absolute unity of all things in general. From the merely formal idea of things I do not know, I infer a Being of beings of which I know even less. This illusory syllogism I shall call the *ideal of pure reason.* (see Section 20.)

A logical paralogism consists of an argument which is formally fallacious, whatever its content may be. A formal paralogism has a formal basis from which a false conclusion necessarily follows. Accordingly, this kind of fallacy has its basis in the nature of mind itself and carries with it an inevitable but not incurable illusion.

We come now to an idea not included in the general list of formal ideas, and which still has to be counted, without altering the list or implying a defect in it. This is the idea, or if you will, the judgment, *I think.* It is easy to see that this idea is the vehicle of all ideas, formal and otherwise. Thus it too is formal, even though without special title, since it serves only to introduce other thoughts to consciousness. Meanwhile, however void of sense it may be, it enables the distinction of two kinds of perceived objects. I, thinking, am an object of inner sense and am called "soul." Then, the object of outer sense is called "body." Accordingly, the expression "I, a thinking being" refers to psychology's object, and psychology is the rational doctrine of soul, supposing that I wish to know only as much about the soul as can be learned independently of experience and deduced strictly from the idea of "I."

The rational doctrine of soul is really an undertaking of this kind; for if the least bit of empirical thought or any percept of my inner states is mixed with the data, it would be empirical and no longer rational. Here, then, is a professed science, built on the single proposition: *I think*. At this point, its soundness or unsoundness should be examined as the nature of formal philosophy permits.

It is no objection that the perception of self always involves an inner experience, so that the doctrine of soul is never pure but is based on an empirical principle. For this inner perception is merely the apperception *I think*, which makes formal ideas possible, such as: *I think substance, I think cause*, etc. For inner experience and its possibility, or perception and its relation to other perceptions, cannot be regarded as empirical knowledge but must be thought of as general knowledge of experience, if there is otherwise no special definition of it. It comes under the head of investigation of the possibility of experience, which investigation is certainly formal. The least object of perception, for example, of pleasure or pain, appearing in a general account of self-consciousness would at once make rational psychology empirical.

I think is therefore the sole text from which the entire wisdom of rational psychology is to be developed. It is easy to see that this thought, if applied to an object (myself), can contain nothing but formal predicates since any empirical taint would spoil the rational purity of the science and its independence of experience.

We have only to follow the categories, except that to begin with, it is a thing, I, a thinking being, that is given. So instead of following the categories in the order of the table, we begin with the category of substance.

I. The soul is *substance*.
II. In quality, it is simple.
III. It is numerically identical, a unity and not a plurality, as in one time, so in another.
IV. It is spatially related to possible objects.

All the ideas of pure psychology arise from combinations of these elements and without any added principle. Substance merely as an object of inner sense implies immateriality; simple substance implies incorruptibility; its identity, intellectual substance, implies personality, and these three together, spirituality. Its relation to objects in space implies action and reaction with bodies. Thinking substance appears as the principle of life in matter, the soul, the basis of animality. And this, limited by spirituality, is immortality.

The four paralogisms of formal psychology refer to these conceptions. It is falsely regarded as pure reason's science of thinking being. Its only basis is the simple "I," which in itself has no content but is the bare consciousness that accompanies ideas. I, or he, or it (the thing) means only the formal subject of the thoughts =X. This subject is known only through the thoughts which are its predicates. Apart from them, we should have no idea of "it," but could only think about "it" in a circle because any judgment of "it" would have already used "it." This ineluctable inconvenience comes of the fact that *consciousness* is not a word distinguishing a particular object but is a formal matter, to some extent involving knowledge, since knowledge is required if I am to say that I am thinking something.

The proposition *I think* (as problematical) contains the form of all judgments and accompanies the categories as their vehicle. It is clear, then, that the conclusions to be drawn from it will involve the mind only formally and that they will forbid any tincture of experience, so that we may not anticipate any advantage from them. Let us then follow *I think* with a critical eye through the various predicaments of pure psychology.

THE FIRST PARALOGISM: SUBSTANTIALITY. The absolute subject of our judgments, represented by "I," which cannot be used to define anything else, is *substance.* I, a thinking being, am the absolute subject of all judgments possible to me, and no "I," or other symbol representing *me,* can ever be used to characterize something else. Therefore, as a thinking being, I am substance.

EVALUATION OF THE FIRST PARALOGISM. The first syllogism of formal psychology offers a supposedly new insight: The constant, logical subject of thought is knowledge of the real subject in which knowledge inheres. It is not possible to know anything about such a subject because a symbol or representation is changed into thought only in consciousness, in which all perceptions of the formal subject must be encountered. Beside the logical meaning of "I," we know nothing about the subject "I" itself, the subject which is the foundation of all our knowledge and thoughts. Meanwhile, the proposition *the soul is substance* may as well be allowed, with a notice that it means nothing, that it discloses none of the usual conclusions of rationalizing psychology, such as the everlasting duration of the human soul through change and death; and acknowledging that the statement that "the soul is substance" is an idea but not a fact.

THE SECOND PARALOGISM: SIMPLICITY. Anything is simple when its action cannot be considered as a composite of the actions of other things. The soul, the thinking "I," is such. Therefore, etc.

EVALUATION OF THE SECOND PARALOGISM. This is the Achilles of dialectical inferences from pure psychology. It is not merely a sophistical play of words contrived by a dogmatist to give his assertions a transient plausibility. The essence of the argument is that if many thoughts are to be one, they must all be contained in the absolute unity of the thinking subject. But no one can prove this just with ideas. For the unity of a thought which consists of many thoughts is collective, and it could just as well apply to a collective unity of various substances.

Thus the celebrated psychological proof is founded merely on the indivisible unity of an idea which only relates a verb to a person. It is clear that the *subject* of the relation is designated only formally by "I," which accompanies the thought without any indication of its character. It calls for something which will be considered simple (a formal subject), since nothing is defined by it. Nothing can be more simple than the idea of a mere *something*. The simplicity of a subject is not knowledge of the simplicity of the subject itself, for no account is given of the properties of what is designated by the utterly empty word "I," which could be applied to any thinking subject.

This much is certain, that by "I," I always think of an absolute, logical unity of subject (this is its simplicity), but not that I actually know my subject to be simple. So the proposition *I am a substance* indicates nothing more than the bare category, of which in this case I can make no specific (empirical) use. I can also say, "I am a simple substance," and the idea refers to nothing of which I am aware. So this idea tells nothing about my *self* as an object of experience because the idea of substance functions only as an organizer, without specific meaning and therefore without an object. It is pertinent only to the conditions of knowledge.

So rational psychology collapses with its supports. There is no hope here or elsewhere of expanding insight with ideas only or without referring to experience, and there is still less hope of increased insight exclusively by way of subjective thinking or through consciousness as such. The fundamental idea of simplicity is such that it never appears in experience, and there is, therefore, no point in saying that it is objectively valid.

THE THIRD PARALOGISM: PERSONALITY. Whatever is conscious of self-identity through various times is to this extent a person. Now the soul, etc. Therefore the soul is a person.

EVALUATION OF THE THIRD PARALOGISM. That my own identity is retained within the field of things and symbols of which I am aware, follows from the ideas involved and is therefore an analytic proposition. But this identity of my subject self, which I know in many forms, is not related to awareness of my self as an object. It therefore does not signify an identity or person, that is, an identity of one's own substance as a thinking being, through all changes of circumstance. To prove this, not merely an analysis of the proposition would be required, but we should need amplifying judgments based on certain awarenesses.

The consciousness of my self as identical through time is therefore a formal condition for the coherence of my thoughts, but it by no means proves the numerical identity of my *self* as a *subject*. Despite the logical identity of "I," such a change could occur in me that retention of self-identity would be ruled out, even though my changed self would still be referred to as "I," the same sound-symbol that was used before the change, recalling my preceding self and passing on the thought of it to subsequent subject-selves.

Although the doctrine of certain ancient schools, that in the world all is flux and nothing is permanent, is not reconcilable with the notion of substance, neither is it refuted by the idea of unity of self-consciousness. We cannot judge from our own consciousness whether as souls we are permanent or not. We reckon only what we are conscious of as belonging to our identity, and so we think that we are the same persons throughout the whole of conscious life. To a stranger, however, such a judgment would not serve, because the apparent permanence in the soul is encountered only as "I," the "I" which accompanies and connects experiences. We can never show that "I" (a mere thought) is not in flux just as much as any other thoughts which "I" links together.

We may keep the idea of personality, however, as we did the ideas of substance and simplicity, as long as it is considered merely formal, that is, representing a unity or identity of the subject-self which is otherwise unknown. Taken this way, the idea is necessary and sufficient for practical purposes, but it is not to be displayed as a means of extending self-knowledge through reasoning, or an advertisement of the unbroken continuation of the subject-self deduced solely from the idea of self.

THE FOURTH PARALOGISM: IDEALITY (in external relations). When the existence of something has to be inferred, as the cause of perceptions, its existence is doubtful. All external phenomena are like this; their existence is not immediately perceived. They are only inferred as the cause of perceptions. Therefore, the existence of all external objects is doubtful. I call this uncertainty the ideality of external phenomena and the doctrine thereof, *idealism*. This is compared with the other doctrine called *dualism*, which maintains the possible certainty of external objects.

EVALUATION OF THE FOURTH PARALOGISM. I distinguish my own existence as a thinking being from the existence of things external to me, among which my body is also reckoned. This is an analytic proposition, but whether this self-consciousness is possible without external things and whether, therefore, I can exist only as a thinking being, without being a man, can neither be known nor inferred from this proposition.

I am conscious of my representations (perceptions, thoughts, ideas, etc.); therefore these exist and I do, too, I who have these representations. But external objects are only phenomena (appearances) and, accordingly, species of my representations, the objects of which become something only by representation. Apart, they are nothing. External things also exist, as I myself exist, and both are real on the immediate witness of my self-consciousness. There is this difference: the representation of my self as a thinking subject depends only on inner sense; the representations which signalize extended beings belong also to outer sense. If external phenomena are regarded as representations caused in us by their objects, which do exist apart from us, it is impossible to see how the existence of these objects can be known except by inference from effect to cause. In this case, it will always be uncertain whether the cause is in us or outside of us.

Knowledge of self as an object is not increased by introspection, because a logical exposition of thought is mistaken for metaphysical definition of the object.

If it could be proved abstractly that all thinking beings are simple substances and that, as a result, personality is inseparable from them and that they are conscious of their existence apart from all matter, that would constitute a great stumbling block, an unanswerable objection to this *Critique*. This would mean taking a step outside the world of sense, into the field of noumena:—for the proposition *every thinking being as such is a simple subject* is abstract and amplifying, because, first, it goes beyond the idea on which it is based and adds mode of being to the act of thinking. Second, to the basic idea it adds a predicate, simplicity, for which experience does not provide. If valid, this would make abstract, amplifying propositions applicable, as principles, not only to possible experience but to things in general and to *things-themselves*. This result would put an end to the whole *Critique* and require a relapse into antique procedure. On closer inspection, the danger is not great.

The procedure of rational psychology is defined by a paralogism, which is illustrated in the following syllogism:

If it cannot be thought otherwise, a subject exists only as a subject and is therefore a substance.
A *thinking being, as such, can be thought only as a subject.*
Therefore it is such, and is substance.

In the major premise, a being is mentioned which can be thought in general, in all relations, and therefore as it appears in awareness. In the minor premise, it is mentioned only as it is, the subject of thought, the unity of consciousness, unrelated to the awareness which would make it an object of thought. The conclusion of the syllogism is thus reached through fallacy.

Let us proceed analytically and consider the proposition *I think*, which already includes existence, under the category of modality. Let us dismember it to find out if and how the "I" defines its existence in space and time through the content of the proposition.

In this case, the propositions of rational psychology would not start with the idea of a thinking being but from a reality. We should then infer what belongs to a thinking being from the way this reality is treated in thought after everything empirical has been removed. This is done as follows: 1. *I think;* 2. . . . *as subject;* 3. . . . *as simple subject;* 4. . . . *as an identical subject in all my thought.*

In 2, there is no requirement that I exist only as the subject and never as the predicate of something else. Subject, here, is a logical idea only. Whether or not it is to be understood as a substance is also undetermined. In 3, however, the absolute unity of self-consciousness, the simple "I," to which all thought is related, comes into its own, although the nature of subsistence of the subject is not established. Self-consciousness is real, and simplicity is implied in its possibilty. But nothing is real in space and also simple. Points are simple but points are only limits; of themselves, they are not parts of space. It follows that it is impossible to explain the nature of self as a thinking subject in terms of materialism.

In the first proposition, existence is taken for granted. This does not mean that all thinking beings exist. This would be saying too much: it would imply that their existence is absolutely necessary. It says only that *I, thinking, exist*. So the proposition is empirical and asserts that my existence is definable in terms of time. To that end, however, as I think of my self, I first need something permanent, something not provided by inner awareness. Simple self-consciousness does not enable me to define my existence, or to say whether I am substance or accident. If, therefore, materialism is inadequate to explain my existence, so is spiritualism, and the conclusion is that there is no way to know what soul is, if it is regarded as a thing apart.

How could it be possible to go beyond experience (living existence) by means of unity of consciousness, which is known simply because it makes experience possible? How could knowledge be extended to the nature of all thinking beings through the empirical proposition *I think*, which is not defined by any kind of awareness?

Rational psychology as a doctrine adds nothing to knowledge of self. As a discipline which limits speculation in this field, it prevents us from throwing ourselves into the arms of soulless materialism, on the one hand; and on the other, from getting lost in a spiritualism without foundation as far as this life is concerned. It also reminds us that it is better to see the refusal of our minds to give a satisfactory answer to curious questions about the great beyond, as a hint: we ought to turn from fruitless and extravagant speculation to fruitful, practical usage, a usage of mind directed always toward objects of experience but deriving its principles from a higher source. Our behavior would then be regulated as if our destination *were* beyond human experience and this life.

This indicates that rational psychology originated in a misunderstanding. The unity of consciousness, the subject "I," on which the categories are based is mistaken as an object of awareness to which then the category of substance is applied. That unity, however, is only unity in thought, and there is no object to accompany it. Thus, the category of substance cannot be applied because it presupposes awareness, and the subject "I" cannot be known. "I," therefore, the subject of the categories, can get no idea of my self as an object to which categories could be applied. In order to apply the categories, mind's pure self-consciousness has to be assumed, but that is what called for explanation in the first place. Similarly, "I," the subject in which the perception of time originated, cannot define my own existence by time.

17 THE ANTINOMIES OF REASONING

There are rifts in the universe of reason

Having demolished man's hope of knowing himself by purely rational methods, Kant turns to a more profound failure. A unified and unassailable theory of the universe cannot be provided by reasoning alone. Errors apart, whatever can be proved about the world as a whole by unaided reasoning, he finds the opposite can be proved just as well. This is the origin of the rifts in the universe of reason, which Kant called antinomies. An antinomy is a pair of apparently contradictory propositions based on the same assumptions. For example, "time flies" and "time does not fly" is an antinomy which may be resolved by showing that the statements refer to experiences of the same person in different circumstances. But when the contradiction stems from a hidden, false, and ineluctable assumption, the matter may be serious and not resolvable by any logic. Kant's citation of four antinomies, four simplifications of contradictory reasoning generally employed in metaphysical controversy, is serious indeed. It is serious to those who study cosmological theories in this or any age. Cosmological theories can hardly be limited to possible human experience, even when human senses are multiplied by instruments of great power.

Did the world have a beginning in time and is it spatially limited? Yes and No, to both questions. Time has not outmoded this antinomy nor the assumption on which it is based. It could be resolved by measurement but only by a person prepared to measure infinite quantities, if necessary. Since nobody can do this, both the Yes and the No can be argued to the extent of one's interest in doing so. Even today, one may choose sides by surveying the weight of evidence, but the weight of evidence cannot conceal the antinomy hidden underneath and still guiding the discussion.

Is matter infinitely divisible? Yes and No. Probably Kant's understanding of matter as phenomenal would indicate that he was here concerned with purely metaphysical conceptions. But the antinomy is familiar today to physicists and philosophers alike and could be resolved only by evidence that the latest division of matter is ultimate or that the ultimate division of matter does not exist. The antinomy arises from the assumption that man can know the answer, that it is within his range of experience.

Is there freedom in the world, that is, are there uncaused causes? Yes and No. The proofs pro and con freedom, which logic offers, have undoubtedly convinced some people and provided others with a rationalization for what they believe anyway. The antinomy arises from the assumption that freedom and causes alike are measurable, objective entities. It is important, however, because freedom is a prime condition of moral life. Kant tells us that the idea of freedom is necessary to account for man's nature as a moral being and that the resolution of the antinomy is not theoretical but practical.

Is God? Is there an absolutely necessary being who is the uncaused cause of all? Yes and No. Kant treats this antinomy by pointing out that two kinds of causes make room for each of the two answers. His presentation, however, demolishes logical argument either as an evangelizing agent or as a deterrent to belief. He will show that the idea of God has uses and that one can argue from the use to the faith if he will. Reason may support the mystic's discoveries but it is no substitute for them and no real danger to them, either.

Formal paralogisms set up one-sided illusions about the subjects of our thinking, but no illusion arising directly from a reasoned idea ever gives support to an opposing assertion. A formal paralogism thus gives spiritualism an advantage, even though the advantage dwindles to a mere wraith in the fire of critical investigation, when its radical defect cannot be denied.

It is quite otherwise when reasoning is applied to the objective organization of the world of phenomena. When an effort is made to establish the principle of unconditioned unity in this field and it is apparently successful, such contradictions develop that all pretensions to a cosmology have to be abandoned. For here we meet a phenomenon new to the human mind, a wholly natural antithesis which needs no subtleties or snares for its work, but into which mind falls naturally and inevitably. To be sure the new phenomenon safeguards mind so that it does not sleep with fictitious convictions, which could result from paralogisms. Instead, one is tempted either to give up in skeptical despair or to adopt a dogmatic and stubborn insistence on selected assertions, without doing justice to opposite arguments. Either way lies the death of sound philosophy, compared to which the death due to one-sided illusions might be called euthanasia.

Before the cleavages and confusions caused by the contradictions in the laws (antinomies) of reasoning appear on the scene, a few remarks are in order to explain and justify the treatment of the subject that follows. I shall call all formal ideas referring to the absolute totality of organized phenomena *cosmic concepts*. Accordingly, as a paralogism of pure reasoning formed the basis of a dialectical psychology, an antinomy of pure reasoning will expose the formal principles of a cosmology which pretends to be pure and rational. It will not show that this cosmology is valid or acceptable, but as one might suppose from its being called a *contradiction in reasoning,* it is irreconcilable with phenomena and is accompanied by deception and illusion.

In order to lay out these ideas with systematic precision and by principle, two points must be remembered.

First. Let us speak of the series *m, n, o,* in which *n* is conditioned by *m,* and *o* by *n*. The series ascends from the conditioned *n* through *m* and *l, k, j,* etc., and descends from the condition *n* through the conditions *o*, and *p, q, r,* etc. If *n* is given, the first series is presupposed and reason requires that *n* is possible only by means of it; *n* however, does not depend on the subsequent series *o, p, q, r,* etc.

I shall call the organization of the series which, on the side of conditions *m, l, k,* etc., begins with the condition nearest the given phenomenon *n* and thence goes up to more remote conditions, the regressive series; on the side of the conditioned from the first consequence to the more remote, the progressive series. The first series moves through antecedents and the second through consequents.

Cosmological ideas are concerned with all the regressive organization of conditions and not with the consequents. The problem of pure reason implied by the progressive series is gratuitous and unnecessary to the complete comprehension of the phenomenon, for which only the antecedents are required.

Second. Pure and formal ideas come only from the mind and not by reasoning. It may be that reasoning sets the mind's ideas free from the inevitable limitations of possible experience, and with them seeks extension beyond the bounds of experience. This happens because reasoning requires, on the side of conditions, absolutely all the conditions for each conditioned entity, the conditions or categories the mind uses to organize the unity of phenomena. So categories get changed into formal ideas to give absolute completeness to the empirical organization by extending it up to the Unconditioned (which is possible theoretically but not in practice). This is required by the principle that *if a conditioned entity is given, so is the whole sum of its conditions as well as an absolutely unconditioned entity*, through which alone the conditioned is possible. Formal ideas are thus, in the first place, only categories extended to the unconditioned and can be arranged in a table in the order of category titles. Not all categories are suited to this treatment but only those for which organization occurs as a series of subordinate, and not co-ordinate, conditions.

In order to arrange a table of ideas according to the table of categories, we first take the two original quanta of all awareness, time and space. Time itself is already a series and, indeed, the formal condition of all series. With reference to the present moment, the past, as an antecedent condition, can be distinguished abstractly and in advance from the future, which is consequent. Hence, the formal idea of the absolute totality of the series of conditions for any conditioned entity refers only to time past. Reasoning requires that all time past should be regarded as the necessary condition of the present moment.

There is no distinction in space between progression and regression because all parts of space exist together, as an aggregate and not as a series. Since the parts of space are never subordinate to each other but always interco-ordinated, one part is not a condition of the possibility of another and so does not, as in time, set up a series. The organization by which the many parts of space are comprehended, however, does make a series, because this comprehension is successive and takes time. In that series, the aggregated spaces, as for example, the feet in a rod, when added to a given space, constitute a condition which limits it. The measuring of space ought therefore to be considered as organizing the series of conditions pertaining to a given entity. There is this difference: in space the side of the conditions is not different from the side of the conditioned. Thus, regression and progression are the same. Each part of space is limited by another but not given by it. Each limited space is regarded as conditioned and presupposes the next space as its limiting condition, and so on. So the formal idea of the absolute totality of the organization of conditions applies to space as well.

Second, matter as the reality of space is a conditioned entity whose parts are its inner conditions and whose parts of parts are remoter conditions, and so on. This is a regressive organization, all of which, absolutely, is required for reasoning. It is possible only by complete division, through which finally the reality of matter vanishes into nothingness, or by becoming simple, ceases to be matter. Here then is a series of conditions and some progress toward an unconditioned entity.

Third, in the categories of real relations between phenomena, the category of *substance* with its *accidents* is unsuited to a formal idea. It offers no inducement for reasoning under regressive conditions. This is also true of the community of substances which is only an aggregate and contains nothing on which to base a series. Substances are not subordinated to one another as conditions of possible existence. This was the case with space, the limits of which are defined only by other spaces. That leaves the category of causality, which offers a series of causes behind a given effect, enabling the ascent from the conditioned to the conditions, and so answers the questions raised by reasoning.

Fourth, the ideas of possibility, reality, and necessity do not lead to series, except as an accident must be considered conditioned and also as the accident points, by a rule of the mind, to a condition which makes it necessary. This in turn will point to a higher condition until reasoning finally reaches unconditioned necessity in the totality of the series.

If the categories which of necessity lead to a series in the organization of a field of awareness are selected, there can be only four cosmological ideas, corresponding to four titles of categories:

1. The absolutely complete composition of all given phenomena.
2. The absolutely complete division of a given phenomenon.
3. The absolutely complete origin of a phenomenon.
4. The absolutely complete dependence of changeable phenomena for their existence.

In the first place, it is worth remarking that the idea of completeness, or totality concerns only the description of phenomena and not a reasoned idea of the whole of things in general. Phenomena are here considered as they are, and the perfect completeness of the conditions of their possibility is assumed for the purposes of reasoning. These conditions constitute a series, or organization which is perfect absolutely and by which phenomena can be described as the mind's laws require.

In the second place, reasoning really requires only an unconditioned entity which belongs to a serial and regressive organization of conditions. What it aims at is, so to speak, a series of premises so complete as to obviate the need of any others. An unconditioned entity is always contained in the absolute totality of a series as imagination sees it. But absolutely complete organization is only an idea, for it is not possible to know in advance whether such an organization of phenomena is possible or not. Thought evolves an idea of completeness whether it is practicable or not. Therefore, according to the categories which represent the completeness of some conditioned entity as a series of conditions, an unconditioned entity is necessarily contained in the absolute totality of the regressive organization of a field of phenomena. This is true apart from any attempt to determine how such totality is possible. So reasoning takes to the road, starting with the idea of *totality* and aiming at the unconditioned, perhaps in an entire series, perhaps in only part of it.

There are two expressions, *world* and *nature*, which sometimes collide. The former means the mathematical sum total of phenomena and the totality of their organization alike in large and small units, through composition or division. When it is regarded as a dynamic whole, this world is also called *nature*, meaning the connection of things as defined through inner causality. Nature is the sum of phenomena, interconnected by an inner causality; it is a self-subsistant whole. In this case, it is not merely an aggregate in space and time but unity among phenomena. Here the condition of an occurrence is its *cause*; the unconditioned quality of a phenomenal cause is *freedom*, while the conditioned cause, in its narrower sense, is *natural cause*. Conditioned entities are contingent; unconditioned entities are necessary. The unconditioned necessity of phenomena may be called *natural necessity*.

I have called the ideas with which we are now concerned *cosmological*, in part because by "*world*" I mean the sum total of all phenomena and because these ideas are aimed at an unconditioned entity among phenomena; and in part because formally, the word "world" means the absolute totality of existing things. We look for the completeness of world organization even though we must regress to it through its preconditions. In spite of the fact that these ideas are *transcendent* and in kind are not superior to phenomenal objects, and in spite of their referring not to noumena but to the world of sense, they still carry organization beyond experience and, in my opinion, are well named *cosmic ideas*. In view of the distinction between the mathematically and dynamically unconditioned entities, to which regression leads, the first two might be called *cosmic ideas*, in the narrower sense of *macrocosmic* and *microcosmic*. The other two are then called *transcendent ideas of nature*. Though this distinction is as yet of no importance, it may become important later.

If reasoning is applied, not only to experience but beyond it, seemingly sensible propositions are encountered which no experience will either confirm or refute. They are all free from contradiction and each will find its necessity established in the very nature of reason itself. Unfortunately, however, in each case, the opposite proposition has grounds on its side which are equally valid and necessary.

Pure reasoning's dialectic must therefore avoid sophistry of arbitrary questions raised in *special pleading*. It is to be addressed to problems actually encountered in the processes of honest reasoning. Then, too, neither a doctrine nor its opposite may involve gratuitous illusions which vanish at once on recognition. This dialectic is to deal with natural and unavoidable illusions, which continue their work even after they cease to deceive and which can never be eradicated even though they have been rendered harmless.

It will refer not to mental unity in experience but to reasoned unity among ideas, the conditions for which involve organization by rules and so belong to the mind. Since it requires absolute unity of organization, dialectic must conform to reasoning. But the conditions for this unity make it too much for the mind when it suits reasoning and too small for reasoning when it suits the mind. Thus there is conflict which is not avoidable, whatever is done about it.

Faked assertions always open up dialectical battlefields where the advantage is with the aggressor, and defeat waits for the defense. As impartial umpires we must avoid deciding which fighter is on the better side and which on the worse. Let them fight it out between themselves. Perhaps when they have tired each other and have done no real harm, they may see the futility of the quarrel and part friends.

The Antinomies of Pure Reason

The first conflict in formal ideas. Thesis: The world had a beginning in time and is spatially limited.

Proof. If the assumption is that the world had no beginning in time, an eternity must have elapsed up to any given instant and an infinite series of states of things must have passed away. The infinity of a series means that it can never be completed by successive additions. Therefore an infinite series is impossible, and a beginning is a necessary condition of the world's existence, which was to be proved.

On the second point, once again let the opposite be assumed, that the world is an infinite whole of coexisting things. Now a quantity not seen as confined within certain limits is conceivable only as the sum of its parts, and its totality is imagined only by repeated addition of unit to unit. Thus, to think of the world which fills all space as a completed whole, the successive addition of parts of the infinite world must be regarded as complete, which means that infinite time must have elapsed in the accumulation of coexisting things; but this is impossible. Accordingly, no infinite aggregate of actual things is either complete or simultaneously presented. Thus the world is not infinitely extended in space but is enclosed within limits, which was to be proved.

Antithesis. The world had no beginning and is not spatially limited; it is infinite in both time and space.

PROOF. Let it be so, that it had a beginning. Then there was a preceding time when the world did not exist, i.e., an empty time, a time when nothing could begin, because there is nothing to distinguish existence from nonexistence in any part of it. Series may begin within the world but the world itself had no beginning, and time past is therefore infinite.

As for the second clause, let us begin by assuming the opposite, that the world is finite and limited in space. Then there must be an unlimited empty space around it. Things will therefore be related within space and to space. Since the world is an absolute whole and we are aware of nothing beyond it which could be its correlate, the relation of the world to empty space would be a relation to nothing. The world, therefore, is not limited in space and is infinitely extended.

The second conflict in formal ideas. THESIS: A composite substance consists of simple parts, and nothing exists that is not either simple or composed of simple parts.

PROOF. Suppose that composite substances do not consist of simple parts. Then if composition is not thought of, no composite part and, by hypothesis, no simple parts of anything exist. Then nothing exists. Either, therefore, composition cannot be thought of as removed, or if it is removed, there is something not composite which remains, i.e., something simple. In the former case, the composition would not consist of substances because then it would be merely accidental. Without composition, the substances would still exist, self-subsistant. Since this contradicts the hypothesis, the view alone remains that composites consist of simple parts.

The immediate consequence is that the world's things are all simple entities and that their composition is merely an external state. Even though these elementary substances can never be isolated from composition, they stand to reason as primary subjects of all composition and, antecedently, as simple entities.

ANTITHESIS. No compound in the world consists of simple parts; nothing simple exists.

PROOF. Assume that a composite (as substance) is made of simple parts. Since all external relations, and so, all compositions of substances, can occur only in space, the space occupied must consist of as many parts as the composite occupying it. Space, however, does not consist of simple parts but of spaces; so each part of the composite occupies a space. The absolutely primitive parts of the composite are simple, and not themselves composite. The simple therefore occupies a space. But all real things occupying space are composites of things external to each other, which are not accidents and could not be external to each other without substance. It follows that the simple would be composed of substances, and this is self-contradictory.

The second proposition of the antithesis, that there is nothing simple, means only that absolute simplicity cannot be established from experience or perception, either externally or internally. Thus simplicity is just an idea without demonstrable reality, and being without an object, it has no point as an explanation of phenomena. For if it were assumed that an object of this formal idea might be found in experience, the experience would have to be free of a field of elements external to each other or compounded into unity. We may not conclude from the absence of such a field that it could not be found otherwise in the awareness of some object; but without such proof, the existence of absolute simplicity cannot be established. It follows, then, that the existence of simplicity is not supported by any perception. Experience will never expose an absolutely simple object. Since, then, by the world of sense, we indicate the sum of all possible experiences, it contains nothing simple.

This second proposition of the antithesis goes further than the first, which banishes simplicity from the awareness of composites; the second excludes simplicity from nature altogether. It could not, therefore, be proved by reference to the idea of an external object but only by its general relation to possible experience.

The third conflict in formal ideas. THESIS. Causality, according to the laws of nature, is not the only causality from which the world's phenomena can be derived. To explain phenomena, it is necessary also to assume that freedom is causal.

PROOF. Let us assume that there is no causality except through natural law. Then everything that happens follows by rule and, inevitably, from a previous state. But there must have been a time when that previous state did not exist and after which it came to be; for if it had always existed, its consequences would have existed with it and would not have just appeared for the occasion. So the cause of a cause is also an event which occurs by nature's laws, and it presupposes in turn an antecedent state with its own causality, and so on. If, then, everything happens by natural law, beginnings will always be merely relative and never primary, and there will be no completed series on the side of causes which succeed one another. But nature's law states that nothing happens without a cause which is completely defined, abstractly and in advance. The proposition, therefore, that causality is possible only by natural law, is self-contradictory if taken in the most general sense, and accordingly it is not the only kind of causality.

We must therefore assume another kind, through which events occur by reason of causes not defined by necessary laws, but from absolutely spontaneous causes, by which a series of phenomena regulated by natural law begins automatically. This means the assumption of a formal freedom without which, as nature goes, no series of phenomena on the side of causes could ever be complete.

ANTITHESIS. There is no freedom; everything in the world happens solely according to nature's laws.

PROOF. Assume that there is freedom in the formal sense, a special kind of causality by which the world's events have occurred, a power from which a state of things may originate, together with the series of its consequences. Since this series had its origin in freedom's causality, that causality itself must have had an absolute beginning which was determined by neither antecedent nor fixed laws. The beginning of an action, however, presupposes that its immediate cause had previously been inactive, but the dynamics of beginning the action presupposes no causal connection with a previous state. Formal freedom thus stands opposed to causal law and makes unity of experience impossible when it operates between the successive states produced by an active cause. It is never met in experience and is thus fiction.

There is nowhere then, except in nature, to look for the connections and order of cosmic events. Freedom (independence) of the laws of nature is undoubtedly freedom from constraint, but it is also freedom from the guidance of rules. For it cannot be said that instead of the laws of nature, laws of freedom will enter the causality of nature's course. If freedom were defined by laws, it would not be freedom but nature. Nature and formal freedom differ, as do *lawfulness* and *lawlessness*. Nature does indeed impose on mind the difficult job of looking ever higher in the series of causes for the origin of events; the cause of events is always conditioned. It promises in return, however, impeccable unity of experience under law. On the other hand, the fiction of freedom promises the inquiring mind rest in the chain of causes because it leads to an unconditioned and self-acting cause which, being blind, breaks the thread of coherent, regulated experience.

The fourth conflict in formal ideas. THESIS. There is a Being which is either a part of the world or its cause, which is absolutely necessary to it.

PROOF. There is a series of changes in the world of sense, in the sum of all phenomena, without which even the idea of serial time, the very condition of the world of sense, would be impossible. But every change is made necessary by a condition which is antecedent to it in time. By the fact of its existence, every conditioned entity presupposes a complete series of conditions extending up to the Unconditioned, which alone is absolutely necessary. Since change is a consequence of the Unconditioned, the Unconditioned must itself exist, and belong to the world of sense. If it were outside the world of sense, the series of changes in the world would have begun apart from the world and the necessary cause itself would not be in the world. But this is impossible. For, a time series begins because of what preceded it in time, and the supreme condition of the beginning does presuppose a preceding time when the thing begun did not exist. So the necessary cause of change and its powers must belong to time and to phenomena, since time is possible only as a form of phenomena. So cause cannot be imagined apart from the world of sense, the sum of phenomena. The world therefore contains something absolutely necessary, perhaps the whole world series itself, perhaps only part of it.

ANTITHESIS. An absolutely necessary being does not exist, either in the world or out of it, as its cause.

PROOF. If we suppose that the world itself is a necessary entity, or that it contains one, there are then two possibilities. Either the series of changes had an uncaused but absolutely necessary beginning or the series had no beginning at all. Then, even though each part of it is contingent and conditioned, the series is still necessary and unconditioned as a whole. The first possibility conflicts with the dynamic law defining the relation of phenomena to time, and the second is self-contradictory, since an aggregate cannot be necessary if no member of it is so.

Assume, then, that there is an absolutely necessary cause of the world which is yet apart from it. This cause would be the highest member of the series of causes of change and would initiate change and its series. In that case, the first cause would have to begin to act, and so it would be temporal and phenomenal. That would make it part of the world, which contradicts our assumption. Therefore, neither in the world nor out of it, is there an absolutely necessary Being to cause it.

18 A REASONER'S SOLILOQUY ON REASONING

The antinomies give way to hope

There is a respectable reason for Kant's occasional reviews of his progress. Periodically he gets a fresh running start, and from the reader's point of view, the reviews are generally better written than his original expositions: they sometimes even approach eloquence. Following the stalemated antinomies which he designed to portray the rationalist-empiricist dispute, he starts again from the beginning to develop a remedy for the stalemate. The remedy is technical but leads to one of Kant's more important contributions, besides providing a testimony to the power of his logic.

The major error underlying the dispute and shared by both parties was in the notion that a coherent account of reality could be accomplished either in terms of mind or of sense, the choice being a prerogative of the philosopher. It should be noticed, however, that rationalism was chiefly Continental, while empiricism was English. Setting the two arguments, equally simplified, to the work of mutual cancellation was an attractive idea, especially if the protagonists could have agreed that Kant's representations were fair. The reader may want to do his own checking on this.

At this point, R. G. Collingwood's statement is as good as any: "It was the merit of Kant to see that each of these opposites succeeded in existing only by implicitly assuming the other, and to show that what they both aimed at was a view in which sensation and thought existed together in an inseparable unity. But this unity was for Kant an attribute of 'consciousness in general,' and this generality of the notion of consciousness marked the collapse of Kant's philosophy into another abstract rationalism, by his failure to identify the 'empirical ego' with the 'transcendental ego,' mind in its immediacy with mind in its ideal perfection." (Speculum Mentis, p. 285.)

Kant's presentation of the phenomenal world as a "regressive series" merely means that beginning from here and now, the world will consist of one thing after another, each dependent on the next and "conditioned" by it, and that perception will range for each person from his particular point of space and time outwards, if not infinitely, then indefinitely. There are two kinds of series. One is "mathematical," by which I understand Kant to mean that it involves space only; the other is "dynamic," involving time, and therefore change or movement. (See p. 138.) According to Kant, the dynamic series is entirely composed of phenomena and may be governed from outside the series. At least one of the governing factors may be empirically unconditioned. This is his clue to the reconciliation of empiricists and rationalists.

There is a passage in which Kant refers to formal objects which are the not-sensed causes of certain perceptions. These are Kant's "things-themselves" about which he insists that we may think, even if we know nothing about them. This means that Kant, too, reaches beyond the limits of experience, a trespass for which he has elsewhere soundly castigated the dogmatists.

For the present, let us consider taking sides in the conflict of reason, consulting no logical criterion of truth but merely our own interests, so that we may understand why the participants in this quarrel have preferred one side rather than the other, without any marked insight into either side. We may then be able to explain, among other things, the fiery zeal of one party and the cold confidence of the other, and why one side won joyous plaudits, while the other has met with implacable prejudice from the first.

By comparing the principles from which each of the two parties starts, we may fix a point of departure from which to carry this preliminary inquiry on to completion. In the *antitheses*, the assertions exhibit uniformity in methods of thought and in maxims. Pure empiricism is applied to the explanation of the world's phenomena and to the discussion of formal ideas of world totality. The statements of the *theses*, on the other hand, in addition to the empiricism involved in the series of phenomena, presuppose intelligible origins, and accordingly their maxims are not so simple. Their distinguishing characteristics impel me to call the method of the theses the *dogmatism of pure reason.*

In the definition of cosmological ideas, we find the following to the credit of the theses, or their dogmatism.

First, there is a certain practical interest which would be shared by any sensible person who knows where his own interests lie. That the world once began, that my thinking self is simple and indestructible, that I am free and above nature's compulsions, and finally that the order of things in the world is due to a primordial being, from whom all unity and purpose comes—these are just so many foundations of morals and religion. The antitheses rob us of these supports, or at least seem to do so.

Second, reasoning also involves a speculative interest on the side of the theses. If formal ideas are assumed and used as they are in the theses, it is possible completely to understand the whole chain of conditions, and so, the derivation of the conditioned object. For here we start from the unconditioned, and this the antithesis does not do. It is thus at a disadvantage. To the question about the organization of conditions, it offers no answer that does not lead to endless renewal of the inquiry. According to the antitheses, every beginning requires another one beyond it, each part needs a smaller part, every event is preceded by another event which is its cause, and the conditions of existence are always based on still other conditions, without ever touching bottom or resting on any self-sufficient thing or primordial being.

Third, this side has the advantage of popularity, which is not the least of its claims to favor. The common mind has no difficulty at all with the notion of an unconditioned beginning of all organization,* because it is more accustomed to going on to the consequences than to turning back to causes. The idea of an absolute First is no bother but rather a source of comfort, a fixed point to which one can return at will. There is no satisfaction in the restless climb from conditioned to conditions, when one foot is always in the air.

In the definition of cosmological ideas, on the side of empiricism or antithesis, first, there is no practical interest in the principles of pure reason such as there is in morals and religion. On the contrary,

* But see pp. 275 ff.

pure empiricism seems to deprive both of all power and influence. If there is no great Original, distinct from the world, if the world is without a beginning and therefore without an Author, if our wills are not free, if the soul is divisible and perishable like matter, moral ideas and principles lose their validity and fall with the theory which supported them.

On the other hand, empiricism offers advantages to the speculative interests of the reasoner, very attractive advantages, far surpassing dogmatic offerings touching reason's ideas. According to empiricism, the mind is always on its own home grounds, the field of purely possible experience where its laws may be traced securely, and intelligible knowledge may be endlessly broadened. Here, every object may have its spot in awareness, both for itself and its relations to other things. Or objects may be represented by concepts, the images of which also have room in similar awareness. It is not necessary to leave the chain of nature's order and resort to ideas whose objects are not known, because they are thoughts and are not visual or audible. The mind is never allowed to leave its work, on the pretext of having finished it, and to wander over into the gardens of idealizing reason or formal ideas where observation is no longer necessary to the discovery of nature's laws, where it is necessary only to think as poets do, sure that nature's facts will not betray; nor will any evidence restrain the mind from bypassing facts and subordinating them to the higher authority of reason.

The empiricist will never allow, therefore, that any epoch of nature is absolutely first or that any horizon is ultimate. Neither will he permit a transition from objects which he can analyze with observation and mathematics, and define in organized awareness, to those objects of thought which neither sense nor imagination can ever make concrete. He will not concede that there is any power in nature which operates independently of nature's laws (i.e., there is no freedom) and which may thus encroach on the mind's business, which is to investigate the origin of phenomena by immutable rules. Finally, he will not admit the search for causes outside of nature, in a great Original. Nature offers its objects and instructs us in their laws. We know nothing beyond that.

If the empiricist with his antitheses cared only to cure the rashness and presumption of those who mistake reason's true vocation, and boast of insight and knowledge where insight and knowledge have long since ceased to be, his principles would be proverbs of moderation. If he would put a stop to calling practical interest speculative and linking physical knowledge to formal ideas under the pretense of extending it, when formal ideas tell us only that we know nothing, then the empiricist would have taught us modesty of assertion and how experience, that eminent teacher, could help us to the greatest possible extension of our minds. If this were the case, our own intellectual presuppositions and faith would still be available to support practical interest, and they would not appear pompously as *science and rational insight,* because the only objects of true speculative knowledge are those provided by experience. The synthesis which aims at a new species of knowledge independent of experience and beyond its limits has no substratum of awareness on which to operate.

It often happens, however, that empiricists themselves become dogmatic about ideas and boldly deny what goes beyond the field of awareness and are guilty of immodesty, which is all the more reprehensible for the irreparable damage thus done to the practical interests of reason.

Finally, it is astonishing that empiricism should be so unpopular. One would think that even ordinary people would eagerly adopt a proposal promising satisfaction within the range of their experience and the considerations that arise from it. One would think that they would prefer this to a formal dogmatism which requires them to rise to ideas which are over the heads even of the best-practiced thinkers. But this it is that moves ordinary people to their choice. Dogmatism gives them a position over which learned people can claim small advantage. They understand little or nothing about such matters, but no one else can boast that he knows much more; and even though they cannot express themselves in scholarly fashion, people can, nevertheless, argue plausibly and endlessly, playing with ideas about which nobody knows anything and about which, therefore, anything can be said. They have nothing to say, however, to investigations of nature and then can only confess their ignorance. Thus indolence and vanity recommend dogmatism. People accept what becomes familiar through common use. They want something that will allow them to go to work with confidence, and therefore formal and idealizing reasoning is popular, while empiricism is not.

Human reasoning is naturally architectonic and implies that knowledge belongs in systems. It therefore entertains only such principles as do not hinder the systematization of knowledge. The principles of the antitheses, on the other hand, are such that they make the completion of an edifice of knowledge wholly impossible. Beyond every state of the world there are others which are older, and parts lie within parts. Thus the architectonic of reasoning which requires unity (not empirical unity but abstract and prior unity) recommends the assertions of the theses.

If a man were free of special interests and indifferent to their consequences, and could consider the assertions of reasoners, thinking only of their matter and grounds, and then if the only way to escape perplexity were to accept one or the other of the conflicting doctrines, he would vacillate perpetually. Today he would be convinced that the human will is free; tomorrow he would be thinking that human freedom is only self-deception, because of nature's unbreakable chain. If he is called to action, however, this play of speculation would disappear like the shadow images of a dream, and he would choose his principles to suit his practical interests.

It is appropriate that a reflective, inquiring being should take time to examine his own reasoning, putting aside all partiality and submitting his observations to the judgment of others. No one can be blamed for putting the pros and cons of his reasoning before a jury of his peers (who are also fallible men) where they may be defended, safe from threats.

It would be preferable not to demand dogmatic answers, if it appeared in advance that the answers would only increase one's ignorance, or lead from one puzzle into another, or into greater darkness, or perhaps to contradictions. If the answers are to be *yes* or *no*, it would be smart to pass over the probable reasoning behind the answers and to consider first what is to be gained either way. If it should turn out that sheer nonsense results from both answers, there is reason for a critical examination of the question asked. The question may be based on footless presuppositions and may be one that toys with an idea whose falsity shows up better in its applications and results than in its own terms. This is the chief use of the skeptical method of dealing with the questions pure reason puts to pure reason. At small cost, it gets rid of much dogmatic waste by providing sober criticism, a true cathartic, which effectively purges illusions and the pretended omniscience that goes with them.

If, therefore, I know in advance that a cosmological idea is always either too large or too small for my mind, that would be an advantage, for I should then know that the cosmological idea is empty and meaningless. It is supposed to deal with an object which we experience and which conforms to a possible mental idea, but the world as an object does not fit the idea, however one might try to make it do so. This is really the case with all cosmic ideas, and this is why reasoning, as long as it deals with them, is involved in antinomies.

First. For suppose that the world had no beginning. The supposition is too large to conceive because it involves a regressive series* that covers the whole elapsed eternity of the past. Or suppose that the world had a beginning. It is then too small to cover one's conception of the extent of time as we think of it. For a beginning is not unconditioned; there was time before that, and so the mind's empirical laws oblige one to look higher and further. The world with a time limit is clearly too small.

It is the same with the double answer to the question about the spatial extent of the world. If it is infinite, it is too large to experience. If it is finite, it is fair enough to ask what defines its limits. Empty space is not a self-sufficient correlate of things nor a final definition, much less an empirical condition, or a part of possible experience. How can there be experience of absolute emptiness? Still, to get the absolute whole of organized experience, the Unconditioned must also be part of it. A limited world is therefore too small for this purpose.

Second. If each material object consists of an infinite number of parts, the regressive series in division will always be too long for the world we see; if the division of space were to stop at any member of the series (it being simple), the result would be too short to contain the idea of the Unconditioned; for the end member could again be subdivided. Similarly, endless causality and an infinitely remote necessary Being are too big to conceive.

In all these cases, we have said that the cosmic idea is either too large or too small for the regressive series as we experience it, and also for our minds. But why not turn the statement around and say that our experience is too small for the idea in the first case and, in

* See pp. 102 ff.

the second case, too large, and so put the blame on the empirical series rather than on the cosmological idea? This is why: Our ideas get reality only from possible experience; without it, they refer to nothing and so mean nothing. Thus possible experience is the standard by which to judge whether an idea is a phantom thought or actually applies to something in the world. A thing is said to be too large or too small for something else when the first is required for the second and has to be adapted to it. We say that the coat is too short for the man, and not that the man is too long for the coat.

There is therefore reason to suspect that the sophistry and contradictions accompanying cosmological ideas depend on an empty and fictitious conception of the object of these ideas. This suspicion should put us back on the trail of the illusions that have so long led men astray.

In the *Formal Aesthetic* (or *Transcendental Aesthetic,* cf. above, Section 6), it has been sufficiently proved that things perceived in space and time, together with objects of possible experience, are simply phenomena, representations, or experiences. Whether they appear as extended entities or as series of changes, they have no independent existence outside our thought. I call this doctrine *formal idealism.* (Cf. below, Section 20.)

In formal idealism it is admitted that objects of external awareness in space are real, and that changes in time perceived by the inner sense are also real. For since space is the form of what we call "outer awareness," and without objects in space there would be no experience whatever, we can and must assume the reality of sized entities. We do the same with time. But space, time, and phenomena are not things; they are experiences and do not exist outside mind. Even the inner, sense awareness of mind, as an object of consciousness which is experienced as a succession of different states in time, is not an independent Self or a formal subject, but a phenomenon, perceived by a being we do not know. The existence of this inner phenomenon as a self-sufficient being is not admissible because it is governed by time, of which things-themselves are utterly independent. But the objective existence of phenomena in space and time is guaranteed beyond doubt, and if dreams and phenomena are simultaneously experienced, there are empirical laws which enable their distinction.

Objects of experience themselves are never perceived except as experiences, and apart from experience they do not exist. That there may be inhabitants of the moon must be admitted even though no one has ever seen them; but this means only that as we progress we may come across them. Everything is real if it is perceived according to the laws by which experience progresses. Objects of experience are therefore real if they are empirically connected with my consciousness, but that does not make them real of themselves, apart from the progress of my experience.

Sense awareness, strictly speaking, is only sensitivity. The senses are affected in certain ways by perceptions which are related to each other in the pure awareness of space and time. Perceptions, so connected and defined by the laws of experience, are called *objects*. We know nothing about the non-sensed cause of these perceptions since it does not appear as an object of awareness. This object would be perceived neither in space nor in time because these pertain to sense perception only, and apart from space and time, awareness is unimaginable. We may, however, call the purely mental cause of phenomena in general a *formal object* so as to have something mental corresponding to sense perception. The extent and connections of all possible perceptions may be attributed to this formal object, and it may be said that it is prior to all experience.

But the phenomena which conform to the formal object are not things-themselves; they occur only as experience. They are perceptions which indicate a real object only when they occur under the rules regulating unity of experience. So we say that the real things of time past are perceived in the formal object of experience. They are real objects in time past only if conceived in a regressive series of possible perceptions; it may be as highlights of history or as the spoor of cause and effect, and governed by empirical laws. In a word, the course of the world leads to a time series in the past as the condition of the present, a series not itself actual except as the continuity of possible experience. Thus the unimaginable periods of time preceding my existence serve only to extend the chain of experience backwards to the conditions which have determined this present time.

The antinomy of pure reason is based on the following dialectical argument: Given any conditioned entity, the whole series of all its conditions comes with it; but we perceive sense objects, and they are conditioned; consequently . . . (sic). Before the fallacies involved in this sophistical syllogism are exposed, it is necessary to correct and define some of its terms. The major premise takes "conditioned entity" in the formal sense of pure category, while the minor premise uses it in the empirical sense of a mental idea applied to phenomena. The demonstration of this error, common in the arguments based on cosmological assertions, should justify the dismissal of both the parties of thesis and antithesis for making unfounded claims. But that would not end the quarrel, as it would if one or both of them had been proved wrong in their conclusions. Nothing could seem clearer than that if one asserts that the world had a beginning, and the other says that it had none, one of the two must be right. There is no way to settle the dispute to the satisfaction of both parties except to convince both that since they have been able so beautifully to refute each other, they are really quarrelling about nothing at all. A certain formal illusion has been mocking them with a mirage of reality, when there is nothing real there.

Since the world does not exist of itself, independently of my perceptions of the regressive series, it is neither an infinite nor a finite whole by itself. It exists only as an empirical, regressive series of phenomena. Since, then, this series is always conditioned, it is never complete and the world is not an unconditioned whole and so is not either finite or infinite in size.

The antinomy of pure reasoning which arose from cosmological ideas disappears when it is shown to be the dialectical product of a dispute over an illusion. It came of applying the idea of absolute totality to phenomena. Absolute totality pertains only to things-themselves; whereas phenomena exist only in my perception and as a regressive series. If the world is a whole, existing by itself, it is either finite or infinite. The proofs of thesis and antithesis have shown that both alternatives are false. It is therefore false that the world by itself is a complete whole. And it follows from this that phenomena are nothing apart from our perceptions, which is just what formal idealism means.

The principle of reasoning is really only a rule, prescribing a regressive series of conditions for given phenomena, forbidding that there should ever be an absolutely unconditioned entity at which the series ends. It is therefore not a principle of the possibility of experience, or of knowing sense objects, or a principle of mind, by which experience is confined within limits described by awareness. It is not a *constitutive* principle of reason enabling the extension of ideas of the sense world beyond the bounds of experience. It is rather a principle of the greatest extension and broadening of experience, a principle which forbids accepting any empirical limit as absolute. It is, therefore, a principle of reasoning which serves as a rule to postulate what ought to happen in the regressive series but not to anticipate what the object will be like when the series reaches it. I call it a *regulative* principle of reasoning. The principle of the absolute totality of conditions in phenomena themselves is, on the other hand, a *constitutive* cosmological principle. I have tried to indicate its nullity in the distinction just drawn, and to avert an otherwise inevitable attribution of objective reality to an idea which is only a rule.

Here as well as in other cosmological problems, the regulative principle of reasoning is based on the proposition that in the empirical regressive series, there exists no experience of an absolute limit or absolutely unconditioned state. The reason is that in experience, the limitation of phenomena by a void or empty place, in which the regressive series comes to an end, is impossible.

The proposition practically says that in the regressive series there are no conditions which are not, in turn, conditioned. It contains the rule about termination that however far I go in the ascending series, I must still inquire for a higher member of the series, whether I know about it from experience or not.

Nothing further is now needed for the solution of the first cosmological problem except to decide whether, in the regression to the unconditioned greatness of the cosmos in time and space, the unlimited ascent is to be called infinite or indefinite regression.

The general conception of the series of all the world's past states, including everything that coexists in it, is merely a possible empirical regression, which I think out indeterminately in privacy. This is the only way the conception of such a series of conditions for a given perception can arise. The cosmic series can, therefore, be neither greater nor smaller than the possible empirical regression on which the idea of it is based. Since the regression presents neither a determinate finiteness nor a determinate infinity, the size of the world itself cannot be assumed to be either finite or infinite. The cosmic whole is just an idea and never appears as a whole in awareness. Thus I cannot argue from the size of the cosmos to the size of the regressive series, defining the latter by the former. On the contrary, I must first construct an idea of the size of the cosmos from the size of the empirical regression, of which we know only that empirically we have always to move on from any given member of it to another which is higher and more remote.

The size of the totality of phenomena is therefore not absolutely measured, and it cannot be said that the regression is infinite. This would be to anticipate members before they turn up in the series and to set the number of them so high that, practically, it would be out of reach. To measure the world, even though negatively, without observing the regressive series, is impossible. Since no awareness brings the world as a whole to me, I cannot know its size except by the regressive series. Hence we cannot tell the size of the world from appearance or say that it involves a continuous, infinite series. All we can do is to try to get an idea of its size, by the rule defining a series of phenomena. This rule says only that no matter how far we go with the series, we may never assume an absolute limit. We continue to subordinate each phenomenon to the next, as its condition, and then move on to that condition. This is the *indefinite* regression. It does not predetermine the size of the world as its object and so is clearly distinguishable from infinite regression.

I cannot say, therefore, that the world is infinite either in space or time. The idea of size, or of infinite size, is of course empirical; so it is impossible to apply it to the cosmos as a sensed object with a view to measurement. Nor shall I say that the regressive series extends from a given perception, through all space and past time to infinity, for this would presuppose an infinite world. Neither can I say that the series is finite: an absolute limit is also empirically impossible. There is nothing that I *can* say about the cosmos of sense as an object of experience. There is only the rule by which experience occurs and progresses, apposite to its subject.

If I divide up my awareness of something whole, I am working from something conditioned by its parts to the conditions of its possibility. Then further division into parts makes a regressive series of conditions. The absolute completion of the series would appear only when at last I get down to *simple* parts. But if all the parts continue to be divisible, however far the series goes, then the regression from the conditioned to the conditions is infinite. The regression must not then be called *indefinite regression,* as it was in the case of the cosmological idea mentioned above, in which we worked from the conditioned outwards to conditions that were not parts of it but were added as the series went on. In spite of this, we may not say of an infinitely divided whole that it consists of an infinite number of parts. For although all the parts are contained in the awareness of the whole, the division into parts is not included. The division is a continuous process of dismemberment, as the regressive series becomes actual. Since this regressive series is infinite and an aggregate, the members or parts at which it finally arrives are all contained in it. But an infinite series is never actually complete and therefore does not contain an infinite number of parts, nor is it a composite of them.

This remark is easily applied to space. Every part of space appears as an individual whole in awareness. Space is always space, however subdivided; its parts are therefore infinitely divisible.

The remark can further be applied to an external phenomenon, a limited body. Its divisibility is the divisibility of space, for space is the condition of the possibility of an extended body. A body is infinitely divisible but does not therefore consist of an infinite number of parts.

Indeed, it might seem that since a body appears as substance in space, it will differ from space in the applicability of the law of division. It will be granted at once that dismemberment of a body would never wipe space out clean, for space without something self-sufficient to fill it would not be space. Even if composite matter should be done away entirely in thought, the very concept of substance would forbid that nothing should remain of it. Substance is the basis of all composites and must persist in some elementary form even when its bonds with space, which made it a body in thought, have been taken away. But this will not apply to the substance of a phenomenon, which is not a thing-itself or conceived by means of one of mind's pure ideas. For the phenomenon is not a material subject. It is nothing but an enduring sense image in awareness, in which no unconditioned entity is ever encountered.

We have thus far overlooked an essential distinction between objects, or the mental ideas that reason would like to upgrade. According to the table of categories, two of the pure ideas imply a mathematical organization of phenomena and two, dynamical. Up to now this oversight has made no great difference because when the formal ideas turned up, it was under phenomenal conditions, and in the case of the two formal mathematical ideas, therefore, the object was phenomenal only. But now we come to mind's dynamic ideas, and we must consider to what extent they suit reason. The distinction between mathematics and dynamics at once becomes important. It opens up an entirely new view of reasoning's trial. Previously, we dismissed this trial because both sides based their argument on false grounds, but now it appears that there may be in the dynamic antinomy an hypothesis generally compatible with the requirements of reason. The judge may be able to make good the faults of the litigants' pleas, of which faults both sides were guilty. Then the trial could be settled to the satisfaction of both parties, on a new basis, which would not have been possible in the case of the mathematical antinomies.

A series of conditions will, no doubt, appear to be homogeneous if it is examined at length merely to see if it is adequate to the idea it serves, or whether the idea is too large or too small for it. The mind's ideas on which dynamic series are based involve either the organization of purely homogeneous elements, which is presupposed in either the composition or division of quantities, or of heterogeneous matter, which is possible dynamically in the case of causality or in relations between necessary and contingent matters.

Thus it happens that the mathematical connections of a series of phenomena may involve only those sense conditions which are themselves part of the series. The dynamic series of sense-conditioned phenomena, on the other hand, may include heterogeneous conditions which are not themselves part of the series but outside it, since they are purely mental. So reason is satisfied, and the unconditioned gets priority over phenomena without disturbing the conditioned character of the phenomena involved or, contrary to mind's principles, cutting the series off short.

Since, then, dynamical ideas permit the phenomena of their series to be conditioned from without, and by conditions which are themselves not phenomenal, the results are wholly different from those of the mathematical antinomies, in which both dialectical assertions had to be declared false. Since dynamic series are made up of phenomena, they are invariably conditioned throughout. If they are connected to something empirically unconditioned and at the same time not-sense, mind is satisfied, and so is reason. Thus the dialectical arguments for the unconditional totality of mere phenomena fall flat, but reason's propositions, now given a correct interpretation, may prove to be true. This could never have been possible with cosmological ideas based on mathematically unconditioned unity, for no condition of the phenomenal series could be found except one which is itself a phenomenon and so a member of the series.

19 "OUGHT" IS FREEDOM'S FIRST LAW

Necessity does not exclude freedom

The relation of causal necessity to freedom is not really a modern problem. The Greeks had considered it well, but when the Renaissance burgeoned into scientific interest, something suggesting an act of God occurred to change the whole perspective. Where once spontaneity and freedom had loomed large, nature's primary dynamic principle, causal necessity, captured the imaginations of Europeans, at least, by offering a universal law not dogmatically conceived. As Kant reviewed the matter for the eighteenth century, the world of sense consisted of a series of phenomena which regressed outward from the observer indefinitely, and each phenomenon was causally related to the one next to it. He gave careful notice that within the sense world, there could be no exception to causal law; but there were others who felt that there should be no exception to it under any circumstances, and they ruled out freedom entirely.

Churchmen, of course, continued to defend the metaphysical notion of freedom. In some sense, all religion is the celebration of a significant free choice. The decision to die for an idea, for example, is distinguished evidence of the presence of freedom. In this case, Kant might have said, death is a phenomenon strictly within the causal series; its ultimate cause, however, is not a phenomenon but a formal idea, extrinsic to sense and the world of discourse, nonspatial, nontemporal, and inscrutable. This explanation would seem to cover the facts, but from the point of view of devotees of causal law, it violated a basic rule of explanation by introducing unexplained and unexplainable terms.

Kant would never have considered getting around this difficulty by ruling out either freedom or necessity and so hiding the problem in a closet; but after painstaking consideration, he found no solution for it within pure reason. The solution had to be reserved for practical reasoning, an accommodation of thought to fact. It was a fact that not all known phenomena could be accounted for within causal series. There are phenomena which require "formal," or "intelligible" causes, causes that are beings outside the world of sense and which he called "things-themselves," or "noumena." The point about them is that they are beyond the reach of causal law where necessity rules, and accordingly, they are "free." A prime example of free causes is a man's noumenal, or formal self; of itself, it can originate a series of phenomena. Thus, there are phenomena which are produced co-operatively by formal and phenomenal causes. They do not exclude each other. This book is an example.

It will be remembered that the third antinomy (p. 109) affirmed and denied causal freedom; the fourth (p. 111) affirmed and denied the necessary Being who is free. These antinomies appear to have permanent significance in the thought of mankind, as the still unresolved conflict of science and religion testifies. Kant conscientiously disavows any intent to prove the existence of an absolutely unconditioned Being by pure reason. Having forbidden mental operations that stray beyond the limits of experience, his conclusion in this matter was bound to be negative. He could only say that no law forbids that the world of sense should depend on a free and intelligible Being and that any judgment ruling out intelligible beings because they do not fit into a phenomenal series is presumptuous. This is indeed negative and cautionary, but once again a Moses in Kant stands on Pisgah looking over into a promised land that is not for him.

The problem of freedom has no meaning on the level of nature where, by today's reckoning, at least, a statistical necessity prevails. Freedom comes to the world only in human terms which add something new, something not previously discovered: a sentient being, able to resist coercion via the senses. That this discovery should pose a problem not logically solvable may be due, as Kant the logician suggests, to the fact that the subject of discourse cannot be simultaneously its object. Or it may be simply that no one can *ever see himself except by reflection. The verification of the human noumenon, and consequently of freedom, is indirect.*

As things go, two kinds of causality are conceivable, the causality of nature and that of freedom. The former is the regulated connection of one state of the world of sense with an antecedent state. But this phenomenal causality is also subject to time conditions and a state antecedent to it. Even if it had always existed as a cause, it could not have been the first step towards producing the present effect. Any cause is therefore also an effect, and it must once have begun, and so it too had a cause.

On the other hand, freedom in the cosmological sense means that a state may begin spontaneously to exist. It would be independent of any cause which would define it by nature's time laws. In this sense, freedom is a purely *formal idea* to which experience contributes nothing. Within nature, the general rule governing the possibility of experience is that everything has a cause; even causality, when it occurs, must have a cause, and the whole field of experience, however extended, becomes simply *nature*. But this does not account for the absolute totality of conditions affected by the causal relation, and so the idea of spontaneity enters, according to which automatic action is possible without an external cause to set it going, as nature's causal law could require.

It is worth noticing that the practical idea of freedom is based on this formal idea, in which the real difficulty about freedom inheres. In the practical sense, *freedom is willful independence of coercion via sense-borne impulses*. All willing is sensuous when prompted by feeling; only when feeling is compulsive, is it animal. Human willing is moved by sense-borne impulses but not as among animals; for in man a sense-borne impulse does not necessitate action; he has self-control which makes him independent of sense drives.

Obviously, if all causality in the sense world were only natural, each thing would be governed by another under fixed laws. Phenomena governing willing would produce natural effects and require appropriate actions, and the denial of formal freedom would involve the elimination of practical freedom. Formal freedom presupposes that even if something that should have happened did not happen, whatever restrained its phenomenal cause was not compelling enough to exclude human willing as a cause. Human willing alone can start a series of events. Independent of nature, and even when opposed by nature's power and influence, it can make things happen; such things will, of course, be well within the time order and will obey nature's laws.

In this case, what happens illustrates what always happens when one reasons beyond the limits of experience. The problem is not physiological but formal. The question about the possibility of freedom bears on psychology; but being based on dialectic arguments of pure reason, its solution lies within formal philosophy. To enable a satisfactory solution, which no practitioner of formal philosophy can decline to attempt, a remark about formal procedure is desirable.

If phenomena were things-themselves, and space and time were merely the forms in which things exist, conditioning and conditioned entities would all be members of the same series. Then the old antinomy would appear, the antinomy common to all formal ideas: the series is both too large and too small for mind's needs. The dynamical ideas to be discussed in this and the next section have this peculiarity, that they apply not to the size but to the existence of an object. Consequently size will be neglected in the series of conditions, and only the dynamic relation of the conditioning to the conditioned entity will be considered.

The difficulty appears then in the problem of *nature* and *freedom*: is freedom possible at all and if it is possible, is it compatible with the universal law of causality in nature? Are these the alternatives, that every event issues either from freedom or nature, or that within the same event but separately, both freedom and nature may operate? It is an established and unexeceptionable principle of the *Formal Analytic* that unchangeable natural laws connect all events in the world of sense. The question then is whether freedom is excluded or whether an effect, while conforming to nature, may not be based on freedom. The injurious influence of the common but fallacious assumption of the *absolute reality* of phenomena appears at this point. If phenomena are things-themselves, freedom is impossible. In this case nature would be the complete and self-sufficient cause of every event. The condition of each event would appear only in a series, and a condition with its effect would occur only as required by natural law. On the other hand, if phenomena are taken only for what they are in fact, as perceptions and not things-themselves, as being connected according to empirical laws, *their* causes must be other than phenomena. Then these causes, being mental, such as *willing* or *ideas*, are not defined by causes which are phenomena. They are outside the series of empirical conditions even though their effects appear in it. Thus the effect can be considered free, i.e., not necessitated, because its cause is mental, and also as a necessary (not free) effect because it is in the series. Thus abstractly put, the distribution may seem subtle and obscure but it will be clear in its application. My purpose in all this is merely to point out that if one should insist on the objective reality of phenomena, freedom would be destroyed. Those who follow the common view have never succeeded in reconciling nature and freedom.

By "mental" (intelligible), I refer to the element in sense objects which is not phenomenal. If, therefore, one phenomenon causes another, and its power to do so cannot be detected via the sense, there are two possible views of its causality. It is mental if its activity is regarded as a thing-itself, or noumenon. It belongs to sense only when its result is a phenomenon. Such causality must, therefore, be conceived both as empirical and mental, both terms referring to the same effect. Such a twofold conception of the causal properties of an object contradicts none of the conceptions, or phenomena, or experience already laid down. For since they are not things-themselves, phenomena must be based on formal objects, i.e., things-themselves, which they represent to the senses. There is nothing to prevent attributing causality or the appearance of it to a formal object or cause which is not phenomenal, even though its effect is encountered only in phenomenal form.

Every immediate cause must have a character or rule for its causality without which it would not be a cause. Accordingly, in the first place, every sense object is empirical, and its action as a phenomenon would connect it with all other phenomena completely, harmoniously, and according to unvarying natural law. Since its action could be derived as well from other phenomena, it constitutes with them a series in nature's order. In the second place, a sense object must have a mental character which causes it to act like a phenomenon, although mental character is not a phenomenon itself and is not subject to sense conditions. The first may be called the character of the thing as a phenomenon, and the second, the character of the thing-itself.

Being mental, this active object will not be time-conditioned; time is for phenomena and not for things-themselves. There can be neither a beginning nor an end of its action. It is not subject to the law which defines change by requiring every event to be preceded by a phenomenal cause. In a word, this object's cause, being mental, has no place in the empirical series which makes an event part of the world of sense. Its mentality is not directly recognizable. It is not perceptible except as it appears in experience, but it must be conceived empirically, just as a formal object has to be thought of as if it were a phenomenon even though we know nothing about it directly.

In order to discover the phenomenal causes or conditions for nature's events, the principle of causality between phenomena is required. If this is adopted, without hedging, mind's requirements are met. One is then empirically justified in regarding all events as natural, and physical explanations go smoothly. Even if it is fiction, mind's requirements are not hurt by the assumption that some natural causes are mental. The action of these causes is not governed by empirical conditions but by mind, and as long as the phenomenal activity they promote meets the requirements of causal law, there is no violation of nature. As a cause of phenomena, the acting object would thus be tied to nature by the unbreakable dependence of all its activity on natural law. It is only when we move from the object's empirical character to its formal character that we discover that this object (with all its phenomenal causality) contains purely mental conditions in its noumenon (thing-itself). As long as we follow nature in the matter of causes, it makes no difference what grounds or connections the phenomena may have with the formal object. These are important only in pure thought, and although pure thought may affect the phenomena, they will still be explainable in terms of natural causality. Their principal explanation will derive from their empirical rather than from their mental character, since the formal cause of their empirical character is completely unknown except as it is signalized in sense.

Let us apply this to experience. Man is a phenomenon of the sense world and a natural cause within natural law. Like everything else in nature, he has an empirical character. We know about that character through the capacities and skills he reveals in action. There is no reason to think that any property of lifeless or animal nature is conditioned except by sense. Only man, who knows the rest of nature through sense, knows himself by pure apperception, by actions and inner controls which are not attributable to sense impressions. Thus, to himself he is at once a phenomenon and a purely mental object. Mind and reasoning make him so. Mind is to be distinguished particularly from all empirically conditioned functions. Its objects appear as ideas which govern mind, causing it to use its own pure ideas empirically.

That mind is causal or that we think it is, is evident from the *imperatives* which we impose on our capabilities in all matters of conduct. "Ought" expresses a kind of necessity and a connection with mind found nowhere else in the whole of nature. Mind comprehends only what is, what has been, and what will be in nature. It cannot be said that anything in nature ought to be other than what it is in any of these time relations. "Ought" means nothing when applied to the course of nature. It is just as absurd to ask what ought to happen in the natural world as it is to ask what properties a circle ought to have. We are justified only in asking what *is* happening in nature and what the properties of a circle *are*.

"Ought" expresses possible action, action caused by an idea. In natural action, the cause must be a phenomenon. The action to which "ought" applies must first be possible within nature. Nature's conditions, however, do not in any sense govern willing itself but only its effects and consequences in the field of phenomena. No matter how many natural reasons or sense impulses urge me to *will,* they cannot rouse the "ought"; they stir up only a willing that is far from necessary and always conditioned. "Ought," on the contrary, as an expression of mind, sets the measure and goal of willing: it forbids or authorizes it. What is willed may be merely an object of sense (something pleasant) or of pure reason (something good), but mind will not back down before sense or follow the order of phenomenal things, but spontaneously it creates order with its own ideas and adapts experience to that order. Accordingly, it reveals that some things which have not been done and may never be done are necessary, on the assumption that mind can cause action. If it may not, ideas would never bear tangible fruit.

Let us then stop at this point and assume that it is possible for mind to cause phenomena. In this case, should mind's action be called free if it is necessarily and precisely governed by its empirical character? Its empirical character is, of course, governed by its mental character as thought. But the latter is revealed only through sense phenomena and is not known directly. Action, then, as attributed to the causality of thought, is not an immediate consequence of thought but only of the effects of thought on the phenomena of inner sense. Pure reasoning, however, as a function of mind is not subject to time or the conditions of the temporal series. It does not start acting as a cause at any given time. If it did, it would come under nature's laws governing phenomena, and its causality would be like nature's but it would not be free. If, therefore, mind can cause phenomena, it is a function which can set up the sense conditions for an empirical series of effects. Mind's causality does not belong to sense and has no starting time. Thus, what hitherto did not appear in any empirical series now shows up: *the cause or condition of a series of events may be empirically unconditioned.* For pure mind, as a cause, is outside the series of phenomena and it is not subject to sense conditions, nor is it governed by time of any antecedent cause.

Mind is therefore the permanent condition of all willful action, the action by which man is distinguished. Before it occurs, each action is predetermined in man's empirical nature. There is no *before* or *after* as far as mental character is concerned, the character which is man's mental part and of which empirical character is only the sense schema. Every action is the immediate result of the mental character of pure mind without reference to either time or phenomena. Mind is therefore free to act and is not dynamically governed by a chain of antecedent causes, either internal or external. But freedom should not be conceived merely as negative independence of empirical conditions, in which case it could not cause phenomena. It should be described positively, as the power to originate a series of events. In reason there is no beginning; there is no antecedent condition: it is the unconditioned condition of every voluntary act. Its effect may be a beginning in a phenomenal series but is not absolutely first there.

Formal principles are not proved by examples. Thus, merely to illustrate the use of the regulative principle of mind, take a voluntary action, such as a malicious lie by which someone causes a certain amount of confusion in society. We at once try to get at the offender's motives to see how much he is to blame for the lie and its consequences. In the first place, a search of the sources of his empirical character shows that he was badly brought up, kept bad company, had a bad disposition, and was shameless, trivial, and thoughtless, not to mention other occasional causes of bad conduct. This is carried out as we might do the study of a causal series which produced a given effect. Then, although we may believe that the offender's lie was influenced by all these circumstances, we nevertheless blame him, not because of his unhappy disposition, nor because of the circumstances by which he was moulded, nor even because of his record.

We assume that all these matters can be left out of consideration, as if his series of past conditions had never happened and his lie were unconditioned by any antecedents, and as if the offender had started a new series of effects with his single act. The blame is based on mind's law that mind is a cause which could and should have controlled his actions, no matter what the influences of his empirical conditioning might be. Mind is not to be regarded as a concurrent cause but as complete in itself, even when sense urges are opposed to it. The act is to be attributed to the agent's mental character. The moment he lies, he is guilty. No matter how the act was conditioned, mind is completely free and the lie is due to its default.

This imputation shows clearly that mind is considered unaffected by sense conditions and that although the effects by which reason is revealed may change with circumstances, mind itself does not change. There is no antecedent state to determine what follows it. Mind is not in the series of sense conditions governing natural phenomena; it is present in all human actions, all the time, and in all circumstances. It is always the same. It is not temporal, and as for new states, it controls them but is not itself in their control. We cannot ask, therefore, why mind did not behave differently, but only why its causality did not turn out other phenomena. This question is unanswerable. A man with another kind of mind *should* have developed another kind of empirical character. To say that in spite of his life history, the offender could have avoided the lie, means only that the lie was immediately within his mind's power and that mind is not conditioned as temporal phenomena are.

By investigating the causality of voluntary actions, therefore, we have arrived at a mental cause, and that is all. We know that this cause is free, i.e., independent of the senses and that it thus may be an unconditioned cause of phenomena. Why mind turns out just these phenomena, and this particular empirical character, under just these circumstances, is beyond our mental powers to decide. This is comparable to the impossibility of saying why a formal object of external sense awareness appears only spatially and not otherwise. Our problem, however, was this: Do freedom and natural necessity conflict when they meet in action? We have already sufficiently answered this question by showing that the conditions of freedom are very different from those of nature's necessities, that nature's laws do not affect freedom, and that the two may act together without mutual interference.

Please observe that in this argument there was no intention of establishing the reality of freedom as a cause of phenomena in the sense world. Such an argument would have been neither formal nor limited to ideas, and it would not have succeeded in any case, since nothing can be inferred from sense experience which is not thinkable under its laws. It was not even our intention to prove the possibility of freedom; this would not have been a success either. It is clear, abstractly and in advance, that a *real cause cannot be established merely from ideas*. We have dealt with freedom only as a formal idea, by which we meant that mind might originate a series of phenomena as from an unconditioned entity. But this way mind gets involved in an antinomy because of its own laws, the laws it prescribes for the empirical use of mind. That this antinomy is based on pure illusion and that nature does not contradict the causality of freedom was all we cared to prove or could prove.

Thus far we have considered changes in the sense world as a dynamic series in which each member is subordinated to the next as its cause. Now this series is to serve merely as a guide to the existence of the highest possible condition of change, namely, a *necessary Being*. Our concern here is not with unconditioned causality but with *the unconditioned existence of substance itself*. Thus the series before us is really only a series of ideas and not of awarenesses, in which one is the condition of the next.

It is easily seen, however, that since phenomena all change, and so are conditioned, there cannot be an absolutely necessary and unconditioned member in the series. If phenomena were things-themselves, and the conditions and the conditioned did belong to the same series of awarenesses, it would be impossible that there should be a *necessary Being* which conditions the existence of phenomena in the sense world.

The dynamic regressive series should be distinguished from the mathematical. The latter is given to combining parts into a whole or dividing a whole into parts. Conditions are parts of the series and homogeneous to it, and they are therefore phenomena. In the dynamic regression, however, we are not concerned with a whole and its parts, one way or the other, but with the derivation of a state from its cause, with deriving the contingent existence of substance from necessary substance. In such a series, the conditioned and the conditions need not together form a single empirical series.

There remains to us still another avenue of escape from the apparent antinomy of freedom and nature. The two conflicting propositions might well be true simultaneously but along different lines. Everything in the world of sense might be contingent and empirically conditioned, even though the whole series might have a nonempirical condition, i.e., an unconditionally necessary Being. Since this is a mental condition, it would not belong to the series, not even as the highest member, nor would any member become unconditioned because of it. It would leave the whole world of sense, with all its members, as ever, empirically conditioned. This way of representing an unconditioned entity as the foundation of phenomena differs from the discussion of freedom's unconditioned causality in preceding paragraphs. There we saw that freedom, the thing-itself, the cause, belonged to the series of conditions. Only its causality was considered mental; but here the necessary Being must be thought of as outside the series of the sense world and as mental only. In this way it can be guarded against being subordinated to the law of contingency and dependence which applies to all phenomena.

Relative to the present problem, the regulative principle of mind is this: Everything in the world of sense has an empirically conditioned existence; none of its properties are unconditionally necessary; for every member of the series, a corresponding empirical condition must be expected and sought in possible experience; it is not justifiable to derive the existence of a member of a series from a condition outside the series or to regard any member of the series as absolutely independent or self-sufficient. At the same time, no law forbids the whole series to depend on some mental Being which is free of empirical conditions and yet makes phenomena possible.

This discussion is by no means intended to prove the existence of an unconditionally necessary Being or even a purely mental condition for the existence of phenomena. To this end, the scope of mind was limited lest it should lose the guiding thread of experience and stray over into transcendent explanations which have no concrete meaning. So now we limit mind's empirical use to prevent presumptuous judgments on what is and what is not possible and so that mental entities may not be declared impossible just because they do not serve to explain phenomena. Thus we have shown only that the complete contingency of natural things and their empirical conditions is compatible with the assumption of a necessary but purely mental condition. When there is no real contradiction between the two assertions, both may well be true. Even if mind's *absolutely necessary* creature should turn out to be impossible, the impossibility could not be inferred from the total contingency and dependence of things in the world of sense or from the principle which forbids basing an appeal to a cause outside the world on a contingent member of it. Mind is its own guide in empirical matters, as in formal matters.

As long as the ideas used in reasoning are focused only on the totality of conditions in the world of sense and their use for reasonable thought, they are both formal and cosmological. But when we put the unconditioned Being, with which we are chiefly concerned, outside the world of sense and therefore beyond experiencing, all relevant ideas become *transcendent*. They no longer serve only to make good the empirical use of mind, which is their function even though it is never wholly discharged. Rather, these ideas get separated from experience and create their own objects, though not from the stuff of experience. They do not depend for their reality on the completion of the empirical series but only on abstract thought. The objects of transcendent ideas are simply mental and may be accepted as formal objects if it is admitted at the same time that we know nothing more about them. They cannot be conceived as defined by their own inner predicates, for they are independent of empirical ideas. There is not the least justification for the assumption that there are such objects. They are just thoughts.

Nevertheless, the cosmological idea underlying the fourth antinomy urges this assumption. The existence of phenomena, which are not self-explanatory but always conditioned, requires nonphenomenal support, that is, the support of a mental object which puts an end to their contingency. Once a self-sufficient reality outside experience is assumed, however, phenomena look like merely contingent modes of mental objects of mental beings. Thus there is only analogy and the use of empirical ideas from which to conceive mental beings, of which really nothing at all is known. Since contingent things are known only by experience, and we are now concerned with matters not related to experience, we shall have to get our knowledge of those matters from pure ideas of things in general, ideas which are necessary in their own right. Thus the first step we take beyond the world of sense in search of new knowledge requires investigation of the *absolutely necessary* Being, and from ideas of it, to derive ideas of all other mental things. This is the matter of the next chapter.

20 THE IDEAL OF PURE REASON

Skepticism provides a denial of denials

Man's fundamental ideas, Kant might have said, are like airplanes that never get off the ground. The idea of the soul ends in paralogism. The idea of cosmos ends in antinomies. The idea of God stays where it is: an idea with no actual object. This is the outline and produce of a monumental skepticism.

A false judgment is a denial of truth and must be explicitly denied before the truth can take place. So Moses and Confucius began with denials of the illusions of their generations on behalf of the moral law, and Jesus denied the "righteousness of the scribes and Pharisees" on behalf of the kingdom of God. It is the work of a prophet to deny all recognizable denials of truth: he is primarily a skeptic who also has an affirmation to make. Prophet or not, it is not unusual to find a philosopher cast as a skeptic, and the final chapter in the Dialectic exhibits Kant in a truly massive denial of three proofs of the existence of God. These proofs were intended to show that God is an object of human knowledge. They only succeeded, however, in exhibiting an ancient human frailty: man's chronic tendency to mistake metaphors for indicators of objective facts. Kant denied these proofs, as he said, to make room for faith.

In the preliminary paragraphs, the supreme being, God, is defined as an individual bearer of all perfections, a perfection being a positive predicate or description of something which cannot be incompatible with any other positive description. This does not, of course, work out in our experience; a thing may not, for example, be at once round and square or wet and dry. But the perfections of God all fit together in perfect unity and he may, accordingly, be comprehended by us by analogy if not directly; he is obviously not within the scope of human recognition. We may take Kant's implied word for it that the philosopher himself had never experienced such a being, and further take his word for it that no being so defined could be an object within any human experience.

At this point a new word is required. "God" means the completion of an infinite series or aggregate of perfections, all within an individual. This is Kant's "ideal" of pure reason. It is more than an idea, and it is "ideal" because experience does not touch it. So God, in Kant's thought, is a formal ideal and logically necessary but not therefore actual.

In spite of this, the three standard "proofs" of God's existence come up for consideration. Before discussing them, it is worth noticing that God may exist and yet not exist for a given person; there may be nothing in one's private experience that suggests his whereabouts. The three "proofs" aim at God's existence only; any implication that he exists for anyone in particular is wholly gratuitous. The proofs are essentially logical and the attack on them has to be made through their logical defects.

The ontological proof is basic. I have an idea of a perfect, infinite being. The idea of perfection includes that of existence. Therefore the perfect, infinite being exists. Kant attacks this by saying that "exists" is equivalent to "is." "God is" is a judgment with no predicate because "is" is merely a copula that should be connecting a subject with a predicate. "Is" or "exists" adds nothing to 'God'. To get God's existence, I must go beyond my idea of a perfect, infinite being. That I may not do in view of the whole preceding argument of the Analytic. In other words, the major premise is analytic: the subject is God, a perfect being. The conclusion is amplifying: the idea of God includes existence. There is a clear non sequitur in the argument.

The cosmological proof is capable of various statements but is also, according to Kant, grievously defective. Basically, it is a statement that phenomena ultimately require an uncaused cause, i.e., God. But, says Kant, within experience all causes are themselves caused; an "uncaused cause" is therefore a contradiction in terms; and in any case, outside of experience "cause" means nothing. In this, he is running true to the argument of the critical philosophy.

The physico-theological proof, which Kant likes best of the three, says that design is evident in the world. There must therefore be an intelligent designer. Kant thinks, however, that the designer at best would be a more or less frustrated architect and not a creator. The technique by which the cosmological and physico-theological proofs are demolished consists in showing that they are reducible to the onotological proof. Since the latter has been refuted, all three are considered worthless. The consolation is offered, however, that atheism, deism, and anthropomorphism can be done away similarly. Meanwhile, the Supreme Being remains an ideal to crown all knowledge. His final word on the matter will come with his moral theory.

We have already seen that it is impossible to conceive a thing apart from the senses and by using pure ideas only. Nothing could ever be objectively real under such circumstances, for pure ideas are only forms of thought. Applied to phenomena, however, they become concrete, taking from the phenomena what they need to that end. They are generally further from objective reality than categories because they are utterly separate from phenomena, through which alone they could become concrete. They have a perfection which is impossible to empirical things; one can reason through them to systematic unity, a unity which may be approached but never attained in experience.

Still more remote from objective reality are what I call *ideals*. These are not merely concrete but *individual instances* of pure ideas. Working under abstract and prior laws and by means of its ideals, *reason** is aimed at the perfect definition of objects but achieves conception of them only in principle, as formal ideas, because the empirical conditions needed for any other result are absent.

The proposition that *everything that exists is completely defined* means not only that one of every pair of *actual* contradictory predicates applies to the thing defined, but that one of all *possible* predicates applies to it. Predicates are thus compared logically with each other, and the thing-itself is formally compared to the totality of its predicates, i.e., to all that can be said about it. The above proposition therefore means that perfect knowledge of a thing is complete knowl-

* Not *reasoning* (see Section 15.)

edge, and from this alone a definition, positive or negative, can be made. There is, of course, no actual instance of a perfect definition; perfect definition has to come via an idea that belongs to reason, which alone can prescribe to mind the rules for *perfect* accomplishment.

Suppose then that a formal substratum, or store of material from which all predicates may be drawn, supports the perfect definition of things: it has to be the idea of all-inclusive reality. Negations are then only limitations put on the all-inclusive reality, of which thought would not make sense if this conception of the "All" were not correct.

But *all-inclusive reality* thus conceived is really the thing-itself, perfectly defined, and so the highest reality is conceived as an individual because it is defined by the one predicate which belongs to being. It is therefore a formal ideal and the basis of perfect definition of everything else. It is the highest and most perfect reality. It is essential to the existence of all things, and the condition to which all thought of the content of objects is traceable. It is, moreover, the only true ideal of which mind is capable. This is the only case in which a general idea of a thing is defined in and through itself and known, therefore, as the definition of an individual.

It is obvious that in the effort to achieve perfect definition of a thing, reason does not require the existence of a being satisfying its ideal but only the idea of such a being. This is required only for the purposes of deducing the totality of limited things from the unconditioned totality of perfect definition. The ideal is therefore the archetype, or prototype of every thing, from which each thing, an imperfect copy of the ideal, derives the substantial possibility of ideal perfection, even though it never gets near to its goal.

It is possible for things to exist only as they are derived, with the exception of the all-inclusive reality which itself must be regarded as the Original. Negation is, then, the only predicate by which things can be distinguished from the "All," and so it always means limitation, the limitation of greater realities and finally of the highest reality. Negation therefore presupposes the highest reality and is derived from it. The many and various things in the world limit the highest reality, which is their common substratum, just as figures are all so many ways of limiting space. Thus the object of the ideal, which exists only for reason, is the *primal being*; regarded as above all else, it is the *Supreme Being,* and when it is the condition of all others, the *Being of beings.* None of these terms, however, indicates an actual relation of their objects to other things but only the relation of an *Idea* to *ideas;* we are still in utter darkness as to the existence of so pre-eminent a being.

We may not say that the primal being consists of a number of derivative beings, since the latter presuppose the former, and so cannot constitute it. The prime being must be thought of as simple (not compounded).

The derivation of all other beings from the primal being cannot therefore be considered a limitation or a division of it. That would be to treat the primal being as an aggregate of derivative beings, which is impossible in view of the foregoing, even though it was represented as such in our first rough sketch. The highest reality would serve the possibility of all things as a cause rather than as their total. The variety of things then would not be derived by limiting the primal being but would be a result of its outreach. Even our senses and all the reality in phenomena belong to the idea of the Supreme Being, as they could not if they were merely ingredients of it.

If this idea of the Supreme Being is treated as a reality, the original Being can be defined by means of it as one, simple, all-sufficient, eternal, etc., or in a word, it can be defined as unconditioned perfection in whatever circumstances. This is the idea of God in its formal sense, and thus, as I have already indicated, reason's ideal is the object of a formal theology.

Such use of the formal idea, however, is a transgression of the limits of its purpose and definition. It was used in reasoning only as the idea of the "All," and as the basis of a perfect definition of things in general, with no requirement that the "All" should be actual, objective, or a thing. This would be mere fiction in which a variety of ideas is gathered up into the one ideal or individual being, and there treated as real. We have no right to do this, nor even to assume its possibility as an hypothesis. The consequences of such an ideal could have no bearing on a perfect definition of things in general, which was the sole purpose of idea in the first place.

This Ideal of the highest reality, though only a symbol, is first conceived as an object, and then treated as one, and finally, as reasoning naturally tends towards perfect unity, personified, as presently we shall see. The regulated unity of experience does not depend on phenomena or sense but on the mind's organization of the field of experience in self-consciousness. Thus the unity of highest reality, and the perfect definition or possibility of all things *seems* to reside in a supreme mind or intelligence.

Only three kinds of proofs of the existence of God are possible within speculative reasoning. The paths that can be followed to this end are as follows. (1) Beginning with definite experience and the peculiar character of the world of sense as it is known to us through experience, you climb up through causal law to the ultimate cause, which is extrinsic to the world. (2) You base the proof on an indefinite experience, or on anything empirically given. (3) You ignore experience altogether and assume the existence of a supreme cause abstractly and in advance, just from ideas. The first kind of proof is physio-theological, the second, cosmological, and the third, ontological. There are no other proofs, and there can be no more.

I shall show that reason goes nowhere on either the empirical or the formal path and that it spreads its wings in vain when the effort is to get beyond the world of sense on speculation's power alone. These proofs will be examined in the order opposite to that of their natural development, as set forth above. It will be shown that even though its first impulse comes from experience, the reasoning effort is guided to its ultimate goal by a *formal* idea. I shall therefore begin by examining the *formal* proof, and see afterwards how much the addition of empirical elements will strengthen it.

After this discussion, it is evident that the idea of an absolutely necessary Being belongs to pure reason and that its objective reality is far from being proved by the fact that our reasoning requires it. It serves only to direct us to a certain unattainable perfection and is thus a limit to mind, rather than a means of its extension to new objectives. But a strange anomaly confronts one immediately; for while the inference from actual existence in general to an absolutely necessary existence seems imperative and correct, the intellectual conditions by which such an idea is conceived are wholly to the contrary.

In all ages, people have discussed an absolutely necessary Being with a view to proving that it exists, without trying to understand whether and how such a being is conceivable. There is, of course, no difficulty about giving the idea of this Being a verbal definition by saying that it is something for which nonexistence is inconceivable. This sheds no light, however, on the conditions which make its nonexistence inconceivable. We need to know what those conditions are and whether the idea of such a Being means anything or not. For nothing is explained by using the word "unconditioned" to throw away the conditions always required by mind to conceive the necessity of something. Even after all that, one would still wonder whether "unconditioned necessity" has any meaning.

What is more, many people have believed that this adventitious but familiar idea had been explained with copious illustration and that further inquiry into its intelligibility was unnecessary. They said that every geometric proposition, such as "a triangle has three angles," is absolutely and necessarily true, and then went on to talk about other things beyond the reach of mind, as if they understood very well what they were talking about.

These alleged illustrations are taken, however, from judgments and not from actual things. The unconditioned necessity in a judgment is not the same as the unconditioned necessity of a thing. The absolute necessity in a judgment is only a conditioned necessity of a thing or of some predicate in the judgment. The proposition cited above does not say that the three angles are necessary but only that if there is to be an actual triangle, three angles will have to be found in it. This *logical necessity* has evinced so great a power of illusion that, given an abstract idea of *something* such that the idea of existence is included, we feel safe in concluding that the *something* really does exist. There is the condition, of course, that I accept it as actual, and so, by the rule of identity, its necessary existence. To repeat, we conclude that the *something* is itself absolutely necessary because its existence is implied in an idea voluntarily accepted, but on condition that it *is* accepted as actual!

If I remove the predicate of an identical judgment and keep the subject, contradiction results; so I say that the former necessarily belongs to the latter. If I erase the subject as well as the predicate, there is nothing left to be contradictory. To assume a triangle and reject its three angles is contradiction, but there is no contradiction involved in rejecting both the triangle and its three angles. The same treatment applies to the idea of an absolutely necessary Being. Eliminate its existence and you eliminate the thing itself and all its predicates; how then could there by any contradiction? Externally there is nothing to cause contradiction, for nothing external requires it; internally there is nothing at all, since its internal properties were eradicated along with the thing itself. That God is almighty is a judgment of necessity. If you accept deity, or an unlimited Being, you may not reject its almightiness, for this conception is identical with that of God. But if you say there is no God, then neither his almightiness nor any other attributes apear, for they were all erased with the subject and no trace of contradiction remains in the thought.

Thus we see that if both subject and predicate are eliminated, there will be no internal contradiction, let the predicate be what it may. The only remaining tactic would be to say there are subjects that may not be ruled out; they do remain. But this is only to say that there are absolutely necessary subjects, *which I question*, and you have to prove. For I cannot conceive of a thing which, if erased with all its properties, would leave a contradiction behind it. Contradiction is, moreover, among pure ideas, the only test for possibility.

Notwithstanding all these considerations, to which no one can object, I may be challenged with a case offering factual proof that there is one and only one idea, the eradication or nonexistence of whose object would entail self-contradiction. This is the idea of the Supreme Reality. *It* possesses all reality and, assuming the possibility of such a Being, is, no doubt, justified. Admit this, for the moment, even though the absence of self-contradiction in an idea is no *proof* that its object *is* possible. So reality involves existence, and existence is accordingly involved in the idea of a thing that is possible. If then this thing were removed, its internal possibilities would depart with it; but this is self-contradictory.

The answer is that when only the possibility of a thing is under consideration, a contradiction is involved in introducing the notion of existence, however it is disguised. To allow the introduction of that notion would be to concede the point at issue, although the winner would gain nothing from it; it would only produce a tautology. This is the question: Is the proposition that a thing exists analytic or amplifying? If it is analytic, the proposition adds nothing to the thought of the thing; in this case, the thing is as the thought has it. But if you have assumed that possibility means existence, that makes for wretched redundance. The word "reality" has a different sound when applied to the idea, unlike the sound of "existence" in the predicate, but this will not help. For if you place a thing and its predicates within the subject because you accept it as real, you only repeat it if you then put it in the predicate as well. If, on the contrary, you admit, as sensible people will, that all existence propositions are amplifying, how can it be asserted that the predicate of existence cannot be removed without contradiction? This is an advantage peculiar to analytic propositions and characteristic of them.

I had hoped to put a direct end to this grubbing argument with an accurate definition of existence, but the illusion produced by mistaking a logical property for a real one which defines a thing, is almost past correcting. Everything can be a logical predicate or property of something else; even a subject may be predicated of itself. Logic is indifferent to the content of ideas. But when a predicate which defines the idea of a subject is added to it, the idea is enlarged. The predicate must not, therefore, have been contained originally in the subject.

It is plain that *being* (to be, is) is no true predicate or conception which is addible to the idea of a thing. It is merely assertion of an object or of certain definitions of it. Logically, it is the copula, or connective in a judgment. The proposition *God is almighty* contains two ideas, each of which has its object, God and all-power. The little word *is*, is not an additional predicate but simply relates the predicate to the subject. If now I take the subject (God) with all its predicates, including almightyness, and say, *God is* or *there is a God*, no new property is added to the idea of God. There is only an assertion of the subject and its predicates, or perhaps the subject is made over into the object of my idea. The contents of both ideas are the same and nothing has been added. The proposition, moreover, expresses only a possibility, even when I think of its object as actual and absolute. Reality thus means no more than possibility.

A hundred real dollars contain not one cent more than a hundred possible dollars. The latter is my idea. The former is its object. If the object contained more than the idea, the idea I have would be inadequate. My finances, however, are improved more by one hundred real dollars than by their mere possibility as expressed in an idea; for the object's existence is not contained analytically in my idea but has to be added to it, amplifying it and thus defining my mental state. The actual hundred dollars is not increased at all by the additional idea of existence.

No matter what a thing's definitions and predicates may be, saying that it exists makes no difference. Otherwise, my idea would not match its object, and I could not say that the exact object of my idea existed! If I attribute to a thing all real properties except one, the missing property is not replaced by my saying that this defective thing exists. It would exist with the defect I think it has, or what exists would not be what I think. When, then, I think of the Being of highest reality (having no defects), the question always remains whether it exists or not. For even though nothing is missing from my idea of the possible content of a thing, something is missing from the relation of my idea to my whole mind when I do not know whether the thing can be experienced. And this points to the source of our difficulty. If we deal with a sense object, there can be no mistaking its existence for an idea of it. For through the idea, we consider that the object meets the conditions of possible experience generally. *By existence it is conceived as being embedded in the context of experience as a whole.* The idea of the object is not in the least enlarged by being connected with the content of experience. All that has been added to thought is one more possible perception. If, however, an attempt is made to consider existence by means of a pure category, it should be no surprise that existence is indistinguishable from possibility.

Whatever content the idea of an object may have, to attribute existence to it one must go beyond the idea. With sense objects, this occurs through perception and according to empirical laws. With objects of pure thought, however, there is no such means of discovering their existence; it would have to be known abstractly and in advance. Consciousness of existence, whether immediately through perception or via inferences connecting something to perception, is part of the unity of experience. Existence outside this field should not be declared impossible, but it is an unjustifiable assumption.

The idea of a Supreme Being is in many ways useful, but of itself, it extends our knowledge not at all. It tells us nothing of the possibility of a Being outside our experience. Of course, the analytic criterion of possibility, the absence of contradiction, applies to it; but the celebrated Leibniz was far from achieving what he proudly claimed: the establishment of the possibility of a sublime, ideal Being by pure thought. He failed because the real properties of a thing are not specified in advance, and accordingly, abstract prediction of their organization is not possible; and even if real properties were specified, still no prediction could be made because in amplifying propositions, experience is always the criterion of possibility, experience in which no object of a pure idea ever appears.

The attempt to establish the existence of a Supreme Being by the famed ontological argument of Descartes is likewise so much labor lost. A person trying to extend his insight by accumulating ideas would be like a merchant trying to get rich by adding zeroes to the totals of his cash account.

The cosmological proof, which Leibniz called proof *from the contingency of the world*, is at any rate natural, and speculatively more convincing. It goes like this: If anything exists, an absolutely necessary Being must exist. But I, at least, exist; so an absolutely necessary Being exists. The minor premise asserts experience, and the major premise, a general inference from experience to necessary being.

This inference is too well known to require complete exposition. It is based on the evident formal law of causality in nature: that everything contingent has its cause and if this cause in turn is also contingent, it too must have a cause, until the series of successively subordinate causes ends in an absolutely necessary Cause, without which it could never be complete.

The proof thus begins with experience and is not wholly abstract or ontological. It is called cosmological because the world is the object of all possible experience. *Because* it stays away from any special properties of the objects of experience by which this world can be distinguished from any other, it differs also from the physico-theological proof, which depends on special characteristics of the sense world.

The proof then proceeds: There is only one way to define the necessary Being and that is by one of each pair of all possible contradictory predicates. It must therefore be defined completely within its own idea. There is, however, only one idea that completely defines a thing, abstractly and in advance, and that is the idea of the supreme reality, which, therefore, is the one idea through which necessary Being may be conceived. So a Supreme Being necessarily exists.

The cosmological argument involves so many miscarriages of thought that it would seem that speculative reason must have rallied its total resources of dialectic skill to produce a maximum of formal illusion. The assay of the proof is therefore postponed a while, until a list is made of the devices by which an old argument is dressed up to look new, and appeal is made to the agreement of two witnesses, namely, pure reasoning and experience. The only real witness, however, is pure reasoning, which changes costume and voice to appear as the experience.

For a secure foundation, the proof starts from experience and to show that it is different from the ontological proof, which puts its trust entirely in pure ideas. It uses experience to make one step only—the step to the existence of necessary Being. The empirical part of the proof, however, has nothing to offer about the properties of necessary Being, so reason takes off to look around among pure ideas for the kind of properties such a Being ought to have, i.e., to see which among all possible things logically implies the property of absolute necessity. The requisite property is found only in the idea of the supreme reality, and the conclusion is, therefore, that the supreme reality is an absolute and necessary Being.

The assumption here is that the idea of supreme reality is adequate to the idea of absolute necessity in existence, that is, that the latter can be inferred from the former. This is, of course, the proposition that was set forth in the ontological proof, and it is now borrowed as a basis for the cosmological proof although it was intended that the latter should avoid it. For absolute necessity is an entity derived from pure ideas. Now if I should say that the idea of the supreme reality is similarly derived and the only one apposite to necessary being, I should have to admit that the latter may be derived from the former. The force of the so-called cosmological proof derives from pure ideas and the ontological argument. The appeal to experience is superfluous; it served to lead us to the idea of absolute necessity but did not demonstrate absolute necessity in any definite object. For when this was required, experience had to be abandoned at once and search made among pure ideas to see which of them implied the conditions for the possibility of absolute, necessary being. If the possibility of such a Being was thus discovered, its existence followed; for this is what was said: Among all the possibilities, there is one that involves absolute necessity, and the existence of such being *is* absolutely necessary.

Thus speculative reasoning's second path, which was chosen to prove the existence of the Supreme Being, is as illusory as the first, but adds the fault of a fallacy by speciously proving something not at issue; it also promises a new route but takes a short cut back to the point of departure on the first path, which was to be abandoned for the new way.

I have just said that there is a whole nest of false assumptions hidden in the cosmological argument, assumptions easily discovered and destroyed by formal criticism. I shall merely list them here, leaving it to the skill of the reader to follow up the illusions and root them out.

We find, first, the formal inference of a cause from a contingency. The principle that every contingent thing has a cause is valid but only in the sense world. It means nothing otherwise. Unlike causality, the pure idea of contingency does not produce an amplifying proposition, but neither has causality any meaning or criterion except in the sense world. In this argument causality is intended to go beyond sense experience.

Second, there is the inference of a First Cause, based on the impossibility of an infinite series of ascending causes within the sense world, an inference forbidden by logic even within experience; here the series extends beyond experience, which is doubly forbidden.

Third, the reasoning by which the series is completed, the removal of conditions without which an idea of necessity is impossible, and the assumption that the series is complete because one can think of no further terms: all these show false pride.

Fourth, there is the confusion of the logical possibility of an idea of unified reality (i.e., the absence of inner contradiction) with the formal possibility of it which requires that organizing it shall be practicable, a principle which again requires the world of experience, etc.

It may be allowable to assume the existence of an all-sufficient Being as the cause of all possible effects, in order to facilitate the achievement of coherent explanations by reasoning. But to assert that such a Being necessarily exists is no longer the modest expression of a permissible hypothesis. It is bold assurance of apodictic certainty; for to know absolute necessity, one must know it with absolute necessity.

Both of the proofs thus far attempted are formal, and independent of experience. Even though the cosmological proof started with it, it referred to no particular feature of it, relying instead on pure reason to reveal the existence of things generally known by experience. The proof abandoned even the leads of experience when it needed the support of pure ideas. Why then do these formal proofs contain dialectical but natural illusions, such as those which connect necessity with supreme reality, and turn mere ideas into self-sufficient entities? Why is it that when among existing things something has to be assumed necessary, we shrink back from the existence of such an entity as from any abyss? How can our reasoning be delivered from this equivocal approval and disapproval, and by being self-consistent, achieve the quality of calm insight?

If I must attribute some necessity to all existing things and yet not to any single thing by itself, the conclusion is inevitable that necessity and contingency are not properties of things-themselves. For if they were, they would be mutually contradictory and so could not be objective. They may be regarded, however, as subjective principles, useful in reasoning. In this case, "necessity" would require a reason for everything and allow no satisfaction with any explanation that is not complete, wholly abstract and prior. "Contingency," however, would forbid the hope of such an explanation or the assumption that any part of experience is unconditioned. It would require that the way ahead be always kept open. In this sense, the two principles are revelatory, regulative, and compatible, since they concern only formal reasoning.

The first indicates that we ought to philosophize about nature as if there were a necessary first cause of every existing thing, if only to bring systematic unity to our knowledge by always looking for an imagined first cause. The other warns against any single definition of a thing's existence being mistaken for the first cause or being regarded as absolutely necessary; the way is always to be kept open to further progress, all definitions meanwhile being held as conditional. If then all perceived objects are to be regarded as conditionally necessary, experience could not possibly turn up anything absolutely necessary.

Granting that absolute necessity is intended only as a principle by which to achieve the greatest possible unity among phenomena and to serve as their ulitmate cause, and that contingency requires that empirical causes be considered always as derived, an absolutely necessary entity can exist only outside this world.

These remarks will indicate that the supreme being is merely a regulating principle of reasoning, which requires that all the connections of the world of sense shall be treated as if they came of all-sufficient, necessary causes. The supreme being is to be used to promote system and coherence in explanations of the world under general laws. It does not involve asserting the existence of any absolutely necessary Being. It is inevitable, however, that by a formal and surreptitious representation, this principle should sometimes appear to be constitutive, and that unity should seem to be a self-subsisting entity. The same thing happens with space. Although space is only a principle of sense, serving originally to make all the forms which limit it possible, it is taken as an absolutely necessary and independent entity and, abstractly and in advance, it is treated as if it were an actual object. This is the present case. The systematic unity of nature cannot be used empirically as a principle of reasoning unless it is based on the idea of a Supreme Being as the highest cause, which Supreme Being, in turn, is regarded as an actual object and is declared necessary because it is the supreme condition. In this way a regulative principle is made constitutive, and the substitution becomes evident the moment that Supreme Being, which was absolutely necessary as far as the world was concerned, is considered a thing-itself. This necessity entails no idea and exists in my reasoning only as a formal condition of thought, not as a material and independent condition for the existence of anything.

Since, then, neither the idea nor the *general* experience of things can provide what we need, there remains one more field to try. Let us see if *definite* experience with things as they are, their constitution and order, does not provide the basis for a proof through which a secure conviction of the existence of a Supreme Being may be achieved. This proof is called physico-theological.

The world presents on an immeasurable stage so much variety, order, purpose, and beauty, disclosed alike in the infinite and infinitesimal parts of it, that the little knowledge gathered by our poor minds, and even all language, pales before its inconceivable marvels. Here, numbers lose their power to measure, thoughts lose their definiteness, and judgment of the whole is dissolved in speechless amazement, but it is not less eloquent therefore. Everywhere the chain of cause and effect, of ends and means, and the regularity of creation and dissolution, are to be seen; and since of itself nothing came to be what it is, everything points to something else as its cause, which as usual requires further investigation.

Nevertheless, the "All" itself would sink into the abyss of nothingness if we could not assume something to support it, something more than endless contingency. There must be a self-subsistent entity, original and independent, which is the origin of the universe and keeps it going. Seeing how great the world is, how great does that cause need to be? We do not know much of the world's content. We know still less how to estimate it in comparison to all existence. Still, causality requires an external, Supreme Being. What, then, is to hinder us from attributing to that Being a degree of perfection that sets it above all other possible existence? This is easily done, though only in the slender outlines of abstract ideas, by telling ourselves that this Supreme Being unites all possible perfections in a single substance. Such an idea meets the requirement of reasoning for economy in principles. There are no contradictions within it, and it could never conceivably be contradicted by experience. It would also favor the extension of reasoning by pointing to order and purpose.

This proof will always deserve to be mentioned with respect. It is the oldest, clearest proof, and the most agreeable to common sense. It enlivens the study of nature on which it depends and from which it constantly derives new impetus. It suggests purposes and intentions which observation does not ordinarily reveal and thus extends the study of nature under the guidance of special unity, a principle which is apart from nature. This knowledge reacts in turn on its cause, that is, on the idea that led to it, and so raises belief in a supreme Author to irresistible conviction.

It would be therefore be both vain and uncomfortable to try to diminish the authority of the proof. Its reasoning is supported by a mighty and ever-increasing mass of evidence, even if it is only empirical, and it will not be subdued by the doubts cast up by subtle, abstract, and dreamlike speculations. One is roused from grubbing indecision by a single glance at the wonders of nature, the majesty of the world; one is lifted from height to height, from condition to condition, up to the highest, the unconditioned Creator of all.

There is no objection to the usefulness and reasonableness of this procedure. It is rather to be encouraged and praised. The claims to absolute certainty which are made for it are not, however, to be approved. Neither is its unsupported claim to favor agreeable. It cannot hurt so good a cause, then, to tone down the glib persuasion, put forth on its behalf, to moderation and modesty of belief which, even if it does not command unconditional submission, suffices nevertheless to comfort. I assert, therefore, that the physico-theological proof can never of itself establish the existence of a Supreme Being but must leave that to the ontological proof, to which it is only an introduction. After all, the ontological proof contains the only possible and apposite argument, and human reasoning can never do without it, *supposing that there is speculative proof of the supreme existence.*

The main points of the physico-theological proof are as follows.

(1) Everywhere in the world there are clear signs of intentional order carried out with great wisdom in a universe indescribably varied in content and infinite in extent.

(2) This purposeful order is foreign to things as they are, and wholly contingent. Their nature forbids their co-operation in such variety and to definite ends unless they are chosen and designed by a rational, order-making principle to play a part agreeable to fundamental rules.

(3) There exists, therefore, a sublime and wise cause (perhaps more than one) which is the cause of the world, not as blind and almighty nature might do it, being fruitful, but as mind might do it, freely.

(4) The unity of this cause may be inferred certainly from the unity displayed in the reciprocal relations of the parts of the world, like the unity of the members of a skillfully built structure. Such unity may be inferred *certainly* as far as observation can verify it; beyond this it may be inferred *probably*, as the principle of analogy provides.

Without intending chicanery over the conclusion of natural reasoning, i.e., the conclusion that nature's products are analogous to those begotten of human skill, violence is done to nature by requiring that it work, not in its own way but in ours, as houses, ships, and clocks must do. The inference is that there is a similar cause which is mind and will, and which is fundamental to nature. From it comes the notion of the possibility of an inner freedom in nature, the freedom that first made human art and then reason itself possible, and which is derived from another superhuman freedom. This is a kind of reasoning that might not withstand the sharp criticism of formal philosophy. If we do have to name a cause, however, it must be admitted that we cannot improve on the method of analogy with purposeful human products, the only ones with whose causes and effects we are fully acquainted. There could be no justification for abandoning known causality for vague and nondemonstrable principles of explanations about which we really know nothing.

This argument, from the purpose and harmony of nature, might prove that *form* is contingent but the world's *substance* is not. To prove the contingency of substance, it would be necessary to show that obedient to universal laws, things could not achieve order and harmony by themselves if their substance were not likewise a product of wisdom. To prove this would require grounds very different from those taken from the analogy of human art. The most that could be proved in this case would be that the world has an architect whose style is cramped by the crudity of his materials. The argument would not unveil a creator to whose thought everything is subject, nor would it by any means be adequate to demonstrate an all-sufficient original being. For the proof of contingency of matter, recourse to formal argument is indicated. But this was to be avoided.

The inference is that the order and design observable everywhere in the world is contingent and that a cause proportional to it exists. The thought of that cause teaches some very definite things about it, i.e., it cannot be other than omnipotent, omniscient Being who, in brief, is also perfect and all-sufficient. But no very definite notions emerge from predicates like *very great, astounding, immeasurable power,* and *virtue;* these never tell us what their subject is really like. They merely represent the size of a world relatively, which the observer compares with himself, and which would be equally grand whether the object is magnified or the subject reduced. Such words yield no definite ideas about the size or perfection of the object in question except when the object includes all possible perfection, and then only its *allness* is completely defined. I hope that no one will undertake to comprehend the relation of the world as he sees it, both in extent and matter, to omnipotence, or world unity to the absolute unity of its author, or world order to the highest wisdom, etc.

Physico-theology gives no definite notion of the world's ultimate cause. It will not serve as a foundation for a religion which is, in turn, based on theology. Even though the journey to absolute totality is utterly impossible by the empirical road, this is, nonetheless, just what the physico-theological proof undertakes. What then are the means that have been used to bridge so wide a cleft?

When one has been led to wonder at the greatness, the wisdom, the might, etc., of the Author of the world and can get no further, one abandons the empirically conducted argument and resorts again to contingency, which was the original inference in the first part of the argument from the order and purpose of the world. It is only from this contingency, and by way of formal ideas, that an absolutely necessary Being is inferred. Then from the absolute necessity of the first cause, it is only a step to a completely defined or definable conception of the all-inclusive reality. Thus the physico-theological proof being stopped in its undertaking, suddenly falls back on the cosmological proof, and since this is only the ontological proof in disguise, the physico-theological proof really fulfilled its mission with pure reason alone, although at first all relation to pure reason was disclaimed and argument was to be based only on the clear evidence of experience.

Accordingly, the physico-theological proof depends on the cosmological proof and this in turn depends on the ontological proof of the existence of one original, supreme Being. Since, then, these three are the only ways open to speculative reasoning, the ontological proof, from the clear ideas of pure reason, is the only possible proof, supposing that there can be any proof of a proposition so sublime and reaching so far beyond human experience.

If it is preferable to doubt the foregoing arguments of the *Analytic* rather than to be robbed of one's conviction that the proofs which have been trusted so long are valuable, doubters will at least not refuse my request for a satisfactory account of the illumination they trust, when they fly so far beyond experience merely on the wings of pure ideas. Let me beg at once to be excused from new proofs or improved workmanship on old ones. The choice is limited, no doubt, since all speculative proofs come down to the ontological proof in the end. I shall not be afraid of the fecundity of dogmatic defenders of reasoning delivered from sense limitations. Even though I do not consider myself much of an antagonist, I shall not decline an invitation to discover the error in any attempt of this kind and so to dispose of its claims.

I know, however, only too well that the hope of better luck springs eternal in the breasts of those accustomed to dogmatic convictions. Thus I restrict myself to one just demand: Let my opponents justify generally, from the nature of mind or other sources of knowledge, their beginning to extend knowledge solely by abstract and prior considerations, then their pushing beyond the reach of experience where there is no possible way to establish the objective reality of ideas. Whatever the mental process by which an idea is conceived, the existence of its object is not analytically contained in it; for to know that an object exists means to know that it exists apart from our thoughts. It is, however, wholly impossible to start from an idea and discover new objects or transcendent beings without following the actual empirical connections without which no phenomena would ever exist.

Speculative reasoning is wholly unequal to so vast a project as the discovery of a Supreme Being. It has, nevertheless, great usefulness in the correction of our knowledge of that Being which is derived from other sources, so that it is self-consistent, and consistent with all other intelligent points of view, and purified from matter incompatible with the idea of the Supreme Being, and free from all other empirical limitations.

Formal theology is therefore important negatively, despite its disabilities. It can be a permanent censor of any reasoning done with pure ideas only, which ideas require formal standards. Suppose, for example, that on practical grounds the hypothesis of a highest and all-sufficient Being, the supreme intelligence, is declared valid and uncontradicted. It would be of the greatest importance to be able to define this conception of the necessary and most real of all beings exactly and formally. It would be important to remove ideas incompatible with highest reality or any purely phenomenal matter. In its wider sense this means getting rid of anthropomorphisms.

At the same time, all contradictory assertions, such as those of atheism, deism, or anthropomorphism, could be done away. Critical treatment like this would be easy, because the same principles by which the inadequacy of human reason to the assertion of a divine

Being was demonstrated, would apply equally to prove the invalidity of the opposite assertions. For where would anyone by purely speculative reasoning acquire the insight that there is no Supreme Being, or all-inclusive Cause? Or where is knowledge to be had that the properties we ascribe to the Supreme Being, properties analogous to the dynamic realities of a thinking being, are misplaced? Or how does one come to know, as anthropomorphism suggests, that the divine Being would be subject to the limitations inevitably imposed by sense on all the minds with which we have had experience?

The Supreme Being is just an ideal for the uses of speculative reasoning, but it is a flawless ideal and an ideal which finishes and crowns all knowledge. Its objective reality can be neither proved nor disproved by pure reasoning. If then there should be a moral theology to make good the deficiency, formal theology which previously had been so problematical could prove indispensable. It could define required ideas, constantly censoring the reasoning so often led astray by sense and not always compatible with its own ideas. Necessity, infinity, unity, existence apart from the world (not being a world soul), eternity unconditioned by time, omnipresence unconditioned by space, the almighty, etc., are thus purely formal predicates, and purified ideas of them are necessary to every theology but are derived only from formal theology.

Part Two

THE METAPHYSICAL FOUNDATIONS OF MORALS

21 THE MORAL LAW IS PURE WISDOM

Duty, imperatives, and the moral law

In 1785, four years after the publication of The Critique of Pure Reason, *Kant produced articles on the philosophy of history, volcanoes on the moon, book reprinting, the concept of races, and finally his basic work on morals, or ethics:* The Metaphysical Foundations of Morals. *The latter may seem a little easier than the first* Critique *because the reader will feel more often that he can identify its thought in his own experience, but the wind of Kant's doctrine is still not tempered to the shorn lamb.*

Throughout his works, Kant's frequent references to matters of theology and ethics inform us that he also was habitually concerned with religion as people generally think of it. The earnest integrity of his thought bears witness to the deeper religious concern of the man. Certainly this first of his works on morality was no afterthought: it must be regarded as integral to his system of thought. The critical principles established by the usage of the first Critique *are present in full vigor in* The Metaphysical Foundations of Morals. *It also ends on a negative note. Having discussed at length the "mind world" and the "kingdom of ends" with eloquence and assurance, he rules them off-limits, so to speak, because he wants to "save much feeble wing flapping by those who mean to hunt transcendent ideas in the empty spaces of the 'mind world' "! At first sight, this is something of a let-down.*

His moral principles presuppose The Critique of Pure Reason. *Mind is still nature's lawgiver, and man, the moral lawgiver is free: "He is free under nature's laws because he obeys only those he himself makes." Even the structural principles of his philosophical building remain essentially unchanged. What the categories are to pure thought, the categorical imperative is to willing. It shapes and aims man's willing by telling him what he "ought" to do: he* ought to give effect to the highest good, in good will itself. Indeed, the prime use of reasoning is to design good will.

Kant's ethical thought is as impersonal as his thought about thinking. This can be made clear by contrast: Christian ethics refers to a specific person at a specific place and time for illustration and definition. There is nothing specific about any of Kant's thoughts. The principles of his ethics are deduced from pure thought which is as formal, impersonal, and general as possible. They remain aloof from any examples of actual moral laws that might be adduced to illustrate them. Presumably a law is moral when it satisfies the categorical imperative. Furthermore, "nothing more evil could ever happen to morality than to assert its derivation from examples." What man is, is not what he ought to be. This leads to a touching passage dealing with the failure of morality as a teaching discipline. Moral teachers fail, he finds, because their "ideas are too often impure," i.e., they try to reinforce their arguments with evidence taken from experience, and they weaken their case by so doing.

Will is defined as man's power to act by principles he makes for himself, and this signifies his humanity, in contrast to the nature of nonrational creatures who obey laws they neither invent nor comprehend. When, however, the categorical imperative calls a man to duty, and he says, "I will," his willing needs moral law stated as a formula. To this end, Kant develops a series of formulas: (1) Let my personal rule of action be fit for general law; (2) Let me treat people as ends and never as means; (3) Let my acts reveal autonomous willing; (4) Let me act as a lawgiving member of the kingdom of ends.

Some of Kant's thoughts on morality and religion obviously derive from the Scriptures. There, the law is to be obeyed because it is God's law; Kant's argument for obedience is formally similar. As for good will, the unqualified good, given passion it could become love. The categorical imperative looks like a philosopher's improvement on the Golden Rule. The kingdom of ends is a bloodless version of the kingdom of God, where "reason" rules instead of Christ. Kant had indeed read the Bible and adapted many of its moral *notions to the requirements of his critical philosophy, but this does not mean that he thought morality depended on religion. There is nothing beyond the reach of psychology in his moral philosophy.*

It turns out that morality requires freedom, in which a man may develop his characteristic necessity: a respect for law in general, and in particular for moral law, which he makes. That he should be concerned to do his duty when duty is still "only an idea" and that this choosing and this willing should result in human freedom is inexplicable. It is indeed a mystery that immaterial ideas cause people to act in characteristic ways. Kant then refers to a "special kind of causation" which is required to explain effects "admittedly real in everyone's experience." His reasoning, however, tells him that any such idea as a special causation is intolerable and he finds that he has thus arrived at the limit beyond which, rationally, no man may go. What his private thoughts were at this point when he gazed but would not trespass, we shall never know. In public, he preferred to be a philosopher beyond reproach. Having given out the principles of his trade, he stopped where they ended.

Philosophy based on experience is said to be empirical; but if its doctrines are abstract and prior, it is said to be pure. Pure and merely formal philosophy is then called logic, but logic becomes metaphysics when it is focused on definite mental objects.

This is the origin of the idea that there are two kinds of metaphysics, the metaphysic of nature and the metaphysic of morals. Physics, for example, is both empirical and theoretical, and so is ethics; but the empirical part of ethics should be called *practical anthropology*, while its theory is properly called *morals*. . . .

Since my present concern here is really with moral wisdom, I limit my question to this: Isn't the construction of a pure moral philosophy, a philosophy freed of all empiricism or matter assignable to anthropology, of the utmost necessity? It must be evident from the common idea of duty and from moral laws that such a philosophy is possible. Everyone will admit that a law, to have moral force and to be the basis of obligation, must carry with it absolute necessity. The commandment "Thou shalt not lie" would not hold for men if there were any other intelligent beings not obligated to observe it. It is the same with all other genuine moral laws. The basis of moral obligation must be sought, consequently, not in human nature or man's circumstances but abstractly and in advance, in the ideas of pure reason. A precept based on experience may be universal in some respects, but if it is empirical at all, even only in motive, it may be a practical rule, but it is not a moral law.

In practical knowledge, therefore, moral laws and principles are distinguished from others which are to any degree empirical. Moral philosophy depends altogether on pure knowledge. It gets nothing from anthropology but instead gives mankind abstract and prior laws because men are rational beings. These laws require, no doubt, judgment which has been sharpened by experience, to enable the selection of the cases to which a law may be applicable and to procure for it access to human willing and so to secure its effect on conduct. So many inclinations urge a man, that he cannot easily work out a moral idea in a specific case even though he is capable of pure practical reasoning.

Pure and authentic moral law occurs, however, only in pure philosophy, and this is of the utmost importance practically. A metaphysic must therefore precede moral philosophy. No mere mixture of pure and empirical principles deserves the name of philosophy. Much less does a mixture deserve the name of moral philosophy because it spoils the very purity of moral meaning; it defeats its own purpose. Commonplace theory offers this kind of confusion, whereas philosophy is distinguished by treating separate sciences separately.

1. *Good will tempers goodness*

Within this world or out of it no one can think of anything unqualifiedly good except good will. Intelligence, wit, judgment, and other namable gifts of mind, or courage, resolution, endurance, and other qualities of temperament, are without doubt good and desirable in many respects, but they can also be bad and hurtful if the will or character that puts them to use is not good. It is the same with fortune's gifts. Power, wealth, honor, health, general well-being, and contentment with one's lot and all that promotes happiness, may give rise to pride and presumption unless good will corrects the influence of such conditions on the soul and adapts the trend of a man's behavior to the purpose of his life. No intelligent and impartial bystander can approve the spectacle of a person who enjoys unbroken prosperity but exhibits no trace of pure good will. Good will alone makes one worthy of happiness.

There are personal qualities which help good will and make its work easier. They presuppose good will and are therefore not independently valuable. The esteem in which they are justly held is thus qualified: moderation in affection and passions, self-control, and sober reflection. They are not only good in many respects but they seem even to constitute in part a person's inner worth. They are, however, not to be described as unqualifiedly good, however highly the ancients may have honored them; for without principled good will, they may be evil indeed. Cold-bloodedness in a villain makes him not only more dangerous but more ugly to behold.

Good will is not good because of the achievements it inspires or because it is a peculiarly fit means to an end, but only because it is *willing*, and thus is good in itself alone. It is to be rated far above anything accomplished by means of it to some desired end or ends. Suppose that by special bad luck or because of the niggardly provision of a stepmotherly nature, one lacked the power to go through with a purpose of good will, and one's maximum effort in that direction therefore failed so that good will alone remained; it would still shine like a jewel with its own light, as something the whole value of which consists in what it is. Good will, in this case, is more than a mere wish; it is the straining of every means within one's power to a good end. Neither usefulness nor fruitfulness can add to its value or diminish it. At the same time, by usefulness, good will appears to advantage in the day's work; usefulness makes it attractive to tyros but neither recommends it to connoisseurs nor fixes its worth.

There is, however, something strange in the idea of the absolute worth of willing apart from any use. Notwithstanding that the idea fits common sense, the statement that reason governs willing could be suspected of high-flown fantasy and a misreading of nature's purpose. Let us study the idea from this point of view.

2. *Reasoning designs good will*

We assume that the bodily organization of a creature designed to live contains no organs except those best adapted to their purposes. Suppose, then, that a reasoning, willing being is intended by nature to take good care of himself, or, let us say, to be happy. Nature would make a bad choice if reasoning were chosen as the vehicle of this purpose. For whatever must be done to this end, the rules for doing it would be laid down securely by instinct. Instinct achieves nature's purpose far more surely than reasoning. By virtue of the power of reasoning, however, this happy creature could contemplate his own lovely nature, admiring it, congratulating himself, feeling thankful to the beneficent cause that gave it but not thankful that his desires are subject to such weak and deceptive guidance as reasoning affords; for reasoning bungles nature's designs. In a word, nature would have prevented reasoning from crashing into action with such weak insights or presuming to plan either happiness or the means of attaining it. Nature not only chooses the ends but also the means, and entrusts both to instinct.

In fact, we find that the more a man of cultivated reason applies himself deliberately to the enjoyment of life and happiness, the more he misses true satisfaction. One result is that many people feel a certain misology or disgust with reasoning but are not candid enough to confess it. When they strike a balance on the advantages derived from it, they find in fact that it does not increase their happiness but multiplies their burden. Sooner or later they come to disdain common people but to envy them for living closer to their instincts and because their lives are so little affected by reasoning. I am not thinking here of the inventions of common luxuries, or even of the sciences, which after all seem to be intellectual luxuries.

It must be confessed of those who would like to tone down or even to stop eulogizing reasoning for the happiness and satisfaction it is supposed to afford, that their judgment is not sour, neither are they ungrateful for the goodness in the government of the world. Their judgments may be based on the idea that man's existence has a purpose, other and more worthy than happiness, for which reasoning is intended and that this is the supreme condition to which all private ends must be subordinated.

Reasoning is not competent to lead willing to its objects or to the satisfaction of man's many needs, needs that reasoning only tends to multiply. Instincts were planted by nature for the sure guidance of willing. Reasoning, nonetheless, is also a practical function, intended to influence willing by making it good, not as a means to further good but as an end, good in itself. For this purpose reasoning is absolutely necessary in a world where otherwise nature has distributed capacities in proportion to the work to be done. Good will need not be considered the only good or the complete good, but it is the supreme good and the condition of all other good things, including the desire for happiness.

Under these circumstances, the development of reasoning is necessary to the creation of good will. It is also consistent with the attainment of happiness, which is always conditional. These two ends do indeed seem to interfere with each other in many ways, at least in this life, but that does not impugn nature's wisdom. Indeed, happiness may even be eliminated altogether without derailing nature. The establishment of good will being reason's highest function, the very achievement of it brings peculiar satisfactions which come of fulfilling a wholly reasonable purpose, even if it does run counter to one's inclinations in the process.

3. Thought discovers duty

We now develop a notion of willing which is valuable for its own sake and nothing further. This notion, which is already native to a sound, natural mind, needs only to be clarified rather than taught. It is of first-rate importance in estimating the worth of any human action, because it is the condition of all the rest. Thus let us take up the idea of duty. This will include good will, but with certain subjective limitations and hindrances which do not in the least obscure it. Instead, it stands out by contrast with them, shining only the more brightly.

I omit at this point all behavior recognized as contrary to duty. It may be useful for this or that purpose but the question whether a deed is done from a sense of duty does not occur, for by hypothesis it conflicts with duty. I also set aside deeds consonant with duty, to which people have no immediate inclination and which require other motivation. It is easy to decide whether something is done from a sense of duty or from self-interest. The distinction is harder when the deed is consonant with duty but also follows on a person's immediate inclination to do it. For example, it is a dealer's duty not to overcharge an inexperienced customer. Where much business is done, a smart merchant sells to everybody at the same fixed price, and a child may do as well with him as anybody else. This is honest service but it would not for a moment make one believe that the merchant behaved so from a sense of duty or on the principle of honesty. His own advantage required it. We do not suppose that he was partial to customers in general, so that just because he loved them all he would not give one an advantage over the other in price. So his action was done neither from duty nor from immediate inclination but just from self-interest.

On the other hand, self-preservation is a duty, and everybody is immediately disposed to it; this is why the anxious care expended by most people to this end is intrinsically worthless and the policy on which they act is amoral. They take care of themselves as duty requires. On the other hand, suppose that adversity and hopeless misery take away a man's taste for life. He is then unhappy, but he is still strong-minded, and more indignant over his fate than cast down or despairing. He wants to die but keeps his life, not because he loves it, or wants to, or from fear, but from a sense of duty: *his* policy is moral.

It is our duty to do good when we can, and more than this, there are many souls so sympathetically disposed that without a motive, either of pride or self-interest, they take pleasure in spreading joy around, delighting to satisfy others by their efforts. I maintain that in such a case, their deeds, however dutiful and amiable, have no moral worth but may be paired off with other inclinations such as the desire for honor. This is indeed honorable, and if, fortunately, it is in the public interest, or in line of duty, their conduct will deserve praise and encouragement but not respect. Its principle is not moral, for morality requires such behavior to come of a sense of duty and not by desire.

Take the case of a philanthropist whose mind is beclouded with sorrow, so much so that his sympathy for other people is completely extinguished. He still could do good to others even then, but because he is absorbed in his own grief, their needs touch him not at all. Now suppose that without any inclination to do so, he breaks out of his dead impassivity and does good simply for duty's sake; then for the first time his work has genuine moral worth.

Again suppose that a certain upright man has small sympathy for others. From his own experience he has acquired special patience and endurance. He thinks that other people should do the same, and so is cold or indifferent to them. He is not nature's meanest product, and even if he is not cut out for philanthropy, is there not a source within him from which worth beyond the reach of a merely good-natured man might come? By all means! Incomparably the highest moral character comes of doing good, not from good feeling, but from a sense of duty.

At least indirectly it is one's duty to keep happy, for discontent under the pressures and cares of unsatisfied needs may easily become a strong temptation to transgress duty. Furthermore, duty aside, people generally have a powerful, composite, inner urge to happiness, within which all other urges are summed up. This composite urge to happiness is often such that it stultifies separate urges. But people are unable to define their idea of the sum-of-satisfactions which goes by the name of happiness, and it is not to be wondered at that a separate urge carrying definite promises which are to be kept at a definite time can supersede a wobbling idea of general satisfaction. Or it is no surprise that a gouty person, for example, chooses to enjoy this and suffer that, calculating that he should not pass up a momentary present pleasure for some unstable expectation of happiness supposed to reside in future good health. Even in this case, if the general desire for happiness does not control his willing, and health does not seem important in his calculations, one recourse will remain to him as it does to all others. It is the law that happiness is promoted not through an urge or inclination but via duty, and in doing his duty his conduct would acquire moral worth.

The passages of Scripture in which love of neighbors and even of enemies is commanded are, without doubt, so to be understood. For love, as an affection, cannot be commanded, but doing good for duty's sake can be, even if one does not feel like doing it or is repelled by a natural and uncontrollable aversion to it. This is practical and not psychological love. It comes from willing and not from the set of one's feelings, or from principles of action and not from tender mercy. Only *love in practice* is subject to orders.

The second proposition is that dutiful action gets its moral worth not from the purpose for which it was done but from the personal policy that brought about the decision to do it. Thus moral worth depends not on the achieved object of an act but on the principle or character of the will behind it, irrespective of the desires involved. It is clear from the preceding passage that deeds get no unconditional moral worth from their purposes or from the effects which prompt willing. Where then is the worth of a deed if not in the relation of will to the effect hoped for? It can only be in the principle or character of willing without reference to the ends to be achieved. For between its formal, abstract and prior principle, and the material motive that appears only in retrospect, willing has come to a fork in the road when a decision must be taken. It is then that the formal character of willing requires a decision to act from a sense of duty, disregarding all material considerations.

4. *Duty leads to law*

The third proposition is a consequence of the two preceding. It can be expressed as follows: *Duty is the necessity of acting with respect for law.* I may be partial to the object of the action I propose to take but never respectful to it because it is to be the effect of my will and not its motive. Similarly, I do not respect *any* special objective, whether mine or someone else's. At most, I may approve my own or like someone else's, i.e., regard it as to my own advantage. The respected object which can command me has to be connected with my will as a principle and never as its own achieved effect. It must not support my partiality but overcome it and rule it out when a choice is to be made. Only law itself can be so respected and the origin of command. To act from a sense of duty, one's own inclinations must be set aside and with them all the objectives of willing so that nothing remains to control willing except, objectively, the law itself, and subjectively, a pure respect for practical law. The resulting personal policy is that law must be obeyed even when private inclinations are thwarted in the process. Notice that *a personal policy is a subjective principle of willing.* The objective principle of willing is the practical law, which would also be a subjective and practical principle of all rational beings if their desires were ruled wholly by reasoning.

The moral worth of a deed, therefore, is not in the effect expected from it, nor in any principle which has to borrow a motive from its hoped-for result. For any effects, such as agreeable circumstances or even the promotion of happiness for others, could have been set up by other causes, and rational willing would not be required to explain them; whereas the highest and unconditioned good is found only in willing. This paramount goodness, which we call moral, consists therefore in the conception of law, as such, and occurs admittedly only in a reasoning being where the conception, and not the effect expected, directs his willing.

It could be objected that with the word "respect," I am taking refuge in vague feeling, rather than giving a clear solution to the problem in reasoned thought. *Respect* is a feeling, but it is not the result of influence. It accompanies a rational idea and so is distinct from feelings such as belong to either desire or fear. The law I recognize, I recognize with respect; which means that consciously I subordinate my will to law without intermediate sense influences. Respect for law is the consciousness of immediate control of my willing by the law. It is the effect of law on the subject and not the cause of law. Respect is really a perception of a value, a perception that suppresses self-love. Law, accordingly, is not to be regarded as an object of desire or fear, though it is analogous to both. Only law may be the object of respect, the law which we impose on ourselves but still consider independently necessary. Self-love is not considered when we subject ourselves to law, and since law is self-imposed, it is a consequence of willing. Respect for persons is really only respect for law (the law of honesty, etc.) which a person may exemplify. All moral interest, as such, consists of reverence for law.

But what kind of law can be called absolutely good without qualification, when it controls volition without any promise of results to be obtained? Since I have taken from volition all motivation which is the result of obedience to law, nothing remains to serve willing as a principle or character but the general conformity of action to law. That is to say, *I ought never to act except so that I would want my policy to become universal law*. Here bare conformity to law in general, without assuming any particular law applied to any particular deed, is the principle of volition and must be its principle if duty is not to become a chimerical idea or a vain delusion. Common sense agrees in practice with this and keeps the principle always handy.

May I, for example, under pressure, make a promise which I intend not to keep? The two senses of this question are easily distinguished: is it prudent and is it right to make false promises? To the first, undoubtedly, the answer may often be "Yes." Of course it is not enough for me to get out of trouble by subterfuge. I must consider well whether a lie may not result in trouble greater than that from which I now try to break free. The consequences of my supposed cunning are not easily foreseen. Loss of credit may hurt me more than the evil I am trying to avoid. Wouldn't it be smarter to follow a general policy and make it my practice to make no promises unless I mean to keep them? Then it dawns on me that this policy is due only to my fear of the consequences.

It is quite a different matter to tell the truth from a sense of duty. In this case, the very idea of what I am to do brings law with it; in the case for prudence, I had to look around to see what the consequences might be for me. To depart from duty is certainly wickedness; to betray prudence may even be advantageous, although it is safer not to do so. The shortest and least trickish way, however, to discover whether a deceitful promise is consistent with duty, is to ask myself whether I could be content to have my policy (getting out of trouble by a dishonest promise) serve as a universal law, for me and for others. Could I tell myself that everyone who gets into trouble and cannot get out of it any other way may resort to dishonest promises? I become aware at once that I can will to lie but I cannot will that lying should become a universal law. Such a law would really forbid all promises. It would, moreover, be futile for me to proclaim my intentions about future actions to people who would not believe me or who, if they did believe me too readily, would soon repay me in my own currency. My policy would thus destroy itself if it were made universal.

No great perspicacity is required to see what I need to do to make my will morally good. Even though I may be inexperienced in the ways of the world and incapable of preparing for all contingencies, I ask myself: Would you make your rule universal? If not, discard it, not because of possible disadvantage to yourself or others, but because it will not fit into possible universal legislation as a principle. Mind at once constrains me to respect such legislation even though I may not see the basis for my respect. This is something for philosophers to investigate. I understand this much, however, that this respect is an estimate of a worth far surpassing any worth man might desire, and that *duty is a man's necessity to act out of pure respect for practical law,* and that every other motive must give way to duty, because duty is the condition of willing that is good of itself, and so is worth more than all else.

5. *Good morals begin in pure thought*

We have thus arrived at a common-sense principle of moral knowledge. It is not commonly conceived in such abstract or general form, but it is always before us as the standard of decision. It would be easy to show how people with such a compass in their hands could decide correctly in practice about good and bad, dutiful or undutiful actions, without further instruction, if, like Socrates, we could only direct their attention to their own principle. Neither science nor philosophy is required for knowledge of what one must do to be honest and good or even wise and virtuous. Indeed, one might have guessed long since that knowledge of what has to be done and therefore must be known is within the reach of even the commonest people.

The great advantage of practical judgment over theoretical appears in common minds, and there, commands admiration. When ordinary people make theoretical judgments, their reasoning simply becomes unintelligible and self-contradictory, involved in a chaos of uncertainty, vagueness, and instability if it gets away from experience or sense perception. In practical matters, however, judgment begins to appear to advantage among common people when they exclude sense motivation from practical law. Then subtleties begin to appear, perhaps some juggling with conscience, claims about right and wrong, or honest efforts to define the value of certain acts for their own instruction. What is more, in the evaluation of action they may turn out to be as right as philosophers could ever promise to be. Indeed, they are almost sure to do better because, in any case, the philosopher has no resource of principle other than what they have, and he can easily get lost in a multitude of irrelevant considerations. Would it not be wiser, then, to follow the judgments of common sense in moral matters or, at most, to use philosophy only to complete and clarify the system of morals and to put the rules in more convenient form for use of disputation, but not to distract common people's minds from their happy simplicity or try to lead them in fresh paths of inquiry and instruction?

I have a letter asking why moral instruction is so ineffective when, rationally, it is so convincing. This is my answer: Teachers' ideas are too often impure, in that they want to make morality look good, and they offer all kinds of inducements to moral behavior. They spoil the medicine by trying to make it strong. Ordinary observation shows that righteous acts done with steadfast mind and no regard for advantage in this world or the next, perhaps even in the face of strong temptation from need or allurement, are far better than similar deeds effected, however slightly, with alien motives. They put these latter acts in the shade, but they uplift a person and inspire the wish to be pure in heart. Even children in adolescence are so impressed, and duty should never be presented otherwise.

It must not be inferred that the conception of duty just presented is empirical because it has been taken from the reasoning of everyday practice. To the contrary, there are many complaints, some admittedly justified, that sure examples of deeds done from pure duty are not discoverable in everyday conduct. To be sure, much that people do is done dutifully but whether any of it has moral worth because it is done from sense of duty is doubtful. Thus there have always been philosophers who have absolutely denied that any human actions actually exemplify a disinterested spirit, and who have therefore ascribed men's deeds simply to more or less refined self-interest. This does not mean that they cast doubt on the rightness of morality as an idea. On the contrary, they speak with sincere sorrow of the frailty and impurity of human nature, which is indeed noble enough to take so reverend an idea for a rule but too weak to carry it out. Reasoning, which ought to legislate, is useful only to take care of man's inclinations either singly, or better, all together, when they are compatible.

It is a fact that in practice it is absolutely impossible to cite with certainty a single case in which the principle of an otherwise dutiful deed was based solely on moral grounds and the conception of duty. Sometimes it happens that the sharpest self-examination turns up nothing except the principle of duty, which was strong enough to move a person to a good deed or to great sacrifice. It cannot be inferred with certainty from this, however, that there is no secret impulse of self-love behind such an exhibition of dutifulness, which impulse really aimed the willing and pulled the trigger. We like to take credit for noble motives when in fact it is not possible to get behind the secret drives of human nature even with the strictest tests. When the topic is moral worth, we should be concerned not with visible behavior but with its visible springs.

In addition, unless the intention is to withhold all truth and applicability from moral ideas, it must be agreed that moral laws are absolutely and necessarily valid, not only for us but for all rational creatures, without condition or exception. It would at once be clear that no experience of ours could produce these laws with this degree of certainty. By what right, then, could we promote a principle that is perhaps valid only under the conditions of human nature to the limited respect accruing to a general prescription for all rational life? How could moral laws regulate the wills of all rational creatures if the moral laws are merely empirical and did not originate abstractly or in advance from pure but practical reasoning?

Nothing more evil could ever happen to morality than to assert its derivation from examples. Each example given must previously have been tested by the principles of morality to see if it is a worthy source of morals and whether it will serve as a pattern even though it does not by any means offer the highest idea of morality. Even the *Holy One of the Gospels* has first to be compared to our ideal of moral perfection before we recognize him for what he is. As he says of himself: *Why do you all call me* (whom you see) *good? No one is good* (the archetype of goodness) *but God* (whom you do not see). Where do we get the idea of God as the supreme good? Simply from the idea of moral perfection, developed by reasoning abstractly and in advance; it is, moreover, an idea indissolubly bound up with the notion of free will. There is no room in morality for imitation. Examples serve only for encouragement. They establish the practicability of what the moral law commands. They make visible what the practical rule expresses in generalizations, but they never justify setting aside their true originals in reasoning, in favor of examples as guides. . . .

From what has been said, it appears that moral ideas originate abstractly and in advance from reasoning, both from ordinary people's reasoning and from high speculation. They cannot be obtained by abstraction from experience and contingent knowledge. Their worth as supreme practical principles depends on the purity of their origin. Both their real influence and the absolute value of moral actions decrease in proportion as empirical considerations are superimposed. Speculatively, it is of the highest necessity that moral ideas and laws should be derived from pure reasoning. It is also of the highest practical importance to present them pure and unmixed, and so to define their domain that these ideas and laws are not dependent on human powers alone, even though in speculative philosophy this may be permitted and, at times, necessary.

Moral laws are to hold good for rational beings in general and must therefore be derived from general conceptions. On this basis, morality has at first to be treated independently, as a pure philosophy or metaphysic, complete by itself, which is easy in so distinct a branch of knowledge; applied to man, however, it requires supplementary anthropology. We know very well that without a metaphysic, it is useless to try to define the moral element of duty for speculative judgment, when duty is involved. In practice and for moral instruction, morals should be based on correct principles. Only a metaphysic makes moral suasion and the grafting of moral principles on men's minds possible, to the benefit of all the world.

All nature obeys laws. Only rational beings can will, i.e., they can act on principles which are individual conceptions of law. Since the deduction of behavior from law requires reasoning, willing is practical reasoning. If reasoning infallibly defines willing, then objectively necessary acts are also subjectively necessary. This would mean that willing is choosing and that the choices are sanctioned by reasoning as being practically necessary, i.e., good with no deference to one's inclinations. If, however, reasoning alone is not adequate to define willing, if willing is subject to inner impulses conflicting with objective forces, in a word, if willing and reasoning do not always agree, as in human beings they do not, then behavior which is objectively necessary, is inwardly causal or contingent. In this case, willing is governed by objective laws and that means *obligation*. The relation of objective laws to morally doubtful willing is conceived as one in which the willing is guided by reasoning, but not being wholly good, it does not obey the principles then laid down.

The conception of an objective principle which makes a certain direction of willing obligatory is called a *commandment* of reason, and the formula of this commandment is called *imperative.*

6. *Willing needs formulas: the Imperatives*

Imperatives are indicated by the word "ought," which signifies the relation of reasoning to willing, a relation in which willing is made obligatory by the objective laws of reasoning but is not governed by them because willing is a subjective function. Imperatives say that something would be good to do or leave undone, but the willing to which this word is addressed does not always follow the prescription. Willing, defined by reasoned ideas, is good practically, however, not from subjective causes but objectively, i.e., from reasons valid for every rational being. This practical goodness is to be distinguished from something merely pleasant, which moves the will by sensation and for subjective causes. It is valid for this or that person but does not apply alike to all people, as a principle of reasoning would.

A perfectly good will therefore comes under objective laws of goodness but is not obligated to action according to those laws, because of its subjective nature. Accordingly, there are no imperatives for divine or holy willing; *ought* also is inappropriate because divine volition is already and of necessity at one with law. Imperatives therefore are only formulas expressing the relation of the objective laws of willing to their subjective and imperfect counterparts, as found, for example, in human willing.

Imperatives command one either hypothetically or categorically. The *hypothetical imperative* indicates the practical necessity of a possible action to some desired end. The *categorical imperative* indicates that an action is objectively necessary of itself, without regard to any purpose that may be contemplated.

Practical laws present possible deeds as good when the person doing them is amenable to reasoning. Accordingly, imperatives are formulas for defining action necessitated by willing that is in some sense good. If an act is good, and a means to something else, the imperative is hypothetical. If the act is good in itself and necessary as a principle of willing that conforms to reasoning, it is categorical.

The imperative thus tells me which of the actions possible to me would be good. It formulates a practical rule for a man who does not always act at once because the action is good. He does not act at once, in part because he does not always know that the action is good and in part because if he did know it, the principle of the action might be contrary to the objective principles of practical reasoning.

The hypothetical imperative says only that an act is good for some purpose or other, possible or actual. In the first case (possible), the imperative is a problematic, practical principle; in the second, it is an assertorial, practical principle. A categorical imperative which declares an act objectively necessary, apart from any purpose or end, is an absolutely certain, practical principle.

When anything is possible only through the capacities of a rational being, it can also be considered the purpose of someone's volition; consequently there are in fact innumerable principles of action for the achievement of all possible purposes. Sciences all have their practical sectors, consisting of problems that presuppose possible human ends and of imperatives which tell how to attain these ends. These may be called the imperatives of skill. Here there is no question of the intelligibility or goodness of the end; there is only the question of what must be done to get to it. A doctor's prescription designed to make a patient healthy and a poisoner's prescription designed to kill him are of equal worth, considering their several purposes. In early youth no one knows what ends will turn up as life goes on; parents therefore try to have their children taught many different things, acquiring skill in many branches . . . some of which may turn out to be of use. Their care in this matter is so great that they commonly neglect to form and correct their children's judgment of the worth of the ends to be selected.

There is one end, however, which can be presupposed for all those rational beings, to whom imperatives apply because they are dependent, and one purpose which all can have and, by a natural necessity, do have: happiness. The hypothetical imperative that sets forth the practical necessity of action as a means to happiness is assertoric. This action has to be necessary, not to some uncertain or merely possible purpose but to a purpose that may be securely and abstractly presupposed for every man because it belongs to his nature. Now skill in choosing the means of one's own happiness may be called *prudence*, in the narrow sense of the word. Thus the imperative that refers to the choice of means to one's own happiness, i.e., the precept of prudence, remains hypothetical. The action is not absolutely commanded; it is a means to an end.

Finally there is an imperative which commands a certain conduct immediately, without basing it on some purpose to be achieved. This imperative is categorical. It is concerned not with the substance of an action or its presumed purpose but with its form and the principle from which it results. The good of the action commanded in this case consists not in its consequences but in the intentions behind it. This is the imperative of morality.

The three kinds of willing based on these three kinds of principle are sharply distinguished by the dissimilarity of the obligations they carry! In order to make the differences clear, I name them in order: they are either *rules of skill*, or *counsels of prudence*, or *commands (laws) of morality*. Only law embodies the idea of unconditioned, truly objective, and generally valid necessity. Commands, moreover, are laws that must be obeyed, or observed even against one's inclinations. Counsel does indeed involve necessity but a necessity under the subjective and contingent condition that this or that person reckons this or that a part of his happiness. The categorical imperative, on the contrary, is not limited by any condition, and being absolutely but practically necessary, it is properly a command. The first imperative may also be called *technical* (concerned with art, the second, *pragmatic* (concerned with well-being), and the third, *moral* (pertaining to free conduct, that is, morals).

7. *The Categorical Imperative*

For the present, the first inquiry is this: Will the bare idea of a categorical imperative provide a formula containing the proposition that alone can be a categorical imperative? When I consider an hypothetical imperative, I never know beforehand what it will contain until its condition is given. But for a categorical imperative, I know at once what it contains. It contains a law and also the requirement that the principle of some act should conform to it. The law is not limited by conditions, and accordingly, the principle has to conform only to the law's universality, and the imperative then asserts that this conformity is necessary.

There is, therefore, just one categorical imperative: *Act only on the principle of which, then and there, you would be willing to make a general law.*

If, then, this imperative can be the principle from which all imperatives of duty can be deduced, we shall at least be able to show what the notion means, even though we leave unsettled for the time being the question whether "duty" is only an empty idea.

Nature, in the most general and formal sense, is the sum of effects obtained by universal law. It is the existence of things as they are governed by law. Thus, the general imperative of duty might go like this: *Act as if the principle of your act would become a general law of nature by your willing.*

Let us enumerate here certain duties, following the customary divisions into duties to self and others and into perfect and imperfect duties. By a "perfect" duty, I understand one that permits no exceptions to accommodate a man's inclinations, and I recognize both inner and outer perfect duties. This is contrary to usage, but it is not necessary to my argument to justify it at this point.

1. Reduced to despair and sick of living, as the result of a series of evils, a certain man was still sufficiently in possession of his reason to ask whether suicide would be contrary to his duty to himself. "Could my principle in this act become a general law of nature?" he asked. "Because I love myself, I adopt it as a principle that I should cut short my life when prolonging it would only increase the misery of it." This, then, is the problem: Can self-love, as a principle, become a general law of nature? It is clear at once that if nature generally sanctioned the destruction of life for the feeling specially designed to compel its improvement, nature would be self-contradictory and soon would cease to exist as such. Suicide, therefore, is inconsistent with the supreme principle of duty and cannot be a general law of nature.

2. Another man felt driven by need to borrow money. Well aware that he could never repay it, he realized also that he could not get a loan without a firm promise to pay at a fixed time. He felt like making such a promise, but his conscience still prompted him to ask, "Isn't it unlawful and inconsistent with duty to get out of trouble this way?" Suppose, however, that he had decided to do it that way; the rule by which he acted would be: "When I am short of money, I'll borrow it and promise to pay even though I know I'll never do it. This principle of self-love or private advantage is a matter of my whole future welfare; but is it right? Let me change the requirements of self-love into general law and put the question this way: How would it be if my rule became general? I see at once that it would never do as a

general law for nature, for it would necessarily be self-contradictory. If everyone who needed something made promises to suit himself and intended not to keep them, promises generally and even the purposes of promises would soon be impossible, because no one would believe he was promised anything and would simply laugh at the hypocritical farce."

3. A third man discovered that he had a talent which, if developed, would make him a useful person in many respects. But he was comfortable, and rather than be bothered with developing and improving his gifts, he preferred to take his pleasure. Still, he asked: "Does my neglect of my talents suit what they call *duty* as well as it suits my inclinations?" He then saw that even though nature generally could get along indefinitely under such a rule, as the South Sea Islanders do, it meant that everybody would just let his talents rust out and devote his life to idleness, indulgence, procreation, and general enjoyment. He could not possibly will that this should be the general rule of nature or the natural instinct in man. For as a rational being, he had to insist that all his capacities be developed, since they served him and were given him for all kinds of purposes.

4. Still, a prosperous fourth man, seeing others struggling with great adversities, when he could have helped them, thought: "What do I care? Let them be as happy as heaven will let them be or as they can make themselves. I don't envy them and I don't want anything they have, but it would be no fun for me to contribute to their welfare or relieve their needs." No doubt that if this kind of thinking were the general rule, the human race could get along and perhaps do better than it does where everyone babbles of sympathy and good will, and even takes the trouble to practice it occasionally, but meanwhile cheats when he can, and sells or otherwise violates human rights. Once again, it is possible that this rule should be universal, and the world still endure, but it is impossible to will that it should be so. Such willing would be self-contradictory; for when it happens that one needs the love and sympathy of others, he could be deprived even of the hope of it by the general law that sprang from his own will.

These are some of the actual, or at least apparently actual, duties to be deduced from that one inescapable principle: *One must be able to will that his rule of behavior should be universal.* This is the general canon of moral judgment. Some action makes it impossible to conceive of its rule as being universal without contradiction, much less to will that it should be so. In other action, the event is otherwise, but it is still impossible to will that the personal policy involved should become universal law, for such willing would be self-contradictory. It is easy to see that the first kind conflicts with duty as it is strictly or narrowly conceived; the second kind conflicts with a broader and more serviceable sense of duty. Thus, in these examples, all types of duties are shown to depend on a single principle.

When duty has been transgressed, self-examination will reveal that in fact no one is willing to have *his* rule of conduct made universal law; on the contrary, all sinners want just the opposite to prevail. Meanwhile we take the liberty (for just this one time) of being the exception to the rule. Here, if we could all see it from the same reasonable point of view, we should discover a contradiction in our willing: a certain objective principle is necessary and general law; and yet subjectively, there are exceptions to it, and it is not generally valid. There is, however, no real contradiction here. An action is considered first in the light of reason and then against a will influenced by inclinations or desires. It is an exhibition of the opposition between inclinations and the prescriptions of reasoning, on account of which a more general law is made less general, and the practical principle of reasoning is adjusted to meet the rule or maxim of conduct halfway. Although, in impartial judgment, this is not a justifiable procedure, it shows, nevertheless, that the validity of the categorical imperative is recognized in practice and that although we do allow ourselves a few exceptions to it, it is only those exceptions which seem unavoidable.

Thus far, the content of the categorical imperative, which contains the principle of duty, has been set forth clearly, but the argument has not progressed far enough to prove abstractly and in advance that such an imperative or practical law actually exists, i.e., a law of such authority that it can command one absolutely to act without other motivation, and a law whose consequence is duty.

It is important to remember that there can be no thought of deducing this principle from special properties of human nature. For if duty is to be the practical, unconditioned necessity of behavior, its principle must be valid for *all* rational beings, for whom imperatives exist. Because it applies to all, it will apply in particular to human willing. A personal maxim or rule can be derived from special human characteristics, feelings, and impulses and even from special human quirks of reasoning not necessarily valid for other persons; but no general law can come from these sources. They may provide subjective principles which move one to act, but they do not provide an objective law on which one *has* to act even when every force within him is opposed to it. The fewer one's private reasons for obedience to the command to duty and the more reasons one has for disobeying it without, of course, weakening the law's obligation or diminishing its validity, the more clearly its sublimity and inner worth appear.

The question, therefore, is this: Is it necessary law that all rational beings should judge their own behavior by policies of their own which they themselves consider fit to be general laws? If this is the law, it must be inferrible abstractly and in advance from the idea of willing generally. . . . Willing is defined as a man's power to act according to his understanding of certain laws. This power occurs only in rational beings. The subjective ground which governs willing is an end or purpose, and if this end is a product of reasoning, it must be valid for all alike. The ground of the possibility of an act is contained in the *means*. The subjective basis of desire is the *spring*; the objective basis of willing is the *motive*. This distinction then is valid for every rational being: subjective ends are based on springs, and objective ends on motives. Practical principles are *formal* when they are rid of all subjective ends or purposes; but they are *material* when they are based on subjective ends and, therefore, on certain springs of action. The ends for which a rational being works are relative and get their worth solely from their relation to his particular desires. They provide, therefore, neither the universal principles necessary to all rational beings nor practical laws.

8. *Man is an end in himself*

Suppose, however, there were something whose very existence had absolute worth, and being an end in itself, it could be a source of definite laws. The source of practical law, i.e., the categorical imperative, would then be found in that something, and in it alone.

Now I say that man and every rational being in general is an end in himself and not an instrument of this or that person's arbitrary willing. Whatever he does, whether for himself or others, he must be considered an end. The objects of human desire have only conditioned worth, for no object would be worth anything if it were not for someone's desires and the needs they nourish. Desires themselves are far indeed from absolute worth or from having any value of their own. Every rational creature must want to be free from them. Thus the worth of everything we make is conditioned. We call creatures of nature that exist apart from our willing and are nonrational, things: they are means, and of relative value. But rational beings are persons, distinguished by their natures as ends in themselves and not as means to some end. They are objects for respect, not for despotism. Persons are not subjective ends which have worth for us because we made them; they are objective ends, and their very existence is an end itself, for which no other end can be a substitute. There is no purpose towards which they could be a means. If this is not so, absolute worth will never appear on earth; for if all worth is conditioned, there is no supreme practical principle of reasoning at all.

If there is to be a supreme practical law and so, for human willing, a categorical imperative, it has to be derived from something that is an end itself and necessarily, then, an end for everybody. It can thus be an objective principle of willing and generally practical law. The core of this law is that *rational nature is an end in itself*. This is how man necessarily thinks of himself and it is thus a subjective principle of human behavior. But every rational being has a similar view of himself so that concurrently it is also an objective principle, and being practical as well, the laws of willing are derivable from it. Accordingly, the practical imperative will be as follows: *Whatever you do, treat humanity in yourself and in other people as an end, but never as a means.* Let us see now if this is practicable, using again the example cited above.

First, consider one's necessary duty to one's self. Let the would-be suicide ask if his contemplated behavior is compatible with the notion of humanity as an end in itself. If he destroys himself to escape wretchedness, he is using a person merely as a means of keeping his life tolerable. But a person is not a thing and certainly not a tool; whatever happens, he remains an end in himself to the last. I therefore may not dispose of humanity in my own person by hurting, spoiling, or killing. To avoid misunderstanding, I must forego at this point a closer definition of this principle by discussing the amputation of limbs to save life or exposing my life to danger in order to save it, etc. This is properly subject matter for ethics.

Second, as for necessary or strict duty to others, the man who has a mind to promise deceitfully should see at once that he is merely using another person as a means to an end that person does not share. For the man I cheat could not possibly like the way I treat him and so would never share my purpose. The violation of other men's humanity is even more obvious in examples of attacks on the freedom and property of others. For then it is clear that the transgressor of human rights intends to use men as his means, not considering that they are rational beings and ought to be honored as ends.

Third, as for contingent and meritorious duties to one's self, it is not enough to avoid violating humanity in one's own person; my behavior otherwise must be congenial to my high view. Now there are capacities for greater perfection which belong to nature's purpose lodged in all people. If these capacities are neglected, humanity might still continue to be an end in itself but its intended advancement would be aborted.

Fourth, as for praiseworthy duties done for others, consider that it is the natural purpose of all men to seek happiness for themselves. Humanity no doubt could continue if nobody contributed to the happiness of anyone else but did refrain from doing them harm. If people do not further each other's ends, as much as in them lies, they agree only negatively that humanity is an end in itself. For if a man is an end in himself, his purposes must be mine too, as far as possible, in order to let this conception of man be fulfilled in me.

That every rational being is an end in himself is the supreme limiting condition of man's freedom of action. It is not, however, a principle derived from experience. In the first place, it is universal and applies to all rational beings, but experience is inadequate to the definition of universality. In the second place, the principle describes humanity not as man's subjective purpose or object but as an objective end and the supreme limiting condition of subjective ends; it must therefore spring from pure reason. This means that practical law can be enacted because of the principle itself and its form, which is sufficiently general to become a law, like a law of nature. Subjectively, practical law is based on an end or purpose, which in this case is the rational being, the end in himself. From this follows the third practical principle of willing, the supreme condition which makes willing agree with universal practical reason: *The willing of rational beings is the willing that makes universal law.*

This principle calls for the rejection of all rules inconsistent with the general legislative feature of willing. Willing is therefore not only subject to law, but it makes the laws to which it is subjected and must be considered the first of subjects, that is, the author of law.

Imperatives, as formulated above, require conformity to universal law on the analogy of nature's conformity, and require the universal supremacy of rational beings as ends in themselves. They exclude from their authority every sign of *ex parte* interest as a motive, because they were conceived as categorical. The assumption of their categorical character was required to explain the idea of duty. It was not proved above nor can it be proved here that imperatives are practical propositions with categorical authority. It could have been shown that some definitive expression in the imperative itself eliminates self-interest from willing when it is inspired by duty. Freedom from any kind of *ex parte* interest is the specific mark that distinguishes a categorical from a hypothetical imperative. It appears in the present (the third) formulation of the principle: *The willing of rational beings makes general laws.*

Once this is understood, self-interest may often be seen binding persons to the law that shapes their willing; but when willing is supreme lawmaking, it cannot possibly be based on anyone's self-interest. If it were, another law would be required to restrict that self-interest to the conditions under which law can be universally valid.

The principle that in all human willing *personal rules turn into universal laws* could very well produce the categorical imperative if all were otherwise correct; but the rule by which universal laws are made *requires the elimination of ex parte or self-interest* and also that the categorical imperative should be unconditional. Or better yet, and to put it in reverse, if there is a categorical imperative, it can shape our willing only if we are ready to make our personal rules universal. Only then are the practical law and the imperative which obeys it unconditional, because self-interest is not involved.

Reviewing the many efforts that have been made to discover the basic principle of morality, it is no wonder that all have failed. Man's duty, it was said, bound him to obey laws, but no one observed that the only laws by which a man is really bound are *the laws he himself makes general*. He is bound to act by his own willing, but nature intended that that willing should also be lawgiving. When moralists thought of people as subject to law (whichever law you please) it was always a law that needed self-interest to make it work. People had to be enticed or forced to obey because the law was not their law. To make them conform, external compulsion was required. This being the inevitable conclusion, all previous effort expended to discover a supreme principle of duty was so much labor lost. The moralists' law did not elicit duty but only behavior inspired by self-interest. Private or otherwise, the imperative of law was therefore conditional and could not rise to the dignity of moral command. I shall therefore call my discovery the *Principle of the Autonomy of Willing* and classify other versions under heteronomy.

9. *He is a member of the kingdom of ends*

The conception of a rational being as one who can see his own personal rules as universal legislation, and judge himself and his behavior from this point of view, leads to another and very fruitful conception which is related to it: the idea of *the kingdom of ends.*

By "kingdom," I understand a systematic union of rational beings under common laws. Since laws define the universal validity of ends, it is possible to conceive the organization of a unity of all ends. It must be abstracted from personal differences and preferences, but it includes rational beings as ends in themselves and also the ends they privately propose. This kingdom of ends is conceived agreeably to the moral principles we have thus far developed.

For rational beings do answer to the law that they and others may never be regarded as means but always as ends in themselves. The result is a systematic union of rational beings under common objective laws, i.e., a kingdom. These laws are designed to relate these beings to each other as ends and means and so to set up a kingdom of ends, which admittedly is ideal.

A rational being belongs to the kingdom of ends *as a member* when he contributes general laws to it and is, at the same time, subject to them. He belongs to it *as a chief* when, as a lawgiver, he is not subject to any other person's willing.

He can be a lawgiver in the kingdom of ends only because for member and chief alike free will obtains. He can be the chief not just because he wants to be the chief, but because he is completely independent, without needs, and his power is unrestricted, adequate to his willing.

Morality consists then in the reference of all behavior to the laws by which the kingdom of ends is established. These laws must be discovered in rational beings themselves and spring from their willing. The principle of their willing is that one does nothing except on a rule that may be universal. Willing is thus regarded as making one's personal rule over into general laws. If one's rule does not answer to the principle of law, duty has to enter as the practical principle of necessary action. Duty does not apply to the chief of a kingdom of ends but it does apply equally to all members.

The practical necessity of acting on the principle of duty has nothing to do with feelings, impulses, or inclinations; it is based on the relation of rational beings to each other. In this relation willing is lawgiving, for otherwise, rational beings could not be ends in themselves. By reasoning, the rules of willing are applied as general legislation to all apposite willing and behavior. This is done not from any ulterior or practical motive or for future advantage but to indicate the dignity of a rational being who obeys the law he helps to make.

In the kingdom of ends, everything has either value or dignity. Value makes it possible to replace a thing with its equivalent; but dignity puts its subject above price and beyond exchange.

Things related to man's general wants or needs have market value; luxury items that meet no need but merely satisfy certain tastes or offer purposeless amusement, command luxury prices; but the condition which makes its subject an end in itself is not of relative worth or value; it has dignity's intrinsic worth.

Morality, therefore, is the condition which makes a rational being an end in himself because it makes him a lawgiving member of the kingdom of ends. It is morality, the morality in people, which alone establishes dignity. Skill, diligence, and work have a market value; wit, lively imagination, and humor command a luxury price; but fidelity to promises and kindness, as a matter of principle rather than instinct, has spiritual worth. Neither nature nor art can replace these if they are wanting. Their worth is not in their effects, advantages, or uses but in the qualities of mind or rules of behavior from which they appear, whether they are visibly effective or not. They need no recommendation from taste or sentiment to gain immediate favor or approval. Without any flair or feeling for effect, fidelity and kindness display the willing that moves in them as something immediately to be respected, and nothing but reasoning is required to impose them on it; certainly coaxing will not do, for where duty is involved that would introduce a contradiction. This evaluation reveals the dignity of mind that goes with morality as beyond price. Even to mention a price for it is profanation.

What then justifies the lofty claims of virtue or high moral-mindedness? They secure to each rational being a share in the lawgiving of the kingdom of ends, making him eligible for membership in it. His own nature destined him to enter this kingdom, for he was born an end in himself. He is free under nature's laws because he obeys only those he makes himself,* and his rules of behavior became general laws. For law sets the worth of everything, but it requires dignity for that function. That is, it must have unconditional, incomparable worth, such that the word "respect" is the only possible expression of a rational being's attitude when he thinks of it. Autonomy then is the basis of human dignity, indeed of the dignity of every rational nature.

The three styles of the moral principle that have been offered thus far are only three formulations of the same law, each one of which involves the other two. Their differences are more subjective than objective and are intended, by means of an analogy, to focus awareness and feeling on a reasoned idea. All personal policies or rules have:

(1) A *form* which is general; accordingly, the formula of the moral imperative is expressed this way: *Rules must be chosen as if they were to be general laws of nature.*

(2) *Subject matter,* which consists of ends or purposes, and on this the formula says that since rational beings are, by nature, ends in themselves, they delimit all the relative or arbitrary ends that appear in personal policies.

(3) A *complete definition of all policies by this formula*: all policies should be made to agree with the kingdom of ends, as with the kingdom of nature. This completes a progression in the order of the

* *Cf.* above, Section 11, where mind is described as nature's lawgiver.

categories of (1) *unity* of form in willing (its generality, (2) *plurality* of subject matter (ends), and (3) *totality* or completeness of the system of ends. In moral judgments, however, stricter methods are better and so we choose the general formula of the categorical imperative as a starting point: *Act by the policy or rule that simultaneously can be a general law.* To get the moral law accepted, however, it is better to take it through the above three stages, and so stay closer to awareness.

We now can end where we began, with the idea of unconditionally good willing. Willing is absolutely good if it cannot be bad, and its rule, if made into general law, never contradicts itself. This therefore is the supreme law of willing: *You are ready to act on your personal policy when you are ready to make it a general law.* On this principle, willing is never at odds with itself, and so stated, the imperative is categorical. The validity of willing as it makes the general law covering all possible acts is analogous to the interconnection of things under general law. This is the formal aspect of nature and permits the following wording of the categorical imperative: *Act only on a personal policy that bids fair to become a general law of nature.* This is a formula of willing that is absolutely good.

Rational nature is distinguished by the goal set before it, the goal that in substance is good will. When willing is absolutely and unconditionally good, however, it is not tied to a goal to be attained. It is independent of all goals, and consequently its goal has to be conceived negatively, i.e., we may never act against it or treat it as a means but must always regard it as a precious motive power of willing. As the subject of all possible goals or ends, it is also the substance of all willing that is absolutely good, and it may not be subordinated to anything else without contradiction. Thus, the principle *treat every other rational being, including yourself, so that in your personal rule of behavior he appears as an end in himself* is basically the same as *act on the rule which is universally valid and simultaneously valid for every rational being.* When I pursue some end, I may make the condition that my rule may be as law to every subject (person), or what is the same thing and the basic principle of all maxims: The subject of all ends, a rational being himself, is never treated as a means to some end. On the contrary, in addition to being an end himself, he is the supreme condition delimiting all means.

It follows indisputably that whatever laws a person may obey, because he is an end in himself, he must think of himself as a giver of general laws through his obedience. He is marked as an end by the very fitness of his personal policies to become general laws. His dignity or prerogative sets him above all other creatures of nature and carries with it the requirement that as a maker of law, he shall choose his personal rules from his own point of view and that of every other person. This is how a world of rational beings becomes a kingdom of ends. People become members of it when they make their own laws. Rational beings therefore enter the kingdom of ends by acting on rules that turn out to be general laws. The formal principle of rules like this is: *Act as if simultaneously your personal rules had to be universal law to all other rational beings.* A kingdom of ends is thus possible on the analogy of the kingdom of nature. The former comes to be through policies or self-imposed rules; the latter comes through efficient causes operating by laws that are externally necessary. Even though nature as a whole is regarded as a machine, still, because rational beings are as ends in it, we call it the kingdom of nature.

The kingdom of ends would exist by virtue of the rules prescribed by the categorical imperative for all rational beings, if those rules were generally followed. No rational being, however, who punctiliously follows these rules can count on everybody else being loyal to them at the same time. Neither can he expect that the kingdom of nature will receive him into its order and be accommodated to him as the kingdom of ends to which he contributes might do. Nature will not favor his expectation of happiness. Still, there is the law, in full force, and it commands us categorically to *act by the rules of a lawgiving member of the kingdom of ends while that kingdom is still merely possible.* At this point a paradox appears. Without any further goal or advantage, the reverence for an idea that is born of man's rational nature and human dignity becomes an inflexible rule of willing. It is this freedom from self-interest that makes man's rules of action sublime and can make every rational being worthy to be a lawgiving member of the kingdom of ends. Otherwise people appear only as subject to the physical laws of their own needs.

Imagine that the kingdom of nature and the kingdom of ends were really united under one head and that the kingdom of ends became actual instead of being a mere idea. The idea of it would then get a certain motive power but no access of intrinsic worth. If this did happen, however, its head, the unique and absolute lawgiver, would have to be conceived as judging rational beings only by the disinterested behavior they prescribed for themselves because of their idea. The essence of things does not change with changes in their external relations. But apart from externals, in that inner something that constitutes the sole worth of man, there is the criterion by which all men will judge one, as the Supreme Being may also be expected to do.

10. *He makes the laws he obeys*

Morality, therefore, is the relation of behavior to the autonomy of willing, that is, to possible general legislation from its maxims. Behavior is morally permissible when it is compatible with autonomy of willing; otherwise it is not. Willing, by the rules which agree necessarily with the law of autonomy, is holy or absolutely good. When willing is not absolutely good, it is still obligated, i.e., dependent on the principle of autonomy (which is moral necessity). The idea of obligation is not therefore applicable to a holy being. The objective necessity to act from obligation is called duty.

It is easy to explain from the foregoing how it happens that even though the idea of duty implies subordination to law, a certain sublimity and dignity is attributed to the person who fulfills his whole duty. He is not sublime because he obeys the moral law but because, having made that law, he then subordinates himself to it. We have also shown that neither fear nor inclination impart moral worth to behavior; that comes only when the motive is respect for law; but the real object of respect is my own idealized will which is moved to action only when its rules are general laws. This is where human dignity appears, in man's capacity to make general laws to which he will be subject.

Willing is a kind of causality inherent in living, rational beings; *freedom* is thus a property of this causality, when it results in behavior independent of the other causes which are foreign to it, just as *physical necessity* is a property of the causation of nonrational beings when they are moved by influences foreign to them.

This definition of freedom is negative, and thus it is not fruitful for the discovery of what freedom *is,* but it does lead to a positive idea which is richer and more productive. The idea of causality implies laws, and by these laws, causes are followed by effects. So although freedom is not a property of willing which depends on physical laws, it is not therefore lawless. On the contrary, freedom is causality of a special kind, operating under immutable laws, for otherwise it would be nothing. Physical necessity is a heteronomy of immediate (efficient) causes, activated by antecedent and alien causes to produce whatever effects are possible under causal law. What else can freedom of willing be, then, but an autonomy, i.e., willing that makes its own laws? But the proposition that whatever its activity, willing is a law unto itself, expresses only the principle that one ought to act on only those maxims that can be general laws. This, however, is just the formula of the categorical imperative and the principle of ethics; free willing, and willing subject to moral laws are identical!

If freedom of willing is assumed, morality and its principle can be deduced from it simply by analysis of the idea. The principle of morality is nevertheless an amplifying proposition: the maxim of absolutely good willing may always be considered as general law. This property of the maxim does not appear from mere analysis of the idea of absolutely good willing. Amplifying propositions like this are possible only when both insights, that of good will and of law, are connected by a third which comprehends both. This *tertium quid* is furnished by the positive conception of freedom and therefore cannot be, like physical causes, of the nature of the physical world. Freedom points to this third something, and we have an abstract, prior idea of it but we cannot show as yet what it is. Some further preparation is required before the deduction of the conception of freedom and the possibility of a categorical imperative from pure practical reasoning can be explained.

It is not enough to attribute freedom to human willing, for whatever reason, unless there is also sufficient reason to attribute it to all other rational beings as well. Morality is a law to us only because we *are* rational beings and because, therefore, it is valid for all. Since it has to be derived from the property of freedom, we must show that freedom is a property of all rational beings. It is not enough to derive freedom from certain alleged fragments of human experience. We have to prove that all rational beings who are capable of willing have it. I now say that for all practical purposes, every being who can operate only by thinking he is free *is really free*, and for that reason. That is to say, all the laws of freedom apply to him as much as if his will had been shown to be free by some theoretically conclusive proof. I adopt the method of assuming that rational behavior is based on the idea of freedom in order to avoid having to prove it theoretically. This is enough for my purpose.

Now I assert that it must be granted that having a will, every rational being can think he is free and act accordingly. It is also understood that rational beings are practical thinkers who pursue their objectives for a reason. A mind in which, consciously, judgments are governed from the outside is inconceivable, for then a person (the subject) would attribute his judgments not to reasoning but to controls. Mind, apart from any foreign influence, has to be the author of its own principles, and accordingly a rational being has to feel free if his mind and will are to function. Therefore, practically speaking, rational beings must think that they are free.

Being intelligent, every rational being considers that he belongs to the world of mind in which, to him, immediate or efficient causation is willing. On the other hand he is conscious of belonging to the world of sense in which his actions are seen as mere phenomena, effects of the sense world's causation. We do not know what this causation is or how it gets results. Human behavior has thus to be considered defined by other phenomena, such as desires and inclinations, also belonging to the sense world. If I were only a member of the world of mind, my actions would be defined solely by the principle of the autonomy of pure willing. If I were just a part of the sense world, they would conform to the natural laws of desire and inclinations, in other words, to the heteronomy of nature. In the first case, morality would be the supreme principle of my behavior, and in the second, happiness. Since, however, the basis of the world of sense and its laws is in the mind world, the law of my willing also is wholly from thence, and I must acknowledge that I am subject to the laws of mind. I therefore regard these laws as imperatives and the acts they require, as duties.

The categorical imperatives are possible, therefore, because the idea of freedom makes me a member of that mind world where, if I had no part in the sense world, my actions would always reveal autonomous willing on my part. But since I am aware simultaneously of being a member of the sense world, my actions *ought* to conform to the mind world. This categorical "ought" implies an abstract, amplifying proposition. To my sense-directed willing there is added the idea of the same willing, now pure and practical, and belonging to the mind world. Reasoning discloses that this second willing constitutes the supreme condition of the first. To sense awareness, mental ideas are added as general forms. This is how abstract, prior, and amplifying propositions become possible. All our knowledge of physical nature depends on them.

11. *Because he thinks so, he is free*

Common sense confirms this reasoning. There is no one who is accustomed to thinking, not even a hardened scoundrel, who does not wish that he could have the qualities illustrated in examples of honest purpose, steady obedience to good rules, sympathy, and general benevolence, all of which are often exemplified at great sacrifice. But the scoundrel's inclinations and impulses hold him back even though he wants to be rid of his burdensome desires. He proves, however, that given a will unburdened by sense drives, he can move over in thought to an order of things wholly different from that of his usual haunts. He can, of course, hope for no gratification of his desires on this course, but he does expect to obtain increased personal worth. He even believes that he *is* a better person when he shifts into the mind world, drawn there involuntarily by the thought of freedom. Freedom means to him independence of the inflexible causation of his senses. Then he is conscious of good will and the moral law which he has acknowledged by transgressing it. What he "ought" to do is what he would do of necessity if he were a member of the mind world, but for him the "ought" is on a par with his membership in the sense world.

The subjective impossibility of explaining free will is like the impossibility of discovering the root of human interest in moral law. The interest is real, nevertheless, and is said to be based on moral feeling. In order to will the imperative prescribed to rational beings, reasoning has to disclose a power to impart to people a feeling of pleasure or satisfaction in the fulfillment of duty; a causality, in which sense is regulated by the mind's own principles, is needed.

It is, however, impossible to understand abstractly and in advance, how an immaterial idea can cause a sensation of pleasure or displeasure. This is a special kind of causation about which, as about all causation, we know nothing abstractly or in advance. We may consult experience but the essence of the cause-effect relation does not appear there. In this case pure reasoning, acting through ideas only and bereft of objects, has to be the cause of an effect admittedly real in everyone's experience; but there is no explanation of how or why a policy, made into general law and become morality, should so interest people. This much alone is certain; moral law is not valid because we are interested in it; for that would be heteronomy and dependence by practical reason on sense or sentiment for its principles. Moral law comes not this way. It interests us because it is valid for persons like us. We are intelligent people, and it sprang from our willing, as from our inmost selves. Reasoning, of necessity, subordinates all phenomenal matters to the nature of the thing-itself.

The categorical imperative presupposes freedom. The question how it is possible can be answered to the extent freedom can be explained and its necessity made apparent. Freedom explains practical reasoning adequately and the validity of both the imperative and the moral law, but no reasoning ever reveals how freedom is possible. From the hypothesis that an intelligent person's willing is free, autonomy follows necessarily and is the condition required to define willing. It is perfectly possible to presuppose free willing, as speculative philosophy can show, without contradicting the principle of the necessary connection between phenomena in the sense world. It is also necessary to show that freedom in practice and thought is the underlying condition of all voluntary behavior. But it is beyond the power of human reasoning to explain how pure thought, without the help of some impulse to action, can be practical, or how the *general* validity of personal rules made into laws could supply such an impulse, or, in a word, how pure thought can be practical. All effort to this end is strictly in vain.

12. *But his freedom is not explained*

The same remarks apply to efforts to explain freedom as the causality of willing. At this point I abandon philosophical explanation and have no other to put in its place. To be sure, I could revel in the mind world as it remains to me. My idea of that world is well supported even though I am not at all acquainted with it and will remain unacquainted, in spite of all my mental powers. The mind world is only something left over when all sense conditions governing my willing have been eliminated, something that as a principle restricts the field of sense motivation, fixing its limits to show that the sense world does not include everything; because there *is* something more. But about this *more,* I know nothing. When matter has been done away and with it all knowledge of objects, there is also nothing left of the pure reasoning which begot this ideal world but forms or practical laws of generalized maxims. With them, there remains the pure world of mind as an immediate or efficient cause governing willing. Unless the thought of the mental world itself should provide them, impulses or motives are totally absent at this point, and we are left with our insoluble problem: How can the ideal world of mind be a motive of human action?

This, then, is the extreme limit of moral study. It is of great importance that the limit should be fixed in order to save fruitless searches in the sense world, to the detriment of ethics, for a supreme moral motive or for some intellectual but empirical interest in the subject. On the other hand it would save much feeble wing flapping by those who mean to hunt transcendent ideas in the empty spaces known as the "mind world." They never get off the ground. They just get lost chasing the ghosts in their own brains. For the rest of us, there remains the pure mind world to which all minds belong, even though otherwise we belonged to the sense world. This is a serviceable idea and permissible for the purposes of rational belief, even though knowledge comes to a dead end at its boundaries. It serves to excite a lively interest in moral law by means of the glorious ideal of the kingdom where rational beings are ends in themselves. We may all belong to this kingdom if we carefully keep to our rules of freedom as if they were natural laws.

And thus, while we do not understand the practical, unconditioned necessity of the moral imperative, we do understand its incomprehensibility, which is all anyone can reasonably expect of the philosophy which pushes its principles to the very limits of human reason.

Part Three

THE CRITIQUE OF PRACTICAL REASONING

22 THE CRITICAL PHILOSOPHY OF MORALS

An insight is justified

Pure reasoning becomes "practical" when one uses it to make up one's mind, to make a practical decision, or to direct and move willingness to accomplishment. It should help one to act intelligently, to get on with the business of life to advantage. It is not practical because experience supports it; quite to the contrary, practical reasoning is as pure as any reasoning can be.

Pure reasoning in its own right is limited to the organization of experience and the critical evaluation of a philosopher's interests. It is formal rather than creative. "Pure" implies negation, and pure reasoning is empty except as it discloses the ideas or forms that wait in mind to organize the raw stuff of experience into knowledge. Causality, for example, is an empty formality until it is applied to nature's objects, and then it becomes the mainspring of the physical world, apart from which no change or movement ever occurs. Man, for example, as he is physical and a phenomenon, is part of the causal order of the world and subject wholly to the relentless succession of causes and effects.

This, however, is not the whole human story. Men disclose their ability to make and obey laws which are, apparently, irrelevant to the processes of physical nature, and do not interdict any of nature's causal laws. The "moral law," peculiar to humanity, is really a description of basic humanity, and intersects the causal order of nature only at the points where there are rational beings. It makes a man, or "noumenal man," an uncaused cause and therefore free, which is to say, free of nature's causal order and its necessity. That there is, nevertheless, reality behind the formal thought of "noumenal man" is inferred from the fact that men do things which are not referable to observed causes. For example, a man may suddenly turn around and go the other way as the result of a thought. This is the essence of Kant's reconciliation of freedom and causality which he had earlier discussed as the third antinomy. (See Section 17, p. 109.)

Pure reasoning cannot deal with freedom or the moral law as phenomena to which the categories of mind are applicable. It is within the province of practical reasoning, however, to justify freedom and the moral law as insights. By this justification, the possibility of moral experience made intelligible under its own special categories, the "categories of freedom," is established. "Mind involves consciousness of a law to which all personal policies are subject, as if a whole order of nature were to be born with our willing. It is a law that contains, therefore, an idea of a nature that is not experienced as actual but which is made possible through freedom. This nature is supersensible, and since we regard it as an object of willing, we attribute to it objective reality, at least practically." This is Kant's insight and its justification.

To some modern readers Kant's attempts to dress up a moral argument in the garments of geometry, as if morality were demonstrable in that manner, will seem curious. He saw no necessary gulf fixed between the certainty of geometrical and moral demonstrations. Manifestly he thought that they could be parallel and that duty could be treated with the same precision as the fall of a stone; moral philosophers need only be guided by the model triumphs of physical scientists. Kant coveted for ethics also the certainty and power he had seen in the application of mathematics to the physical world. (See p. 14.)

What seems clear today, but was not clear in the eighteenth century, is that scientists had already become priests of a kind, absorbed in the unfolding of an old mystery in a new liturgy, full of pride in what had been accomplished in their cult, and boldly confident of what lay just ahead. To many, by comparison philosophy and morals seemed destined to vestigiality. The paradox of science and religion, or of causal necessity and freedom, had become a major lesion in humane concerns. Of this lesion and its importance Kant *was fully aware, and his effort to deal with it is impressive. If it should ever turn out that the paradox of science and religion is largely semantic and to some degree, therefore, voluntary, the intention, if not the results of Kant's practical reasoning will receive new justification.*

The excerpt that follows is approximately one third of the total work first published in 1788, under the title Kritik der praktischen Vernunft. *The omitted portions are redactions of material already included from the earlier works and would be redundant in a volume of this kind. To those who share Kant's insight that freedom is causal and that the moral law is objectively real, the material I have included will be sufficient; without this insight, nothing would convince an adverse critic.*

The theoretical use of reasoning had to do only with objects of mind, and criticism of it was restricted to an examination of the formal knowing process. This aroused suspicion that one might easily go beyond the proper limitations of his mind and get lost among unattainable objects and contradictions—a suspicion which was subsequently confirmed. But it is not so with practical reasoning, the means by which willing is governed. Practical reasoning functions to produce objects that correspond to ideas or to steer one toward his objectives, whether they are within reach or not. It defines causality in man. Reasoning can always go this far and be objectively real if willing alone is involved.

1. *Does pure reasoning govern willing?*

The first question then is this: Can willing be managed by means of pure reasoning alone? Or is experience also required? At this point the notion of freedom appears. Although not based on experience, it is a conception which was justified in *The Critique of Pure Reason.* Accordingly, if we can now prove that freedom is a property of all rational willing, it will appear that only pure reasoning can be practical and that reasoning laced with experience is not practical. To this end an examination not of pure reasoning but practical reasoning is required. Once the fact of pure reasoning is established, it needs no critique. Of itself it provides the criterion for the examination of its own uses. A critical evaluation of practical reasoning, however, will generally prevent us from thinking that reasoning can plot a true course of willing only when it is based on experience: the true uses of practical reasoning appear as soon as it is established. On the other hand, reasoning based on experience is transcendent, and being reputed to be uniquely superior, its requirements and precepts go far beyond its allotted scope. This is just the opposite of the reputation of pure reasoning in speculation.

Pure reasoning is still the foundation of practical reasoning, and the outline of knowledge used in practical reasoning must accordingly follow the outline of its predecessor. There must be an *Elements* and a *Methodology* of reasoning. The *Elements* will contain an *Analytic*, or rule of truth and a *Dialectic** which sets forth the illusions native to practical reasoning and gives their resolutions. The order of subdivisions in the *Analytic* will be opposite to that of *The Critique of Pure Reason*. Here we shall begin with principles and proceed to ideas and thence to the senses, if possible. In the case of speculation we began with the senses and had to end with principles. Now, however, we are concerned with willing. We have to *consider reasoning as related not to objects but to willing and its causes*. We begin with principles of a causality which is not empirically conditioned. We shall try to establish a basis for the control of willing, showing that our conception of it applies to objects, to the person, and to his senses. Of necessity we begin with the law of freedom's causality. This is a pure practical principle and it alone will govern the choice of objects to which it can be applied.

Chapter I. *The Principles of Pure Practical Reasoning*. Practical principles are propositions which generally define willing. Under each principle there are several practical rules or *policies* (maxims) which are subjective when a person regards them as valid only for his own willing. They are objective, or practical *laws*, when they are valid for the willing of all rational creatures.

Comment. If pure reasoning discloses practical principles adequate to govern willing, the principles are practical laws; otherwise they are merely policies. Pathological persons often experience a conflict between their own personal policies and the practical laws whose validity

* Omitted here.

they recognize. For example, someone might make it a rule to let no injury pass unrevenged and yet observe that this is not a practical law but merely his own policy. He might see that if his policy were made a rule governing the willing of all rational beings, it would be self-contradictory. In natural science, the principles of events are at the same time laws of nature. Take, for example, the principle of the communication of motion, that action and reaction are equal. The use of reasoning here is theoretical and determined by the nature of the object. On the other hand in practical philosophy, which deals with the management of willing by reasoning, a man is not inexorably bound by the principles he makes for himself. Practical reasoning involves a person and his desires; his special character may therefore cause variations in any rule.

A practical rule is always a product of reasoning because it prescribes action as a means of getting an intended result. In the case of a person whose willing is not managed entirely by reasoning, this rule is an *imperative*. It expresses the objective necessity of some action by "ought," and means that if willing conformed to reasoning, the resultant action would inevitably occur according to the rule. Imperatives, therefore, are objectively valid and distinct from policies, or maxims, which are subjective. Either imperatives are efficient causes, fixing the conditions of causality in a rational being (meaning the choice of effects and means of attaining them), or they determine whether or not the willing involved is adequate. In the first case, the imperative is hypothetical, involving only precepts of skill; in the second, the imperatives are categorical and practical laws. Policies are principles, therefore, but not imperatives.

When imperatives are conditional or hypothetical; i.e., when they do not control willing directly but only in terms of a desired effect, they are practical precepts but not laws. Laws effect the control of willing directly, whether or not I have the means, or am able to get the effect I want. Either they are categorical or they are not laws at all. They are practically necessary and independent even of pathological conditions, which are connected only contingently with the willing. Tell a man, for example, that he must work and save when he is young so that he may not be poor in his old age. This is a correct and important counsel, but it is obvious in such a case that the youth's willing is being steered toward something the counselor supposes him to desire; whereas the youth may look forward to resources other than his own. He may even expect that he will never be old, or that if he is in need he can make what little he has do.

Reasoning alone can produce a rule involving necessity and does indeed give necessity to the precept just considered, but it is a subjective necessity whose force varies from person to person. For lawgiving, however, reasoning is its own only necessary presupposition. Rules are objectively and generally valid only when they hold, no matter what the subjective or contingent conditions distinguishing one person from another may be. Now, tell a man that he should never make a deceitful promise. This is a rule that concerns only his own willing, whether he can get what he wants by deceit; it is only his willing that is to be governed, abstractly and in advance, by that rule. If it is found that the rule is correct in practice, it is then a law because it is categorically imperative. Practical laws thus apply only to willing, without regard to the aim of its causality. Causality may therefore be disregarded. It belongs to the sense world. Practical laws are pure.

Theorem I. A practical principle is empirical when it presupposes that willing is governed by the desire for the realization of some material object. Accordingly, no practical law will come of it.

If the desire for the object preceded the practical rule and was the condition which made it a principle, the principle is then wholly empirical. For the choice was determined by an idea of the object and by the relation of the object to the person who decides so to satisfy his desire. Call this kind of a relation between a person and an object *pleasure in the realization of an object*. It is a condition by which willing is governed. No one, however, can know abstractly and in advance whether the thought of an object will be pleasant, painful, or neutral. The choice, therefore, has to be empirical, like the practical material principle which presupposes the idea.

In the second place, susceptibility to pleasure or pain can be known only by experience and will vary from person to person. A principle therefore which is based on the susceptibility of a particular person may serve him as a personal policy but it will not be a law, even to him. The objective necessity which has to be apparent beforehand is missing, and accordingly no practical law will come of this kind of principle either.

THEOREM II. Material, practical principles, as such, are all alike in that generally they express the principle of self-love or individual happiness.

Pleasure in the thought of a thing's existence, if it stimulates desire for that thing, depends on a person's susceptibility and the presence of the object. The pleasure is therefore sensual, a matter of feeling and not of mind. Mind relates ideas to objects by means of categories, not to persons by their feelings. Pleasure, then, is a practical principle only to the extent that a person's desire is determined by the agreeableness of anticipating his object's presence. Now any rational being would be happy to feel that his whole life would be uninterruptedly pleasant, and self-love is the principle on which he wills it so. All material principles, then, which make pleasure or pain due to the existence of an object the determining motive of willing, are alike in that they pertain to the principle of self-love or individual happiness.

2. *Willing is not governed by desire*

Corollary: Material and practical rules suggest that the lower desires govern willing. If willing is not controlled by any formal laws, the existence of higher desires is inadmissible.

Comment 1. It is surprising that otherwise acute people distinguish between lower and higher desires according as the idea and feeling of pleasure come from the senses or from mind. When inquiry into the springs of desire reveals anticipation of something pleasant, it does not matter where the idea of it came from but only how pleasant it is. Whether an idea originates in the mind or not, if the pleasure of it moves a person to choose, its power depends on whether a person's inner sense is pleasantly affected by it. Ideas of objects may be dissimilar, whether they come from mind or are derived from reason (in contrast to ideas of sense). Still the feeling of pleasure moving a person to action on behalf of the object of his desires is the same: it comes of expected satisfaction. It can be known empirically when it affects a person's vital force and appears as desire. It differs only in degree from any other motive of willing.

Otherwise, how could two principles of the control of willing based on ideas from different sources be compared in magnitude to the advantage of higher desires? A man may return unread an instructive book, which he can have only once, so as not to miss a hunt; or he may leave in the middle of a fine speech, so as not to be late to dinner; or he could forsake intelligent conversation, which he otherwise covets, for a gambling session; or he may even repulse a poor man, one he otherwise would be pleased to help, because he has only just enough money for his theatre ticket. If his willing is controlled by his feelings of pleasure or displeasure from any source, it is all the same to him, through whatever channel they affect him. In making his choice, he will care only how strong, how protracted, how easy to come by, and how often repeated his pleasure in anything may be. A man who wants money to spend cares not at all whether the gold of it is dug out of a mountain or washed from sand, if it all has the same value. So nobody cares whether life's pleasure comes from mind or sense. The only question about pleasure is: how much, and for how long?

Those who would deny that pure reasoning apart from feeling can govern willing might like to depart so far from their own explanations as to declare that matters formerly under the same principle are now to be explained separately. For example, it appears that there is pleasure in the exercise of power, or in strength of mind that overcomes obstacles, or in the development of one's native gifts. These are correctly called the finer pleasures and enjoyments because they are, more than others, within our reach. They do not wear out, but as they are enjoyed and cultivated the pleasure in them increases. It is foolish to say, therefore, that their control of willing is different or accomplished otherwise than via sense, because this pleasure depends on a feeling native to man, a feeling which is the prime condition for such satisfactions. It is the kind of thing ignorant persons imagine and then believe, when they putter around with metaphysics. With their talking about matter being so fine, so superfine, they get dizzy and think they have conceived a kind of being that is both spiritual and extended.

If we make out that virtue governs willing only by means of the pleasure it promises, we shall not blame Epicurus for saying that this pleasure is the same as that of the senses. There is no ground for asserting that he attributed ideas that excite feeling to the physical senses only. So far as one can judge, he sought the source of many such ideas in the services of the higher mental functions. This, however, did not and could not prevent him from maintaining the principle that intellectual pleasures and those that control willing are all alike. Consistency is a philosopher's chief obligation, and chiefly it is honored in neglect. The ancient Greek schools provide more examples of it than we find in this syncretistic age. Nowadays, systems are devised that pull contradictory principles together by some trick and in shallow, dishonest compromises. They appeal to the public. People generally are content to know something of everything and everything about nothing and so to "ride firm in the saddle."

No matter how much thought and reasoning it costs, the principle that private happiness controls willing is the same whether the happiness comes from lower or higher desires. Either there are no higher desires, or pure reasoning is merely practical; i.e., it controls willing by means of the bare form of a practical rule, without feelings or ideas of pleasure or displeasure—feelings and ideas which are the substance of desire and always the empirical conditions of principles. Reasoning is a function of higher desire only when it alone controls willing but does not control it on behalf of some inclination.

Comment 2. Every finite rational being necessarily wants to be happy and this principle inevitably influences his desires. No one was ever satisfied with his original condition, for such bliss would imply that one knows that he is both independent and self-sufficient. Man's finite nature imposes a problem on him. He has wants, and his wants are the basis of desires which give him feelings of pleasure or displeasure and which determine his requirements for satisfaction. There is no law in all this, however, because one can know about this kind of a material principle of control only by his own experience. A law, by contrast, is objective and involves one kind of control for all cases and all rational beings.

THEOREM III. A rational being may consider that his policies are practical, general laws only if he conceives them as controlling willing, not by their content, but by their form. The content of a practical principle or policy is the object at which willing is aimed.

Comment. Common sense, without instruction, is enough to enable any person to decide when a personal policy is fit to be general law and when it is not. Suppose, for example, that I have made it my policy to increase my wealth by every safe means. Even now, I have in my hand a sum of money to deposit to someone's account. The owner is dead, and he left no written will about it. This is a natural test of my policy. I want to know if my policy will hold as a general law. I apply it, therefore, to the present case and ask what would happen if everyone were to pocket a sum that should be deposited and about which nothing can be proved. I at once become aware that on this principle, a law would destroy itself, for soon there would be no depositee. To be practical, a law must qualify as general legislation. This is an identical proposition and clear enough. If I say that my willing is subject to practical law, I cannot offer my own inclination (as in the present case, an inclination to avarice) as a principle or as a suitable basis for general practical law. In the form of general law, it would destroy itself.

It is surprising that intelligent people have believed that it is the desire for happiness that makes general practical law, because this desire is universal and, therefore, so is the policy by which it controls willing. But whereas the general laws of nature make for harmony, if individual policies are given the effect of general laws, the extreme opposite of harmony ensues, entailing the most ardent contradiction and the complete destruction of both the policies and their purposes. For here there is not one will but many; everyone has his own private welfare in view. Some intentions may agree with others which are equally selfish, but there will be not enough of this kind of agreement to make a law. Innumerable occasional exceptions cannot be covered by any general rule. The resultant harmony would be something like the harmony of a couple depicted in a certain satirical poem, whose marriage was headed for the rocks: "O wonderful harmony!—what he wants, she wants, etc.," or like the pledge said to have been made by King Francis I to Emperor Charles V: "What my brother wants, I want too," namely, Milan. Empirical principles for the government of willing are not suited to external legislation or to internal legislation either.

3. *How is freedom obtained?*

Problem I. Suppose that the legislative form of policies is by itself enough of a principle to control willing: what kind of willing can be controlled by this means?

Since the bare legal form is conceivable only by means of reasoning, it is neither an object of sense nor a phenomenon. The idea of legal form alone as governing willing is, therefore, quite different from the principle of the government of natural events under causal law. In nature, phenomena are the governing principles. Willing, therefore, when controlled only by a universal legislative form, is independent of the law governing phenomena, that is, of causal law. This is called freedom in the strictest or formal sense. Willing, therefore, is *free* when its law is the legislative form of the person's policy.

Problem II. Suppose that someone's willing is free: what law is necessary and suitable to govern it?

Since the substance of practical law is the object of policies, it can be known only by experience. It follows that if the principle governing free willing must be found in law, it has to be independent of the substance of the law. But besides its substance, law has nothing but form. It is the legislative form alone, then, as it appears in a policy, which governs free willing.

Comment. Freedom and unconditioned practical law, therefore, reciprocally imply each other. At this point, I do not ask if in fact they are different, or if unconditioned law is not just a form of self-consciousness that goes with practical reasoning, or whether the latter is not identical with the positive form of freedom. My question is this: Where do we find out about this notion that there is something both unconditioned and practical? Should we look to freedom or to practical law? It does not come from freedom; we have no immediate consciousness of freedom, because originally it is negative conception. It cannot be inferred from experience, because experience provides only knowledge of the laws of phenomena and the mechanisms of nature, which are the direct opposites of freedom. It is therefore the moral law which presents itself first and of which we become immediately conscious as soon as policies of willing come up for consideration. The moral law leads directly to freedom because reasoning presents freedom as a principle of the government of willing, a principle which is wholly independent of sense.

But how do we become conscious of that moral law? We become conscious of pure practical laws just as we come to be conscious of pure theoretical principles. We follow the prescriptions of reasoning. We get rid of all empiricisms and attend closely to the necessity by which reasoning prescribes its principles. The idea of pure willing is inferred from pure practical laws, just as the idea of pure thought comes from pure theoretical laws. That this is the correct ranking of these ideas, that morality first discloses freedom and that the most perplexing problem of speculation comes from the treatment of freedom by practical reasoning, is quite evident. The following considerations are to the point.

It is the mechanism of nature and not the idea of freedom which is the clue to the explanation of phenomena. Moreover, the climb with pure reasoning up the series of causes to the unconditioned, ends in that antinomy of equal and opposite entanglements in matters incomprehensible; whereas mechanism is useful in the explanation of phenomena. No one therefore would be so rash as to introduce the notion of freedom into scientific discussion, if moral law and practical reasoning did not compel it. Experience, however, establishes the correctness of this pattern of ideas. Suppose that someone alleges of his lustful inclinations that the conjunction of his beloved object and the opportunity was irresistible. But could he control his passion if a gallows were erected before the house of opportunity, so that immediately after his lust was gratified he would be hanged? There is no need to speculate on his reply. Then put this question: Suppose the prince ordered him, on pain of the same immediate execution, to bear false witness against an honorable man whom the prince wished to destroy on some plausible pretext; could he then overcome his presumably great love of life? Probably he would not care to say that he would or could do this, but he would without hesitation affirm that it would be possible. He will judge that he can do something because he ought to do it and because he recognizes that he is free, a fact which he would never have known but for the moral law.

The fundamental law of pure practical reasoning is this: Act so that your personal policy in willing can be simultaneously valid as general law.

Comment. Pure geometry has postulates which are practical propositions, but they are only assumptions that something *can* be done if it is required and should be done. These are the only propositions in geometry which deal with existence. There are also practical rules for dealing with problematic conditions of willing, but here the rule says that the procedure to be followed must *absolutely* be thus and so. Accordingly such a practical rule is unconditioned, and conceived abstractly and in advance as categorical and a practical proposition. Willing is controlled by it immediately, absolutely, and objectively, as by a law. In this case, pure practical reasoning itself becomes directly legislative. Willing is considered independent of empirical conditions, and being thus pure is controlled by the form of the law itself. This is the supreme condition of all personal policies.

This thing is strange enough, and there is nothing like it in our practical knowledge otherwise. The abstract thought of possible general legislation is here unconditionally ordained as law while it is still problematical and as yet has borrowed nothing from experience or any external willing. It is not a prescription, however, that something should be done to get a certain effect, for then willing would be physically conditioned. It is a rule that governs willing abstractly and in advance but only through the forms of the policies involved. It is, therefore, not impossible to conceive a law which applies only to the subjective form of principles, and still serves as a principle of control because it has also the general, objective form of a law. The consciousness of this fundamental law may be called a *fact of reasoning* because it cannot be conjured from any of the data previous to reasoning, such as conscious freedom. Freedom is not an antecedent fact. Consciousness of the fundamental law, however, is disclosed as an abstract, prior and amplifying proposition, not based on either pure or empirical awareness. It would be an analytic proposition if freedom of willing could be presupposed, but as a positive idea this kind of freedom would require an intellectual awareness which is not permissible. If it is regarded as an actual law, then, to avoid misunderstanding, note well that its actuality is not an empirical fact but the only fact by which pure reasoning can be shown to originate legislation.

4. *Pure reasoning provides a moral law*

Corollary. Pure reasoning, as such, is practical and gives mankind a general law which we call the moral law.

Comment. The above-mentioned fact is undeniable. It is necessary only to analyze the judgments men pass on the legality of their actions to discover that whatever they may say to the contrary, their own incorruptible and self-impelled reasoning confronts the policy of each deed they do with pure willing; i.e., with willing which abstractly and in advance is considered practical. The general character of its legislation makes morality the supreme, formal, controlling principle of willing, no matter what subjective varieties of willing may appear. Reasoning shows that the moral law is a law for all rational beings capable of willing, or who have power to conceive rules of conduct which govern their own inner causality. Rational beings must, of course, be capable of acting on principle and consequently on abstract and prior practical principles, which alone involve the necessity a principle must have.

Moral law is not limited, therefore, to people but extends to all reasoning, willing, finite beings. It even includes the infinite Being, the supreme intelligence. In the case of people, the law takes the form of an imperative. Because they are rational, pure willing can be expected of them. Because they have needs and sense motives, they are not capable of holy willing, the willing in which policy never conflicts with the moral law. For people, therefore, the moral law is imperative and commands categorically because it is unconditioned. The relation of willing to this law is one of dependence and is called *obligation.* Obligation implies constraint, constraining one to the conduct known as *duty*. Constraint appears in the idea of duty because willing may be subject to psychological effects when free choice is involved. Then wishes of subjective origin appear and they conflict with pure, objective principles of control. The moral constraint of pure practical reasoning is then required and may be called an internal, or intellectual compulsion.

In the supreme intelligence, free willing is correctly conceived as involving no policy that could not at the same time be objective law. For this reason the notion of holiness pertaining to supreme intelligence places it not above all practical law but above all restrictive laws, and so above obligation and duty. Holiness of willing is then really a practical idea. It becomes the archetype towards which man moves but never reaches. It is the ideal which the moral law constantly holds before our eyes and for which that law is called holy. Man's finite practical reasoning then accomplishes its most exalted work in the endless, unwavering progress of personal policies towards virtue, the highest and best product of finite practical reasoning. The assurance of virtue, however, never amounts to apodictic certainty, and when it is only persuasion it is dangerous.

THEOREM IV. The sole principle of all moral laws and of the duties congruent to them is that willing should be autonomous; but no obligation can be based on the heteronomy of arbitrary willing; heteronomy conflicts with the principles of obligation and moral willing. When willing is independent of the subject matter of law (some desired object) and arbitrary willing is controlled merely by the general legislative form a personal policy can take, the principle of morality is exemplified. Independence is freedom in the negative sense, but when pure practical reasoning makes its own laws, this is freedom in the positive sense. The moral law therefore expresses the autonomy of pure practical reasoning, and this means that freedom is the formal condition of all personal policies, the basis on which they can agree with the supreme practical laws. If the subject matter of willing; i.e., some desired object related to law, becomes the occasion of the possibility of practical law, the result will be the heteronomy of free choice, acting on impulses or inclinations and depending only on physical law. This way, willing does not provide its own law but only prescriptions for following psychological laws rationally. Personal policies do not then take a general legislative form or produce obligations; they are opposed to the principle of pure practical reason and therefore to morality, even though what happens as a result of these policies is legally correct.

Comment 1. A practical precept involving a material or empirical condition must never be considered practical law. For pure willing is free, and its laws put it in a nonempirical category. There the necessity expressed by law is not physical but consists of the formal conditions making laws generally possible. The subject matter of practical rules comes out of subjective conditions, from which they get only conditional generalization (if I want this or that, I must do thus and so to get it), but they all turn on the principle of private happiness.

Now it is undeniable that willing requires an object, and therefore subject matter, but this need not be the determining principle or the condition of a personal policy. If it is, the policy could never take the form of general legislation. A choice would then be determined by anticipation of the object, and willing presupposes that the desire behind it is based on the existence of something. This something must be sought among empirical conditions, which never produce the principle of a necessary and general rule. Thus the happiness of others may be the object of the willing of a rational being. If it is the principle on which a personal policy is formed, it must be presupposed that the well-being of others is not only a rational satisfaction but a need such as all sympathetic persons feel. This need, however, cannot be presumed in all rational beings, and in God, not at all. The subject matter of one's policy may stand, but it must not be the determining principle of it if the policy is to be fit for law. Thus willing gets its subject matter under a form of law which limits it but does not presuppose it.

For example, let the subject matter be my own happiness. The rule (in the last sentence of the foregoing paragraph) holds true for every finite being and can be an objective practical law only if I include others with myself. Thence we get the law requiring us to promote the happiness of others. It does not rest on the assumption that this is the chosen object of all concerned. The condition for this law is that the policy of self-love will determine willing only when it takes the general form required by reasoning, and so gets objective validity. Therefore, it was not my object or the happiness of others that determined my pure willing. It was rather the form of law by which I restricted my policies, which were based on inclinations, so as to give them the general applicability of law and adapt them to practical reasoning. It was this restriction and not the incidence of an external impulse which evoked the idea of obligation and extended my policy of self-love to concern for the happiness of others.

Comment II. The direct opposite of the principle of morality occurs when private happiness is made the controlling principle of willing. Moreover, as I have already shown, we must include in this every consideration other than the legislative form of personal policies. The contradiction caused by this principle of private happiness is not merely logical, such as the contradictions which occur between empirically conditioned rules lately raised to the rank of necessary principles of knowing. The contradiction here is practical, and if reason's voice were not so clear about willing, so irrepressible and distinct even to common people, morality would be ruined altogether by it. It can be supported only in the dizzy schools of speculation, where they are bold enough to shut out the heavenly voice for the sake of a theory that gives them no headaches.

Suppose that an acquaintance you have liked tries to justify to you his having borne false witness. First, he mentions his sacred duty to protect his own happiness and recounts the advantages he has gained by lying. He points out how prudent he has been and how he has secured himself against detection even by you to whom he has bared his secret only so that he may deny it at any time. Suppose then that in all seriousness he claims to have done his true duty as a human being. You'd laugh in his face or shrink from him in disgust. And yet, at the same time, if a man operated merely on the principle of self-advantage, you wouldn't mind in the least.

Or suppose a man is recommended to you as a butler to whom you can turn over all your affairs with blind confidence, and in the build-up he is praised as a clever fellow, expert in his own interests and so busy that nothing ever gets past him. Then, lest you worry about his vulgar selfishness until it becomes an obstacle, the good taste with which he lives is praised. He doesn't get his fun by making money or in riotous living but by extending his knowledge, associating with the right people, and sometimes even by helping the poor. With what means he does all this, he isn't fussy (the end justifies the means). He will use other people's money for his purposes as if it were his own, if he can do so without getting caught. By this time you might think that either the recommender was fooling or he had lost his mind. The boundary between self-love and morality is so sharply marked that even the dullest eye cannot fail to see whether something belongs to one side or the other. The few remarks that follow may seem superfluous when the truth is so plain but they also may serve to clear up some common-sense judgments.

The policy of self-love (shrewdness) is advisory; the law of morality commands. Between what one is advised to do and what one is obliged to do, the difference is great.

Common sense would enable anyone to see easily, and without taking thought, what the principle of free or autonomous choice allows. If, however, heteronomy of willing is assumed, it is hard to know what one ought to do as a result, and knowing this much requires vast experience with the world. One's moral duty is plain enough, but what will be to one's lifelong advantage lies covered with impenetrable darkness. Making all due allowances, it takes great shrewdness even tolerably to adapt an applicable and practical rule to life's purposes. Moral law, on the other hand, demands strict obedience. It should not, therefore, be too difficult even for a dullard without worldly shrewdness to judge what this law requires of him.

One may be vexed at his own stupidity when he loses a game, but if he has cheated he will despise himself in spite of winnings when he consults the moral law. The moral law is therefore something quite other than a principle of personal happiness. When a man has to say to himself, "With a full purse, I am worthless," his standard is very different from that of the fellow who says "I am shrewd; I have made money."

Finally, there is something else in the idea of practical reasoning that goes with transgression of a moral law; namely punishable culpability. The notion of punishment is not generally associated with that of sharing happiness. Even though the punisher has good intentions and sets out to correct the culprit, the punishment must still be justified as an injury so that the culprit, even though he sees no kindness behind the severity, will still admit that it serves him right and that he got his just deserts. Justice must characterize every punishment because it is the essence of the conception of punishment. Goodness may indeed be connected with it but the sinner has not the least reason to count on it. Punishment is therefore a physical evil and though not a natural consequence of moral evil should be connected with it by the principles of moral legislation. Consequently, if crime, even when committed with no regard to the physical consequences to him who does it, is self-punished; i.e., results in forfeited happiness, it is plainly preposterous to say that crime consists of a man drawing punishment on himself and so hurting his own happiness. On the principle of self-love, this is the correct conception of all crime: Punishment would be the reason for calling any act a crime; and justice would call for the elimination of punishment and even for stopping natural punishment. No act would be bad any longer; the injury which followed it and made it evil is now prevented. Finally, all rewards and punishments are viewed as so much machinery in the hands of a higher power designed to get people to strive for happiness. This is plainly a mechanical interpretation of willing and so destructive of freedom that it need not detain us here.

More refined but just as false is the theory of those who allege a certain special moral sense. They say that it is this moral sense rather than reason that determines moral law. It connects consciousness of virtue immediately with satisfaction and contentment, and consciousness of vice with distress and pain. Morality is thus reduced to a desire for happiness. Without repeating what has already been said, I shall comment here on the fallacy involved in this theory.

In order to represent a vicious person as plagued by the consciousness of his transgressions, they have to represent the main basis of his character as being to some degree good. Similarly, one who enjoys the consciousness of duty done is represented as already virtuous. The idea of morality and duty must therefore have preceded any thought of this satisfaction and cannot be derived from it. One must first appreciate the importance of duty, the authority of the moral law, and the immediate worth a person gets in his own eyes by obeying it in order to feel the satisfaction that goes with moral conformity. He must also know the bitter remorse that comes with the consciousness of transgression. Content or discontent cannot precede a person's consciousness of obligation as it must if obligation is to be based on such feelings. A man must be at least half-honest to have any idea of such matters. Since freedom makes willing immediately controllable by moral law, I shall not deny that much exercise in morality will at length produce a feeling of satisfaction. What is more, it is one's duty to cultivate and establish this feeling that alone deserves to be called moral sentiment; but the idea of duty cannot be derived from it. If it were, we should have to take a feeling for a law and thus treat law, which only reasoning can devise, as an object of sense. If this is not to be a flat contradiction, it requires that the idea of duty be given up and be replaced by a mechanical play of fine inclinations contending with coarser ones.

If now the formal, supreme principle of practical reasoning, the autonomy of willing, is compared with all previous material principles of morality, they can be exhibited in a table that covers all possible cases, with the exception of that one formal principle. This will make it obvious that it is useless to look for any principle other than the one here proposed. Indeed, all possible principles for the control of willing are either subjective and therefore empirical or they are objective and rational. They are also all either external or internal.

The practical, material principles for the control of willing, the foundations of morality are these:

SUBJECTIVE		OBJECTIVE	
External	*Internal*	*Internal*	*External*
Nurture (Montaigne)	Physical feeling (Epicurus)	Perfection (Wolff and the Stoics)	Will of God (Crusius and other theological moralists)
The Civil Constitution (Mandeville)	Moral feeling (Hutcheson)		

Those on the left side are empirical and obviously incapable of providing a general principle of morality. Those on the right side are based on reasoning. Perfection as an attribute of things, and the highest perfection conceived as substance, or God, can be thought of only in reasoned ideas. Perfection otherwise means completeness in the theoretical sense of the completeness of a thing in its own way; i.e., formal completeness; or it may mean the metaphysical completeness of a thing, with which we are not now concerned. The idea of perfection in the practical sense is the fitness or adequacy of a thing for any purpose. As a human quality, perfection is internal and is simply *talent* and the *skill* that strengthens or completes it. Supreme perfection, conceived as substance, or God, is external, and it is the practical adequacy of this Being (God) for all purposes in general. The idea of perfection, whether internal in ourselves or external in God, can control willing in relation to ends only when those ends are specified in advance. This kind of end is empirical because it is an object which by reason of a practical rule precedes the control of willing. It is practical also because it contains the principle which makes the control of willing possible. It may serve, therefore, as a principle of the *Epicurean* theory of happiness but not for the principle of morality and duty, which has to be derived from pure reasoning.

Thus because talents, and the skills that improve them, contribute to the advantages of life, they may be motives for willing. Or the will of God may be a motive if agreement with it is considered an object and there is no antecedent, independent, practical principle to consider. These matters, however, move one only when they can be expected to yield happiness. Consequently (1) the principles here set forth are material and (2) they include all possible principles. The conclusion follows that the formal practical principle of pure reason, i.e., the bare form of general legislation, is the only principle adequate to furnish a categorical imperative. It was shown above that material, practical principles are incapable of producing the supreme moral law. It is only practical law that makes action a duty and so can serve generally as moral principle, both to criticize conduct and to control willing.

5. *Freedom comes with morality*

This analytic establishes the practicality of pure reasoning, i.e., that pure reasoning can control willing independently of any empirical considerations. This is accomplished because morality is by principle autonomous and because pure reasoning does lead willing into action. It shows simultaneously that this fact is inseparably linked with the consciousness of freedom of willing or better that it is the same thing. This willing, like other efficient causes, is necessarily subject to the laws of causality because it belongs to the world of sense. At the same time, since it belongs to a rational being, it is recognized as being of the intelligible order of things and as being controlled from that order. This is not the result of any special awareness of its particular existence but is due to certain dynamic laws which control causality in the sense world; for freedom, being attributed to man, puts him in the intelligible or mental order of things, which has elsewhere been proved adequately. (See pp. 195 ff.)

If we now compare this *Analytic* with the analytical part of *The Critique of Pure Speculative Reason* a remarkable contrast between the two sections will appear. Abstract and prior knowledge first became possible not from principles but from pure sense awareness of space and time. This was the first datum: it made abstract and prior knowledge possible, though only for knowledge of sensed objects. Amplifying principles cannot be developed from pure ideas without awareness. They occur only as sensed objects are possible to experience; for there can be the kind of knowledge we call experience only when mental ideas organize awareness. All positive knowledge reaching beyond experience and its objects to things which are noumenal was correctly disclaimed on behalf of speculative reasoning. It was nevertheless possible to establish the idea of noumena, or at least the possibility and necessity of thinking of such things. For example, against all objections the assumption of freedom as a negative conception was proved consistent with the principles and limitations of pure theory. Theory, however, gave no extension of definite knowledge to such objects as noumena. Instead it cut off the view of them altogether.

On the other hand, although there is no view connected with the moral law, that law yields a fact which is absolutely inexplicable in terms of any available data of the sense world. Nothing in the whole compass of known theory explains it either. It is a fact which points to a pure world of mind, defining it positively and permitting us to know one thing about it; namely its principal law.

As far as rational beings are concerned, this law gives the sensed world a system or a form taken from the world of mind or supersensible nature, but not interfering with the sensed world's mechanism. A system of nature, in the general sense, is the existence of things under laws. Generally, the sensed nature of rational beings is their existence under empirically conditioned laws and this, from the point of view of reasoning, is heteronomy. On the other hand, the supersensible nature of the same beings is their existence under laws which are independent of all empirical conditions and which belong to the autonomy of pure reasoning. *These laws are practical: they make the existence of things depend on their being known.* Thus, as far as one can see, supersensible nature is nature under the autonomy of pure practical reasoning. The autonomous moral law, therefore, is the basic law of supersensible nature. It is also the law of the pure mind world, of which the sensed world is a counter-image, but neither world interferes with the laws of the other. The two worlds might be called, in order, the archetypal or original world, known only by reasoning, and the ectypal or copied world, in which the idea of the original world is effective as it controls the principle of willing. The moral law in fact moves man over into supersensible nature, in which pure reason would realize the supreme goodness if it had adequate physical power. There the moral law causes human willing to impart its form to the sensed world (i.e., it imparts the pure mind world) as it does to all rational beings. The least scrutiny of one's self shows that this idea serves actually as the pattern for the control of willing.

If the policy I like to follow when I give testimony is tested by practical reasoning, I consider what it would have to be if it were the law of all nature. It is obvious in this case that everybody would have to tell the truth. The general character of natural law does not tolerate argued proof which is purposely false. Thus the policy which I adopt for the free disposition of my life is fixed at once if I ask what that policy would have to be if all nature were to be run by it. Obviously no one could then arbitrarily end his own life, for there would be no permanence in nature if this were the general practice. All other cases would operate similarly. In actual nature, however, freedom of willing as an object of experience does not require the adoption of policies which could be nature's fundamental laws. Personal policies do not even have to fit into such a system. Policies of willing are, on the contrary, like private inclinations; they are not part of the system of nature but are possible only when willing follows pure practical laws. From nature's viewpoint they constitute a body of psychological procedures. At the same time, reasoning brings with it consciousness of a law to which all personal policies are subject, as if a whole order of nature were to be born with our willing. It is a law that contains, therefore, the idea of a nature which is not experienced as actual but which is made *possible* through freedom. This nature is supersensible and since we regard it as an object of willing, we attribute to it objective reality, at least *practically*.

There is a distinction to be made, therefore, between the laws of a nature to which willing is subject and the laws of a nature which are subject to willing. In the former, objects cause the ideas that govern willing; whereas in the latter, willing causes the objects, and the controlling principle of causality is derived from pure practical reasoning.

There are, therefore, two problems: (1) how pure reasoning develops knowledge of objects abstractly and in advance, and (2) how pure reasoning can be an immediate controlling principle of willing; i.e., of the causality lodged in rational beings. [These are the problems of the first two *Critiques*—trans.]

In this inquiry, criticism can and must begin with pure practical laws and their reality. These are not derived from awareness of the sensed world but from the existence of these pure practical laws in the mind world. This means that criticism begins in the idea of freedom, for freedom has no meaning apart from practical laws, and these are possible only when willing is free. Thus if freedom is presupposed, pure practical laws are necessary. Conversely, freedom is necessary because such laws are necessary practical postulates. It is not possible to explain further how we happen to be conscious of the moral law or, what amounts to the same thing, how freedom is possible. Its permissibility as an idea, however, is well established in the theoretical (or first) *Critique*.

The exposition of the supreme principle of practical reasoning is now finished; that is to say, its contents have been indicated and it has been shown to be self-subsistent, wholly abstract, prior, and independent of experience. We have also shown that it is different from all other practical principles. We cannot hope to succeed with the deduction of this principle, that is, with the defense of its objectives and its general validity, nor with getting insight into the possibility of this kind of abstract, amplifying proposition, as we did with the principles of pure theoretical reasoning. The latter referred to objects of possible experience, that is, to phenomena. It could be proved that phenomena could be known as objects of experience only as they fit the categories provided by these laws, and therefore that all possible experience is subject to them. The deduction of the moral law, however, doesn't proceed like this. It has nothing to do with knowledge of the properties of objects. This knowledge has to get into the reasoning from some other source. The deduction of the moral law does, however, concern a kind of knowledge which makes pure reasoning causal because it is basic to the existence of objects, and, therefore, it governs willing.

All human insight fails where fundamental human functions take over. The very possibility of these functions is unintelligible, and accordingly they must neither be assumed nor be arbitrarily invented. The use of them or their assumption in theoretical reasoning is justified only by experience, but to substitute them for missing elements of abstract knowledge is forbidden by the rules of pure practical reasoning. If some entity's reality needs to be justified by experience, its very possibility must also be justified by the principles of experience and this would not be pure practical reasoning. On the other hand, the moral law is an actual fact of pure reasoning, of which we are conscious abstractly and in advance. It is also apodictically certain, even though no example of its exact fulfillment is encountered in human experience. It follows that the objective reality of the moral law is not demonstrable by theoretical reasoning alone; but even then, if it also were to be conceded as not apodictically certain, experience would not save it. It is, nevertheless, a firmly established fact.

6. *Moral law indicates an uncaused cause*

If a speculative deduction of the moral law is thus sought in vain, something else, wholly unexpected, appears in its stead. The moral law serves conversely as the principle by which an inscrutable human capacity is deduced, and not via experience. The moral law must be assumed if speculative reasoning is not to be found self-contradictory when, among cosmological ideas, something unconditionally causal is discovered, namely, freedom. Moral law on its own part, needing no justification, not only proves the possibility of freedom but demonstrates that beings who acknowledge obligation under moral law are actually free. Freedom thus makes the moral law causal and so establishes the possibility of supersensible nature, just as the metaphysical law of the properties of the sensed world becomes the causal law of physical nature. The moral law therefore becomes a causal law, which fact had to be omitted from speculative philosophy or at least regarded as merely negative. This then is how the idea of freedom first gets objective validity.

Abstract justification of the moral law is unnecessary because it is the basic principle of freedom, and freedom is causality in pure reasoning. At first, the possibility of freedom had to be assumed in pure reasoning to fill up a lacuna in the train of thought. In *The Critique of Pure Reason* (see p. 109, the third conflict in formal ideas), the reality of the moral law was sufficiently proved by the fact that it provided a positive definition for the causality which had previously been negatively conceived. This causality was assumed in pure reasoning even though it was unintelligible. To the negative conception of reasoning as governing willing by the imposition of reasoned personal policies, the moral law now adds the condition of a general legislative form. It thus for the first time imparts to reasoning an objective but as yet only practical reality. Otherwise, reasoning has heretofore tended to extravagant flights with its ideas. The moral law thus changes the *transcendent* use of reasoning into an *immanent* use and makes it an efficient cause in the field of experience.

The definition of the causality of beings in the sense world can never be unconditional and yet all series of conditions must ultimately end in something that is unconditioned. This means that there must be a self-determined causality. Thus, freedom as absolute spontaneity was not discovered as a need but as an analytical principle of pure speculative reasoning. Because, however, there is no perfect example of this conception in experience and no discoverable, unconditioned causality, the supposition that a being in the sensed world might be considered a noumenon, and so a free, efficient cause could only be defended. The defense showed that when the cause is an intellectual being, and thus physically unconditioned, no contradiction is involved in regarding its actions as subject to physical conditions when they are phenomenal. This is how the idea of freedom regulates reasoning. It does not, however, indicate the object to which this kind of causality is attributed and the difficulty is met in one of two ways. We may leave to the proponents of mechanism and physical necessity the right to go from condition to condition *ad infinitum* or we may keep the place for this causality open to pure reason so that the unconditioned causal something may be transferred to the mind world.

I was not able to make this idea real in *The Critique of Pure Reason*. I could not transform it into knowledge of a being whose behavior indicated efficient causality, or even the possibility of such a being. Pure practical reasoning now fills this empty place with the notion of freedom and a definite (moral) law or causality in the mind world. This means no access of insight through speculative reasoning. It does mean a gain in the certainty of pure reasoning's problematic conception of freedom: freedom acquires objective reality and is now undoubted, though merely practical. Even the conception of causality, the application and meaning of which properly extends only to phenomena connected with experience (as proved in *The Critique of Pure Reason*), is not extended beyond its wonted boundaries. To extend the idea of causality beyond its ordinary limits, it would be necessary to show how the logical relation of cause and effect can be used to organize awareness that is not sensed, i.e., how a noumenal cause is possible. Theoretical reasoning cannot do this and practical reasoning is not concerned.

According to practical reasoning, human causality stems from pure reasoning, and this makes reasoning practical. The notion of cause is then useful, not for knowledge of objects but to define causality in general. In practical reasoning, then, the conception of causality need not be applied to objects: it is always present to mind because it is abstract and independent of any awareness. Since, therefore, the idea of causality is used only practically, the control of willing may be transferred to the mental order of things, admitting meanwhile that we do not understand the purpose of causality as a means to the knowledge of things. The effect of causality on willing, however, must be definitely known if definite action is ever to result from practical reasoning. The theoretical idea of its own causality as noumenal need not be defined by practical reasoning as a means of knowing the supersensible world. In any case, through the moral law the supersensible world gets significance, even though its significance is only practical.

The moral principle has now been stated as a law of causality set above the conditions of the sensed world. Willing has been conceived as controlled from the mind world to which it belongs. The willing subject (a man) is therefore conceived as belonging not only to the mind world, though in this respect he is unknown, as was shown in *The Critique of Pure Reason*. He has also been defined as causal by means of a law which is not reducible to any law of the physical world. Our knowledge is thus extended beyond the limits of that world, and this is a pretension which in *The Critique of Pure Reason* was shown to be pure vanity as far as speculation is concerned. How then is this practical use of pure reason to be reconciled with its theoretical use, in view of the limits set for all reasoning? What about the application of the category of causality, among others, to objects beyond experience?

No existing thing can be known without the categories. I have been able to deduce the objective reality of the categories only because they refer to objects of possible experience. These pure ideas were saved on this basis. I have also proved that even though they do not define any object in advance, they make thought about objects possible. The categories have a place in pure mind and are referred by the mind to objects of sense or thought. If anything else is needed, it is the conditions under which these categories, particularly the category of causality, may be applied to objects of awareness, objects which are not actual but like noumena, and about which theoretical knowledge is desired. This, of course, was forbidden, as *The Critique of Pure Reason* indicates.

The objective reality of the idea of causality remains, nevertheless, and it may be used even on noumena. In this case, no knowledge accrues from its use because the theoretical idea involved (noumena) is not positively defined. Still, there is nothing impossible about the idea of causality when it refers to a nonmaterial object. This is proved by the fact that even when the object is material, causality still has a secure place in pure mind. Moreover, suppose that it is referred to things-themselves, which are beyond experiencing, from which no knowledge accrues, and which are not definable as definite objects. Even then, the idea of causality might be so defined as to be applicable. This could not happen if, as Hume maintained, the idea of causality involved a generally unintelligible element.

7. *There are immaterial causes*

To discover the conditions under which the idea of causality may be applied to noumena, it is necessary merely to recall why we were not satisfied to apply it only to objects of experience and wished to apply it as well to things-themselves. It will then appear that it was from a practical and not from a theoretical viewpoint that this extension of application seemed necessary. Even if the idea of causality could be applied successfully within pure thought, our knowledge of nature or any actual objects would not thereby be increased. On the contrary, this would merely be taking a long step away from the sensed world into the supersensible, whereas we have enough to do otherwise to follow the chain of causes within the sensed world and to complete our knowledge of principles and fix the limits of knowledge here. An infinite, unfillable gulf, however, will always remain between what we know and the limits of knowledge. Moving off into the supersensible would indicate that we were prompted by curiosity rather than a solid desire for knowledge.

If with Hume I had denied the objective reality of the idea of causality in its theoretically defined uses, as when it is applied either to things-themselves (the supersensible) or to sensed objects, it would have lost all meaning. It would be useless because theoretically impossible and it would therefore be absurd to try to use it practically. The idea of a causality which is not conditioned by experience is, however, theoretically possible even though it tells us nothing and refers to no object of awareness. Its object is indeterminate, but in a practical sense the moral law gives it compensating meaning. Its theoretical, objective reality is not defined by awareness but it has real applications which are concretely represented by personal intentions or policies. This means that it has practical reality which can be specified and this is enough to justify its reference to noumena.

Once adopted, the objective reality of one category in the field of supersensible matters gives objective reality to all the other categories if, as they govern willing, they are of necessity connected with the moral law. Objective reality is then purely a practical matter since it adds nothing to the theoretical knowledge of an object, and for pure mind it yields no insight into an object's nature. In the following pages it will appear that these categories refer only to thoughts, and in thoughts only to the relation of reasoning to willing. Thus, they apply only to practical matters, and beyond this they imply no pretension to any extra knowledge.

Chapter II. *The Conception of an Object of Pure Practical Reasoning.* By the conception of an object of practical reasoning, I mean the free imagination of it as a possibility. An object of practical knowledge therefore refers only to the relation of willing to action by which the object or its opposite is to be realized. The identification of an object of pure practical willing as such, means a decision as to the possibility or impossibility of willing to do what its realization requires, if the power to do it is available. The decision as to the power available will depend on experience. If the object is desired, then before it can be said that it is an object of practical reasoning, we must know whether its realization is physically possible and whether we are *free* to achieve it.

On the other hand, suppose that law can be considered, abstractly and in advance, the defining principle of behavior and that behavior is determined, therefore, by pure practical reasoning. The decision, then, about whether or not a thing is an object of pure practical reasoning will not depend on an assessment of one's physical power. In this case, the question is only whether, if we *are* able to attain the object, we should *will* to do what has to be done to attain it. Accordingly, the moral possibility of the required action must first be defined, for it is the law of willing and not the object that controls behavior.

Good and evil, therefore, are the only objects of practical reasoning. *Good* means an object necessarily desired in accord with some principle of reasoning, while *evil* means an object to be shunned by reason of the same principle.

If the idea of the good is not derived from an antecedent practical law but is to serve as the law's foundation, the idea has to be one that promises pleasure and so causes the subject to do good, thus governing his desire. It is, of course, impossible to say, abstractly and in advance, which idea will be pleasant and which unpleasant; the distinction of good and evil, in this case, will depend on personal experience, on *feeling*, a feeling of pleasure or pain which is a property of inner sense. The *good* will then be anything that immediately causes a sensation of *pleasure* while *evil* similarly causes *pain*.

There is an old formula of the schools: *We want nothing unless we think it good; we are averse to nothing unless we think it bad.* This is often used correctly, but sometimes to the detriment of philosophy because the expressions *good* and *bad* are equivocal, for which terseness of expression is to blame. These words really have a double meaning and so make the meaning of practical laws dubious. When they are used in philosophy, and variant meanings of the same word are discovered, and no substitutes appear, philosophers tend to indulge in subtle distinctions about which subsequently there is no agreement.

Weal or *woe* imply only a reference to a person's condition as *pleasant* or *unpleasant*, or as *gratifying* or *afflicting*. If, on this acount, an object is desired or avoided, this is done because of its effect on one's sensibilities, which means the feeling of pleasure or pain it causes. *Good* and *evil*, however, always refer to willing, as a law of reasoning causes willing to be aimed at some object. For willing is never governed by an object or the idea of it; it takes a rule of reasoning as a motive for action and thus for the realization of some object. Good and evil are therefore properly referred to behavior and not to the sensations of a person. Only the behavior of persons may be regarded as absolutely good or evil, that is, good or evil in every respect and unconditionally. Things are never good or evil.

The Stoic may be laughed at for having cried out during a severe spasm of gout: "Pain, you torment me; nevertheless I will not admit that you are evil!" He was, however, right. The pain was bad—his outcry proved that—but he saw no reason to admit that the evil was his own. The pain did not diminish his personal worth in the least but only the worth of his condition. If he had been conscious of telling one lie, his pride would have been stricken; but the pain of gout served only to lift his pride: he knew that he had done nothing to deserve punishment.

What we call good must be desirable in the judgment of every reasonable person, and evil must likewise be an object of general aversion. This kind of judgment requires reasoning in addition to sensibility; which is also the case with truthfulness as opposed to lying, or with justice as opposed to violence, etc. We may, however, call something *bad* when everyone else thinks it good, directly or indirectly. A man who undergoes surgery may well feel that his operation is a bad thing, while others think it good. When someone who likes to annoy or vex peaceable people at last takes a beating, this undoubtedly seeems bad to him but it is approved by everyone else, even though nothing more ever comes of it. Even the beaten one must reasonably acknowledge that the punishment was right because the relation of good conduct to good fortune, which reasoning portrays, was sustained in his case.

Weal and woe are indeed of great importance in the judgments of practical reasoning. We are physical beings and happiness may therefore be a matter of great consequence if it is estimated reasonably, not by those transient sensations that go with it but because of the way it influences our whole existence and the long-term satisfaction it affords. It is not, however, the only matter of importance. Man, a creature of the world of sense, is needy, and in this connection his mind has a function it cannot abdicate. It must take care of his sense nature and make practical policies affecting his present and future happiness. He is not, however, so completely animal as to be indifferent to what mind has to say for itself or to use it merely as an instrument for the service of his physical needs. Mind could not raise man above the brutes if it served him only as instinct serves them. Mind in that case would be only a particular method by which nature equips man to do what beasts can do, without raising him above their level. To understand weal and woe, a man needs mind in addition to his physical endowments, but he needs it for a higher purpose. He needs mind to know what is good and what is evil; only pure reasoning uninfluenced by sense can give judgment about such matters and distinguish them from physical needs, making the pure reasoning the supreme condition of the latter.

In judging what is good or evil of itself and distinguishing it from so-called weal or woe, consider the following points. A rational principle may be devised to control willing, neglecting any object desired. It would then be merely a legislative form of a personal policy and accordingly, abstractly and in advance, a practical law, as pure reasoning may be practical. In this case, law controls willing directly, and the resulting action is good in itself. A personal policy which always conforms to law makes willing absolutely good in every respect and the supreme condition of all goodness.

In contrast, consider a personal policy which is the result of desire and presupposes an object of pleasure or pain, pleasing or displeasing. It would be reasonable policy to pursue the pleasant object and to avoid the unpleasant. Then behavior would be called good when it agrees with one's inclinations, or indirectly good when some other end, to which one's inclinations are the means, is sought. On this basis, personal policies are not laws but could be called reasonable, practical precepts, since the purpose, the pleasure sought, is not goodness but satisfaction. This is not a conception born of reasoning but an empirical idea of a sensed object. The means to this end, the action taken to attain it, is still called good because it requires rational deliberation. Even so, it is not absolutely good, but good relative to sense or to feelings of pleasure or pain. Moreover, when personal policy is affected by pertinent feelings, the resultant willing is not pure. Willing is pure only when pure reasoning can be practical in it.

This is the place to explain the paradox of the method of a critique of practical reasoning: *The conception of good and evil may appear to be the foundation of the moral law but it must not be defined until the moral law has been stated, and then only in terms of it.* Suppose that we did not know that the moral law is pure, abstract and prior, as it governs willing. Even then, to avoid a gratuitous assumption of principles, we should have to delay deciding how willing is controlled, whether empirically or abstractly and in advance. It is against all the rules of philosophic method to assume in advance the point to be proved. Suppose that we try to deduce the law of willing from the conception of good and evil. Willing would then be controlled by the idea of some object that is considered good; but since there is no abstract, prior, practical law to provide a standard for the idea, the only remaining criterion of good and evil would be the effect of the object, for pleasure or pain, on a person's feelings. Reasoning would then be used, first, to define the pleasure or pain involved against a lifetime of experience with these sensations and, second, to decide how to get at the pleasant object. One knows, however, about pleasant and unpleasant feelings only by experience, and if by hypothesis practical law is to be based on this experience, the possibility of abstract, prior, practical law is excluded at once. This is due to thinking it necessary to begin by finding an object, such that the idea of it as a good thing constitutes an empirical principle by which willing may be controlled.

Before that we ought to have inquired whether or not there is an abstract principle that controls willing. It could be found, of course, only in pure practical law if, without reference to any object, the law prescribes the form to be taken by personal policies. It was, however, an object in terms of good and evil that was made the basis of practical law, and, there being no previous law, it was possible to think of that object only in terms of experience. The possibility of conceiving a pure, practical law was therefore excluded. Earlier analytical inquiry would have revealed that it is not the idea of an object as good or evil that defines the moral law and makes it possible, but on the contrary, it is the moral law that defines the idea of goodness and makes it possible.

This remark explains at once what occasioned the errors of philosophers with the supreme principle of morals. They looked for an object of willing which could be the substance and principle of a moral law. The law, consequently, would govern willing only indirectly through the relation of the object to feelings of pleasure or pain. They should instead have looked for a law that would govern willing directly, abstractly and in advance, and so define the object to accord with willing. Whether those philosophers found the pleasant object which supplied the supreme conception of goodness in happiness, perfection, moral sentiment, or the will of God, makes no difference. Their principle was always heteronomy. Inevitably they had to depend on experience for a moral law because their object, which was to be the immediate activating principle of willing, could not be called good or bad except from its immediate relation to feeling, which is always empirical. Only a formal law; i.e., one in which reasoning prescribes the most general form of legislation as supreme form for personal policies, can be abstractly and in advance a definitive principle of practical reasoning. The ancients acknowledged the error made by moderns by directing all their moral inquiries towards the definition of the idea of supreme goodness. They then set up an object which they later intended to make the definitive principle of willing in moral law. It is only now, much later, after that moral law has been well established and shown to be the definitive principle of willing, that this object can be set before the willing subject; for the form of willing is now known to be defined abstractly and in advance. Moderns, for whom the idea of supreme goodness has gone out of use or seems to have become at least a secondary matter, hide their error with vague words. It is, nevertheless, often seen peering out of their systems as heteronomy in practical reasoning. No moral law with general authority can be developed on this basis.

When the ideas of good and evil are consequences of abstract and prior definitions of willing, they also imply a pure practical principle, the causality of pure reasoning. Hence their original relation to objects is not like that of the mind's pure ideas, the categories. Ideas of good and evil presuppose that their objects are actually present and that they are all modes of the category of causality. The definitive principle of causality is a rational idea of a law, the law of freedom, which reasoning provides for itself and thereby, abstractly and in advance, proves of itself that it is practical. Behavior, on the one hand, is under law, not physical law but the law of freedom, and consequently it answers to the behavior of intelligible beings. On the other hand, as they are events in the sensed world, human acts are phenomena. Therefore, the control of behavior in this second aspect is accomplished in practical reasoning through mind's categories, but not with a view to any theoretical use of them. These categories are used instead to subject man's many desires to the unity of consciousness involved in practical reasoning under moral law; i.e., to pure, abstract and prior willing.

8. *Freedom has twelve categories*

In contradistinction to mind's theoretical forms, i.e., the categories applied to nature, we propose now to consider the categories of freedom. These have an obvious advantage over the former. The categories applied to physical nature are only forms of thought and designate unspecified objects of awareness by means of general ideas. The categories of freedom, on the other hand, define free choice, but awareness is not involved in the definition. Free choice is based on a pure, practical, prior law, which is not true of the categories or ideas involved theoretically in the knowing process. These practical, elementary ideas are based on the forms pure willing takes in mind itself and not on the forms of awareness; i.e., space and time, which are derived from sensibility rather than from reasoning. Pure practical reasoning is thus concerned chiefly with the control of willing and not with a person's practical ability to accomplish his purpose. Thus, practical, abstract and prior principles become knowledge of the supreme principle of freedom and need not wait for awareness to get meaning. This is true for the remarkable reason that they create the reality to which they refer, i.e., the aim of willing, which theoretical ideas cannot do. We must carefully notice, however, that *categories of freedom apply only to matters of practical reasoning.* They are here listed in order, from those categories which are still subject to sense conditions and morally indeterminate, to those that are free of sense conditions and subject to moral law.

TABLE of the CATEGORIES of FREEDOM
as they are related to the ideas of good and evil

I. QUANTITY

Subjective, by personal policies; practical individual opinions
Objective, by principles; precepts
Abstract and prior, subjective and objective principles of freedom; laws

II. QUALITY

Practical rules for action; perceptive
Practical rules for omission; prohibitory
Practical rules for exceptions; exceptive

III. RELATION

To personality
To the condition of a person
Reciprocal, of one person to the condition of another

IV. MODIFYING

Permitted and forbidden
For and against duty
Perfect and imperfect duty

It is clear at once that in this table, freedom is a kind of causality in whatever actions are made possible by it and that it is not subject to the controls of experience. The actions caused by it are phenomena of the sense world, and freedom therefore pertains to all the categories in which it is physically possible. Each category is quite general, so that the corresponding causality can be derived from a principle outside the sense world; i.e., from freedom, a property of thinking beings. Finally and problematically, the *modifying categories* make the transition from practical principles to the principles of morality, for moral principles can be established definitively only by the moral law itself.

I add nothing further in explanation of the table; it speaks for itself. Such a classification by principles is pertinent to all sciences; it makes for thoroughness and intelligibility. It tells that practical inquiries must begin with personal policies based on individual inclinations, with precepts which are valid for a genre of intelligent beings whose inclinations agree, and with the laws which are valid for all people, whatever their inclinations. Thus the whole agenda of moral and practical philosophy is surveyed and the order in which it is to be covered is laid out.

9. *Moral law is typical of natural law*

In the first place, willing gets its object from ideas of good and evil. The ideas themselves are, however, subject to a practical rule of reasoning which, if it is pure, governs the relation of willing to its object abstractly and in advance. Whether an action which is possible in the sense world comes under the rule or not is a matter to be decided by practical judgment. The decision applies the general principle to the particular case. Since, however, a practical rule of pure reasoning implies first the object's existence and then that some action is necessary, it is a practical law, a law of freedom and, as such, independent of experience. This makes it seem absurd to find in the sense world a case which comes under physical nature's law, yet involves an application of freedom's law, and so offers a concrete example of the supersensible idea of moral goodness. Thus, a judgment of pure practical reasoning is subject to the same difficulties as those encountered in pure theoretical reasoning. For the latter, however, there was an escape clause, in that for theoretical use, objects of awareness were required, objects to which pure ideas could be applied. These objects could be specified abstractly and in advance even though they were sense objects. On the other hand, the object of moral goodness is supersensible and there is nothing in sense awareness that corresponds to it. There is, therefore, a special difficulty about judgments which depend on the laws of pure practical reasoning: *freedom's law applies to actions which occur in the sense world, and so belong to physical nature.*

Here again, however, a prospect favorable to pure practical judgment opens up. When I find that an action possible to me in the sense world comes under pure practical law, the possibility of the physical event does not concern me. This is matter for theoretical reasoning under the causal law, which is a pure idea of mind and for which, therefore, there is a schema in sense awareness. Physical causality, or the condition under which it occurs, belongs among ideas of physical nature, and its schema (see p. 56 ff.) is sketched by formal imagination. In practical judgment, however, the concern is not with the schema of an occurrence according to law but with the schema of the law itself, because the willing involved is governed only by the law. This fact connects the idea of causality with conditions other than physical.

Physical law, as a law to which objects of sense awareness conform, must have its own corresponding schema or general imaginative procedure by which abstractly and in advance the senses get the mind's pure ideas defined by the law. The law of freedom, however, which is not a sense-conditioned causality, and the idea of unconditioned goodness which comes of it will not get a concrete application either by awareness or schema. Consequently, for its application to objects of nature, the moral law depends solely on mind and not on imagination. For the purposes of practical judgment, mind can furnish a rational idea with a law but not with a schema. It is only formally a law, but it can be represented concretely in sensed objects and is therefore a law of nature. This law is called a *type* of moral law.

The rule of judgment by pure practical reasoning's laws is this: Ask yourself whether you would regard it possible that the action you contemplate and have willed would answer to the law of the system of nature of which you are a part.

Everyone, in fact, does decide by this rule whether actions are good or evil. He says: What if everyone cheated when he thought it profitable? Or felt justified in ending his life when he got tired of it? Or viewed the need of others with indifference? If you belonged to an order where things happened this way, would you freely assent to it? Now everyone knows that when, secretly, he cheats, not all other people will cheat too; or that if he has no compassion, not all other people are like him. Thus, a comparison of his own personal policy with a general law of nature does not govern his willing. The law is, nevertheless, the *type* or standard by which personal policies are judged according to moral principles. If the personal policy does not stand the test of being a form of general natural law, it is morally inadmissible. This is also the judgment of common sense, by which even the ordinary judgments that come with experience are generally based on natural law. Common sense usually causes judgment to follow nature, except in cases where causality takes the form of freedom, and then the *law of nature* becomes the *type* of freedom's law. Common sense, however, does not enable the right application of a law of pure practical reasoning when the occasion for it occurs unless there is an example to go by.

It is therefore permissible to use the sense world as the type of the supersensible world, provided one's awareness and its consequences are not transferred thither intact, but instead one applies to the supersensible world merely the general form of nature's law. This idea of the law is common in common sense but is not definitely known, or known abstractly and in advance, except when pure practical reasoning is in use. In this respect, all laws are alike, no matter where they get defined.

Furthermore, whereas nothing at all is known of the supersensible world except that freedom born of moral law is inseparable from it; and whereas supersensible objects, to which reason leads when it is guided by that law, have no reality except as they carry out the law's purposes and are useful in practical reasoning; and whereas reasoning is authorized and even compelled to use the mental forms of physical nature as types of judgment, this remark will serve to prevent the inclusion of types of ideas among the ideas themselves. The typing of judgments guards against empiricism in practical reasoning by which practical ideas of good and evil are derived from experience, as so-called happiness is. Without doubt, happiness would serve as a perfectly suitable type of moral goodness, but happiness and moral goodness are not identical. The same remark applies as well to the endlessly useful consequences of willing controlled by self-interest, when such willing is capable of forming a general law of nature. The same typing of judgments guards against the mysticism of practical reasoning which turns a symbol into a schema. Mysticism undertakes to furnish a real, if not visualized, basis for moral ideas, such as an invisible kingdom of God, and so dives off into transcendent matters.

Only the reasoning power of judgment is suited to the use of moral ideas. It borrows from nature only what pure reasoning can conceive by itself in conformity to law. It transfers nothing to the supersensible world unless, conversely, it is also represented in the sense world by a formal rule of natural law. The warning against empiricism is, however, the more important of the two. Mysticism is reconcilable with the purity and sublimity of the moral law; but it is neither natural nor agreeable to man's usual habits of thought to screw up the imagination to an awareness of the supersensible world, and accordingly the danger this way is not great. Empiricism, on the other hand, tears moral intentions up by the roots, when it is from these intentions rather than actual behavior that a man's high worth can and ought to come. Empiricism substitutes empirical interest for duty, and that is something quite different and secretly linked to inclinations. Being thus allied to desire, empiricism degrades humanity by raising desire to the dignity of a supreme practical principle, and because this is agreeable to everyone's feelings, empiricism is more dangerous than mysticism, which is not an enduring condition of many people.

10. *Conclusion*

Two things fill one's mind with ever new and increasing admiration and awe, the oftener and more continuously one reflects on them: the starry heaven above and the moral law within. I need not look for them as though they were covered with darkness or were transcendent, or ponder them as if they were beyond the reach of my eyes. I see them before me and connect them at once with my own conscious existence. The starry heavens begin at the place where I am in the external world of sense and expand my reach out to world after world, system after system, over the endless ages of their periodic motions, from the beginning until now. The moral law within begins with my own invisible self, my personality, placing me in a world of true infinity, which is fathomable only to mind, a world with which I see that my connection is not an accident but is both general and necessary, as it is with all the visible worlds.

The prospect of countless worlds abolishes my animal sense of importance. No one knows how I came to be provided for a short time with this vital force, but I must at last give back the matter of which I am formed to the planet I have inhabited, a planet which is a mere speck to the universe. The moral law, however, raises my worth infinitely, as I am intelligent and a person in whom there is a life independent of animality and the world of sense, at least as far as may be inferred from the definition of the purpose of my existence given by the moral law. It is a definition not limited to the conditions and boundaries of this life but reaching to infinity.

Admiration and wonder may prompt inquiry about these matters but they can never substitute for it. How then is the inquiry to be conducted usefully or made appropriate to its lofty theme? Examples may serve us here as warnings as well as for imitation. The world was first contemplated as the noblest spectacle of human sense and for the penetration of mind, but contemplation ended in astrology. Morality began with the development and cultivation of the noblest property of human nature, promising infinite utility, but it ended in fanaticism and superstition. This is generally what happens with all crude attempts of the kind, when reasoning plays the principal role in the project. The use of reason, unlike the use of one's feet, does not come automatically after much practice. This is especially so when human qualities are involved which do not appear directly in experience. Then lately, it became the style to examine in advance all the steps proposed for reasoning, with a view to confining reasoning to the ruts of well-considered methods. Thought about the structure of the world took a wholly new direction, with incomparably happier results. The fall of a stone, the motion of a sling, analyzed into their elements and external forces and treated mathematically, produced at last a clear and unalterable insight into the structure of the world. There need never be fear that this insight will retreat; its ever-increasing extension may be expected as long as observation continues.

This example suggests that if the moral qualities of human nature are treated similarly, similarly good results may be hoped for. There are examples of moral judgment by reasoning. If these are analyzed into their elementary ideas, separating the rational from the empirical elements, and if repeated experiments are made on common sense, we may learn with certainty what each part separately can accomplish, and exhibit it then in its pure state. In this way the errors of amateur reasoners can be avoided. On the other hand, and far more necessary, the extravagances of genius may be avoided. For as it used to happen with the adepts of the philosophers' stone, nature's true treasures are squandered and imaginary ones are promised, when there is no methodical research. Briefly, science, critically undertaken and methodically conducted, is the strait gate that leads to wisdom's doctrine (philosophy). This should be understood to refer not merely to what one ought to do himself but to that guide of teachers, by which they may build well the highway to wisdom on which all may travel and on which all are kept from going astray. The highway is science, of which philosophy must always be the true guardian, and even if there is no public interest in its subtler researches, there will always be widespread interest in doctrines which are clear because they result from scientific work.

Part Four

THE CRITIQUE OF JUDGMENT

23 JUDGMENT MEDIATES BETWEEN FREEDOM AND NATURE

Beauty and faith involve judgments of purpose

It was in 1790, when Kant was sixty-six years old, that he came to the end of his third Critique, The Critique of Judgment: "With this, then, I put a period to my whole critical enterprise. I shall move on quickly to the doctrinal part, to take advantage of my best remaining years. . . . The metaphysics of nature and morals will then be completed." The issues, at least, had been given a stirring statement.

The matter of the third Critique is criticism, or evaluation of the judgment that nature and freedom, far from being mutually inimical ideas, actually harmonize. This involves teleology, a study of purpose, not in the primitive sense in which individual human purposes are read into nature, but in the sense of the purposiveness or appropriateness that may be observed in nature's parts. No part has a purpose of its own, but each part seems designed to fit into the total scheme or design of a final purpose.

This will not imply that Kant slackened his belief in the desirability of mechanistic explanation wherever it could succeed. Mechanism, as a philosophy of nature, had just scored a maximum triumph in physics. It had done less well in biology and nothing with the characteristic human processes. This lag could be made good either by waiting for more knowledge and improved techniques or via the hypothesis that the human essences are beyond all mechanisms as such. Kant chose the latter, at least provisionally, and sought through judgment an understanding of beauty from purpose and of God as the final end of all creation. He had proved in the first Critique that neither God nor beauty are established by thought; neither are they there because of man's desire or feeling. They appear from significant observations of the purposiveness or appropriateness in nature's parts, which are then judged to be either beautiful, good, or the work of God. Kant calls this "reflective judgment." It is just a way of thinking that is helpful and useful as long as the thought is not mistaken for the fact.

Enroute in his argument, Kant goes into the distinction between beauty and sublimity at length, a discussion for which aestheticians generally are said to have little taste nowadays. To those who come fresh to the subject, however, what Kant has to say will be engaging. Independent natural beauty, he says, discloses a technique of nature which makes it look as if nature operates not merely with purposeless mechanisms but with something analogous to art. Judgment requires that we proceed on the principle that nature conforms to our means of knowing. At first sight, this is not surprising in view of Kant's first major contention that mind is nature's lawgiver. There is, however, more to it than that. Nature is more than an inchoate mass of cosmic putty that submits to mind because nothing makes a difference. It meets mind like an eager partner well-schooled in advance in what the steps in the dance of life will be. This could give rise to misunderstanding if it were not precisely the hypothesis on which scientists must proceed to research. If the world were not amenable to understanding, there would be no science; neither would there be religion in the sense of man and God made one.

Mechanism and teleology are not mutually any more inimical than arithmetic and algebra. For some scientific purposes, mechanistic explanations are not only adequate; they are simpler. (See p. 212.) Falsehood appears in mechanistic theories when their limited applicability, which in practice is quite abstract, is arbitrarily extended to brush aside as fakes humane qualities such as freedom, morality, and spirit; where these factors are not considered fakes, a more capacious theory is required. Teleology is such a theory. It includes purposiveness or appropriateness where mechanism applies, and God's purpose where over-all considerations intrude. That there are difficulties about teleology, Kant's development of the subject *will illustrate very well. It may be doubted whether any single and explicit theory can elucidate adequately the whole of reality.*

In the final summing up of all his efforts to answer the question: "What do I know?" Kant says that knowledge includes matters of opinion, matters of fact, and matters of faith. Matters of opinion, as such, have been dealt with only incidentally. They are matters about which empirical knowledge is possible. For example, I do not know the date on which the Communists will cease to govern China. But it is possible that I shall know, and meanwhile I have an opinion. Matters of fact are instances of ideas of demonstrable objective reality. This has been the principal burden of the whole critical philosophy. Matters of faith are ideas turned up by pure practical reasoning in service to duty. They are out beyond the limits of experience where valid theory applies. Faith, says Kant, is wholly a matter of morals; it is confidence that when duty requires the attainment of a purpose, that purpose can be attained even though no one sees how.

Let us say that there is a gulf between the sense world and the supersensible, a gulf not bridged by reasoning. There would, then, be two worlds, neither of which could influence the other; and yet the supersensible is intended to affect the sense world: freedom provides for the realization in the sense world and in nature of the purpose embodied in supersensible laws. The sense world, therefore, has to be conceived so that its forms harmonize with freedom's purposes. This requires a principle of unity joining the supersensible basis of nature with the notion of freedom, a principle which enables transition between the two worlds.

Among mind's superior facilities there is a middle term between mind and reason; namely, judgment, which has a field of its own and to which no other mental facility is appropriate. Judgment, in general, is the facility by which particular instances of a universal rule are conceived. It is *definitive* when it assigns a particular instance to a given rule, principle, or law; it is *reflective* when the general principle covering the particular instance has still to be found. Reflective judgment is, therefore, guided by a principle that does not come of experience, but is developed as follows. Since the general laws of nature spring from mind, there must also be particular empirical laws covering all instances not covered by the general laws. They are to be thought of as comprised in a unity such as mind gives them. This need not imply the existence of such a mind. This thought is merely an idea used in a reflective judgment and it is not definitive. In this way, reflective judgment gets its own laws.

When an object embodies an idea, the idea is called its *purpose*, or *end*. When an object fits into an arrangement of things that could be possible only according to some purpose, it is said to be formally appropriate, or purposive. The principle of judgment, then, deals with the fitness of objects to purposes in nature. Nature in all its variety is considered as if a mind gave unity to its manifold empirical laws. Purpose or fitness in nature is thus an idea originating in reflective judgment. It is not attributed to the products of nature themselves. It is an idea used for reflecting on the connections between phenomena as provided by empirical laws. It is also quite different from the purpose or appropriateness displayed in art and morals, although these do furnish it with analogies. The principle of the purposiveness of nature is a *formal* principle, as certain proverbs of metaphysical wisdom make evident: "Nature takes the shortest path; but there are no jumps in the sequence of its changes or in the juxtaposition of specifically differing forms; its vast variety of empirical laws, for all that, compose a unity under a few principles" and so forth.

If the origin of these principles is sought along psychological lines their sense is violated. For they tell us, not what happens or how we actually judge nature, but how we *ought* to judge it, and this logical, objective requirement, this *ought*, would not appear if these principles were merely empirical. Hence, as far as knowing is concerned, purpose in nature is the result of a formal principle of judgment. Judgment, therefore, involves a subjective, abstract and prior principle covering nature's possibilities, a principle intended to guide reflection on nature. It is called *the law of specification in nature*. Nature specifies its general laws so that they are appropriate to man's mind. This is not a law prescribed to nature or learned from nature; it describes the basis on which empirical laws are framed because it is the only way knowledge may be had.

The harmony of nature's many laws with the requirements of mind and with man's need for finding general principles for nature, must be considered fortuitous; it is nevertheless indispensable to learning. The discovery of order or harmony is the work of mind, pursued for a purpose peculiar to mind: it brings unity among principles to nature. Judgment, then, attributes that unity to nature, since mind does not legislate it, and a feeling of pleasure results. Since pleasure comes of an abstract and prior idea and is, thus, a general principle of reflective judgment, the feeling of pleasure is defined as an abstract and prior principle, valid for all.

We gladly listen to one who gives us hope that the more we know of nature, the simpler we shall find its principles to be, or to the one who says that as our experience of nature grows we shall see the apparent variety of its empirical laws increasingly exhibiting uniformity. For judgment requires that we proceed on the principle that nature conforms to our means of knowing, without mentioning how far that principle can be extended. Limits are set for the thinking mind, but experience it illimitable.

The purpose of an object of experience may be represented subjectively by the appropriateness of its form to the knowing process of mind or it may be represented objectively by the object's fitness for what it can be. Thus *natural beauty* represents formal or subjective purpose, while *natural purpose* represents the idea of real or objective appropriateness. Natural beauty is judged by aesthetic taste, by the feeling of pleasure it gives; natural purposes, on the other hand, are logical, conceptual matters for judgment by mind and reasoning. On this basis *The Critique of Judgment* is divided into critiques of aesthetic and teleological judgment.

Susceptibility to pleasure derived from reflection on the forms of nature or art indicates not only purpose in the objects, as revealed in reflective judgment, but by virtue of the idea of freedom, it indicates purpose in the percipient of the form or formlessness in the objects. It thus happens that aesthetic judgment is not only related to beauty as a judgment of taste; it is also related to *sublimity* when it springs from spiritual feeling. "The Critique of Aesthetic Judgment" is therefore divided into two corresponding sections.

The following table may facilitate the review of the unified higher mental processes:

(1) *The general list*	(3) *Pure principles*
Thought	Legality
Feeling of pleasure or pain	Appropriateness
Desire	Ultimate purpose
(2) *The processes of knowing*	(4) *These all are applied to*
Mind as understanding	Nature
Mind as judgment	Art
Mind as reasoning	Freedom

1. *Judgment is disinterested and general*

To decide whether or not anything is beautiful, we do not mentally refer the idea of it to the object as we would to get knowledge; it is referred rather by imagination to feelings of pleasure or pain in the person perceiving it, perhaps with some help from mind. Taste, as judgment, is not a means to knowledge and is, therefore, not logical but aesthetic and subjective.

If I am asked whether I consider a certain palace beautiful, I may reply that I do not care for things made just to be gaped at; or I may answer like that Iroquois sachem who said that nothing pleased him in Paris better than the restaurants. I might even, like Rousseau, rebuke the vanity of the great who spend the sweat of the people on unnecessary things. Or finally, I could easily persuade myself that if I were ever on an uninhabited island with no hope of seeing people any more, and there I could imagine splendid buildings merely by wishing for them, I wouldn't even go to that trouble if I already had a comfortable hut.

All this can be conceded and approved, but it is not the point at issue. I want to know whether the idea of an object would delight me even if I were utterly indifferent to its actual existence. It is plain that in order to show that I have taste and to say that an object is beautiful, I must depend on the meaning I can give to the idea of its beauty and not on the real existence of the object. It will be generally conceded that a judgment about beauty which is tinctured with personal interest is partial and not in pure taste. To play the part of judge in matters of taste, one must not be concerned at all for the real existence of the thing in question. To this one must be indifferent.

This point, which is of prime importance, cannot be explained better than by contrasting the pure disinterested delight of a judgment in taste with a partial judgment. Note well, however, that judgment of an object of delight may be disinterested, but still interesting. True judgment brings interest with it, but it is not based on private concern. Pure moral judgments are like this. Personal interests, however, are not built on judgments of taste. It is only socially that taste is considered an interesting personal property.

Delight in pleasant and good things involves personal interest. This is true not only of pleasant things, or of those that are good because they are useful or please because they are means to pleasure; it is also true of absolute goodness, of matters good from every point of view, such as moral goodness, which is of the highest interest. For goodness is the object of willing, of desire controlled by reasoning, but to want something and to delight in its existence; i.e., to take an interest in it, are identical. Pleasantness and goodness refer to desire. The first of these involves delight that is psychologically conditioned by stimuli. The second involves pure practical delight that is defined not only by the idea of the object but by the percipient's connection with it. On the other hand, judgment by taste is contemplative. Indifferent as to the object's existence, it involves comparison of the characteristics of the object with the feelings of pleasure or pain it evokes.

The three adjectives pleasant, beautiful, and good denote three relations of imagination to the feeling of pleasure or pain by which objects and representations of objects are distinguished. Among these three sources of delight, only taste for beauty is disinterested and free, since neither sense nor reasoning requires approval. Taste, therefore, is the capacity to judge an object or its image apart from any personal interest. The object of this kind of delight is beauty, and delight in it is universal.

As for pleasant things, everyone would concede that his judgment is strictly his own. A violet color is soft and lovely to one person; to another it is faded and dead. One man likes the wood winds; another prefers the strings. There is no disputing taste in sense matters: each person has his own.

Beauty is another matter. It would be ridiculous for one who fancied his own taste to say, "This building or that clothing, this concert or that poem is beautiful—to me!" He has no right to call anything beautiful if it pleases *him* alone. Many things might charm or please him and nobody would care; but when he proclaims that something is beautiful, he attributes his delight to other people. He is judging not just for himself but for all, and he is speaking of beauty as a property of things. He demands agreement of other people and blames them if they disagree. In this matter it cannot be said that each person may have his own peculiar taste; for this would mean that there is no taste, no aesthetic judgment eligible to universal assent.

When an end or goal is a source of delight, it brings with it an interest on the basis of which judgment about an object of pleasure is made. A judgment of taste, therefore, is never based on subjective ends or goals. Neither is it defined by an idea of objective purpose; i.e., of the possibilities of the object under the conditions. Taste is thus not defined by an idea of goodness, because goodness involves an aesthetic and not a logical judgment. Taste does not deal with an idea of nature or with this or that cause of an object, but merely with the interplay of a person's imaginative powers as imagination defines them.

2. *Taste is abstract and prior*

This interplay enters into the definition of an object as beautiful, bringing with it a feeling of pleasure; then judgment of taste pronounces this pleasure valid for all. The pleasantness of an idea, therefore, no more defines a judgment of taste than the perfection of an object or the idea of goodness may do. It is the appropriateness in the idea embodied by an object that constitutes the delight which is universally communicable. This, then, is the basis of the definition of a judgment of taste: beauty comes of formal purposiveness or appropriateness in an object.

It is based on abstract and prior principles. It is impossible abstractly to establish the connection between an idea and the pleasure or pain it evokes. This would be a causal relation which can be known only after the fact and by experience. Since, however, the pleasure of aesthetic judgments is contemplative, it involves being conscious of the interplay of one's thought and imagination. This is the pleasure in question because it is the basis on which one decides what to do when his thinking quickens. As for knowledge, here too the interplay of thought and imagination is an inner and final cause, and not limited to any special bit of knowledge. This pleasure is not practical, and yet it involves causality, a causality that preserves the idea when it is embodied and stimulates thought apart from ulterior motives. We therefore linger in contemplation of a beautiful thing because contemplation strengthens and reproduces itself. This lingering is analogous, but only analogous, to the dalliance over physical charm felt in the imagination of an object which repeatedly claims attention when one's mind is passive.

Beauty and sublimity are alike in being pleasant on their own account. Neither presupposes a sensual reaction or a logical judgment. Both involve judgments of reflection. Their delight, consequently, depends not on sense, as it does with pleasant things, nor on definite ideas, as it does with good deeds, although it does refer nonspecifically to ideas. The delight is associated rather with imagination, and signalizes the co-ordination of imagination and reasoning. Thus both judgments are individual, but valid everywhere for everybody even though they report merely a feeling of pleasure in an object rather than any knowledge of it.

3. *Beauty rises from ideas; sublimity from emotions*

There are also remarkable differences. Beauty in nature is connected with the form of an object, and form here means limitation; whereas sublimity is found in formless objects, whose formlessness suggests boundlessness, to which the thought of totality is added. Accordingly, beauty seems to be a nonspecific idea of *mind* and is associated with *quality*, while sublimity is a concept of *reason* associated with *quantity*. Moreover the two delights are different in kind. Beauty is directly attended by a feeling that where it is, life is being encouraged. It is therefore compatible with charm and playful imagination. On the other hand the feeling of sublimity is an indirect pleasure, evoked by a momentary blocking of one's vital power, followed by an even stronger release of it. Sublimity seems to be an emotion, not of play but of grave imagination. It is incompatible, therefore, with physical charm, and as mind is alternately attracted and repelled by the sublime object, delight in sublimity involves not so much positive pleasure as wonder or respect, and is better called negative pleasure.

Here, then, is the inner and more important difference between sublimity and beauty. Look first at sublimity in objects of nature, since art is restricted by the terms of its agreement with nature. Observe that whereas beauty in nature is independent, its form suggests appropriateness by which the object is pre-adapted to human judgment, and this makes it an object of delight. On the other hand a feeling, by no means subtle, may come over one, excited by the very apprehension of a sublime object, a feeling that violates both the form and purpose of judgment. The sublime object would thus be inappropriate to one's imagination and would do violence to it but seem only the more sublime because it does so.

From this it appears inappropriate to call one of nature's objects sublime, even though it may justly be called beautiful. For how can anything with a purpose be singled out for such approval? We can say only that some object lends itself to the representation of a sublimity discoverable in mind, a sublimity no sense form can ever wholly contain. It concerns rational ideas which cannot be suitably expressed but are suggested by their very incongruity with sense imagery. The broad ocean in a raging storm cannot be called sublime. Its appearance may be horrible, but the pressure of ideas evoked by the horror must be high indeed to make one feel that such a scene is sublime; it could be sublime only if one forgets the actual scene and is occupied with ideas suggested by the storm but reaching far beyond it.

Independent natural beauty discloses a technique of nature which makes it look as if nature also operates by laws whose principle is not a property of any mind. It is the principle that purpose, as it refers to the use of judgment on phenomena, indicates that phenomena do not belong merely within nature's purposeless mechanism but to something analogous to art. This principle does not extend our knowledge of nature but it does extend our ideas of nature, so that nature as mechanism is replaced by the idea of nature as art.

There is nothing about what we are accustomed to call sublime that leads to any particular objective principles or forms corresponding to them. Nature excites the idea of sublimity by the chaos of its wildest disorders and desolations when size and power are exhibited. This shows that sublimity in nature is neither as important or consequential as beauty. It discloses no purpose in nature except that when one observes it, it induces a feeling or purpose which is independent of nature. Beauty in nature is to be sought in a principle external to man; sublimity is found within him and is infused into the idea of nature by his own attitudes and ways of thinking. This is a necessary preliminary remark. It detaches ideas of sublimity from those of purpose or appropriateness in nature and makes the theory of sublimity an appendix to aesthetic judgment of purpose in nature. Sublimity wears no special form. The purpose served by the idea of it is developed only by imagination.

4. *Taste is examined by dialectic*

To be dialectical, judgment must be reasoned abstractly and in advance, and eligible to universality. *This* dialectic consists of an opposition, or antinomy among such judgments. There is nothing dialectical about the irreconcilable judgments of sense that declare pleasant and unpleasant matters. Neither is a conflict of judgments of taste dialectical, since no one thinks his own judgment universal. There remains therefore only a dialectic of the principles of taste; for in this field ideas contradict each other naturally and unavoidably on the possibility of judgments of taste. A formal critique of taste will therefore contain a part to be known as the dialectic of aesthetic judgment if an antinomy of principles appears in this area and makes the principles of aesthetic judgment doubtful as to their legality and inner possibility.

The first commonplace of taste is contained in the proposition with which tasteless people generally hope to ward off blame: *Everyone has his own taste.* This means that the principle governing one's judgments of taste is subjective, as in gratification or grief, and that such judgments do not necessarily govern other people.

The second commonplace, used by those who admit that judgments of taste may be generally valid, is that *taste is not for disputation.* This means that the principle governing a judgment of taste may be objective but it cannot be reduced to definite ideas; proofs, therefore, do not affect it, even though it may justly be contested. Contests and disputes probably have this in common: they aim to get agreement out of opposition; but they differ in that the aim in disputes is to accomplish agreement by means of proofs based on objective ideas which are, therefore, introduced as a basis of taste. Where this is considered impracticable, disputes also are impracticable.

An intermediate proposition is missing from between these two commonplaces. It is not proverbial but it is familiar. *There may be contests over taste,* if not disputes. This contradicts the first commonplace. For where a contest is permissible there must be hope of agreement. There must also be principles of judgment which have more than private validity, and so are not merely subjective. This, of course, contradicts the statement that *everyone has his own taste.*

The principle of taste therefore discloses the following antinomy:

(1) *Thesis.* Judgments of taste are not based on ideas, for they would then permit disputation or decision by proofs.

(2) *Antithesis.* Judgments of taste are based on ideas, for otherwise, in spite of any disagreement, there would be no contest because no claim for necessary agreement from others could be made.

There is no possibility of removing conflict from the principles every judgment of taste implies except by showing that the idea to which an object is referred in this kind of judgment has been used in different senses in the two propositions; that a double meaning or point of view is necessary to formal judgment; and that the illusion due to the confusion of meanings is natural and inevitable.

A judgment of taste must refer to some idea, for otherwise general validity could not be claimed for it; but that does not mean that an idea could prove its general correctness. An idea may be either definable or undefined and undefinable. Mental ideas are of the first kind. They can be defined by appropriate predicates of sense awareness. But the formal, reasoned, supersensible ideas on which all sense awareness is based are of the second kind and cannot be further defined. Judgments of taste are applied to objects of sense but not in order to define them, for taste does not involve logical judgment. Taste is a private judgment in which individual images taken from awareness are associated with a feeling of pleasure, and their validity is thus limited to the individual that judges; as who should say, "The object is delightful *for me* but it may be otherwise for other people; everyone to his own taste!"

At the same time, there is no doubt that given the ideas and persons they involve, judgments of taste may cover more territory than other judgments, and accordingly they are extended so that they apply necessarily to everyone. The ideas on which judgments of taste are based are not defined by awareness and are not sources of knowledge. They are not, therefore, material to be offered as proof of the correctness of a judgment of taste, but they are pure, reasoned ideas and elements of the supersensible world, fundamental to sensed objects and judging persons alike, as to all phenomena. Apart from some such view, the case for the general validity of judgments of taste would be hopeless. If it were based merely on some confused mental idea, such as that of perfection, to which a sensed awareness of beauty might be made to correspond, it might be possible to prove correctness in judgment of taste; but this would contradict the thesis.

All contradiction disappears, however, if I say: Judgment of taste is based on the subjective appropriateness of nature to human judgment. This tells and proves nothing about an object because subjective appropriateness is undefinable and, so, unsuited for knowledge. It is, however, valid for everyone for the individual judgment that comes with awareness, because the principle that defines it is part of the supersensible foundation of humanity.

The solution of an antinomy depends on the possibility of showing that the contradiction is only apparent and that the two propositions may be consistent even though the explanation for this eventually transcends our knowledge. The illusion of the contradiction then no longer misleads anyone. It is natural and unavoidable in human reasoning. Why it is an illusion, and remains so, should be clear from the foregoing considerations.

In a pair of contradictory judgments the idea on which the general validity of the two judgments is based has the same meaning for both, but two opposing predicates are applied to it. Thus, the thesis should read: A judgment of taste *is not* based on a *definable* idea. The antithesis should read: A judgment of taste *is* based on an *indefinable* idea; i.e., an idea from the supersensible foundation of all phenomena. There would then be no antinomy.

All one can do is to remove the conflict of claim and counterclaim about taste. It is absolutely impossible to assign a definite, objective principle of taste from which its judgments could be derived, tested, and demonstrated; for to do so would rule out taste altogether. The subjective principle, the undefined idea of something supersensible in man is offered as the only key to the puzzle of taste; its sources are otherwise hidden and unexplainable.

The resolution of the antinomy thus presented depends on conceiving taste as a purely reflective, aesthetic judgment; the two apparently contradictory propositions are then reconciled by saying that both may be true—which is enough. Some people say that taste is defined by *pleasantness* because the idea of pleasantness is individual. Others define taste by the principle of *perfection* because it is general. Both definitions give rise to antinomies absolutely unresolvable apart from showing that the two propositions are false; and if this is so, the idea on which they are based is self-contradictory. It is clear then that the removal of the antinomy of aesthetic judgment takes a course similar to the one followed heretofore in resolving the antinomies of pure reasoning and here, as in *The Critique of Practical Reason,* the antinomies require one to look beyond the sense world to the supersensible, to find that point towards which one's abstract, prior thoughts and insights converge. There is no other way to harmonize reasoning.

5. *Beauty is the face of appropriateness or purposiveness*

There are two form principles which make good reasons for attributing subjective purpose to certain of nature's laws; this is how they become comprehensible and make the systematic connection of particular experiences possible. Many items of nature may appear in such a system, as if they were put there in a form specially adapted to cater to human judgment. These forms, by their diversity and unity, serve to sustain and strengthen mind in judgment. They are called *beautiful forms.*

The general notion of nature, however, provides no reason to believe that natural things serve one another to a purpose or that this kind of causality explains their existence. As in the case of *beautiful forms,* the image of a thing is internal to man and it is therefore suited abstractly and in advance to the internal control of learning with a purpose. Nature, however, is not mental and we have therefore no abstract or prior reason to assume that purposes, which are neither man's nor nature's, could or should constitute a special causality or a special order of nature. What is more, even experience does not demonstrate the actuality of these purposes. It may be that some antecedent mental sleight caused purpose to be read into the nature of things; or the idea of purpose, not being derived from actual objects, was used to make nature more understandable, on the analogy of the connections that link man's subjective images, but not parallel to the processes of knowledge gathered objectively.

Furthermore, objective purpose or appropriateness as a principle is so far removed from the necessary connections in nature that it is often used to prove that nature and its forms are fortuitous. Take, for example, the structure of a bird, the hollow bones, the set of the wings for motion, the tail for steering, etc. They say that all this came about quite accidentally without any need for a special cause, such as purpose. Regard nature as a higher mechanism and its unity could have been contrived in a thousand ways other than by purpose! One has to look outside nature to find any trace of an abstract reason for unity by purpose.

Teleological judgment is, however, correctly brought to bear on the study of nature, not with a view to using purpose to explain nature but to investigate it by the analogy of purpose to causality. This pertains to reflective and not to definitive judgment. The idea that the combination and forms of nature are contrived for a purpose is thus one more principle by which phenomena can be organized when the cause of an object is said to be an idea, *as if* the idea occurred in nature rather than in the observer. It is also introduced when the observer understands the possibility of an object in terms of his own experience of causality, and thus views nature as if through a special facility of mind. Without the analogy of the observer's own experience, nature's causality would have to be regarded as blind mechanism. The method of analogy does not mean, however, that nature's causes operate from designs or intentions to which their own laws subject them. This would be teleology offered not simply as a regulative principle by which to judge phenomena, but as a constitutive or creative principle for deriving effects from causes. Nature's purposes would then derive from definitive rather than reflective judgments. They would not then pertain to judgments as such, like the idea that beauty is formal and subjective appropriateness; and a new kind of causality would be introduced into natural science, borrowed from our own psychology and attributed to other beings without even assuming them to be like us.

To see that something is possible only as the result of purpose, it must be clear that it did not originate in nature's mechanism but from activity controlled by an idea. Its form must not be possible as the result of the operation of natural laws, i.e., mind's laws applied to sensed objects.

Suppose that a person found a geometrical figure, a regular hexagon, traced on the beach of an apparently uninhabited country. Thinking it over, groping for an idea, his reasoning might suggest that the construction of the figure involved reasoned unity. Reasoning also would forbid him to attribute the hexagon to the sand, the nearby sea, the winds, animal footprints, or any other familiar cause, or to an irrational cause. The chance that such a figure should be a coincidence is infinitesimal. It could occur only as the result of reasoning, and if it were a coincidence there might as well be no natural law at all. Nature, moreover, could not produce the hexagon mechanically, but its cause must have been in an idea someone had in mind and could compare with its object. The hexagon would thus appear not as a result of natural purpose but as a result of human purpose and would be a product of art.

A product of nature, the result of natural purposes, is alternately its own cause and effect. This means that each of its parts, in their collective unity, are reciprocally the cause and effect of the others' forms. The idea of the whole product could thus design the form of each part and combine them all into a whole entity. It would do this not as a cause, for that would be artificial. It would effect the combination of the form and matter so that the result would be intelligible to him who judges it.

In such a product, each part is considered as being there because of every other part and also as existing for the sake of all other parts and the whole. Each part is therefore an instrument or organ, not like an instrument of art, which serves a general purpose without ever realizing it in particular. Each part is an instrument or organ which produces other parts, which no instrument of art can do. It has to be an instrument that makes other instruments, and materials for instruments as well. Only on these conditions and terms can a natural product be called an organism or a self-organizing being, the result of nature's purpose.

In a watch, one part is instrumental to the motion of other parts, but one wheel is not the efficient cause of the creation of another; one part is there for the sake of the other but not because of it. The creative cause of the watch and its form is not in the kind of material of which it is made but, externally, in a being who can act on an idea to create something of which he was the cause.

The idea that some thing is one of nature's ends or goals is not constitutive, either for mind or reasoning. It may, however, be used as a guide when organisms are investigated by the remote analogy of human causality and human ends, and for the consideration of their ultimate principle. The idea does not, however, serve to extend man's knowledge of nature or its origins. Its use is limited to the scope of practical reasoning and the analogy of human causality to purpose in nature.

Organisms alone, considered apart from other things, are thus conceivable as ends or goals of nature. They provide the first instance of a goal of nature which is objectively real and not merely practical. From organisms, natural science gets a basis for the idea of teleology, which is a way of judging objects by a special principle, otherwise unjustified, because purpose does not appear abstractly and in advance in nature.

This is the principle and definition of organisms: *An organized product of nature is one in which every element is reciprocally an end and a means.* There is nothing in an organism that has no purpose or is attributable to blind mechanism.

Experience is, no doubt the occasion of this principle, and it is experience in the form of methodical observation. It cannot, however, be wholly a matter of experience because of the generality and necessity it claims for purpose. Even though it is merely regulative, and the purpose it asserts may belong only to the observer's mind instead of to an immediate cause, there must be an abstract and prior principle behind the experience. The principle of organisms described above, then, is considered a *personal policy* for the judgment of purpose in organisms.

We know that those who dissect plants and animals find this policy necessary. For example, in animal bodies several parts may be conceived as concretions required by mechanical laws, like the hide, the bones, and the hair. Yet the cause that gathers the appropriate material, modifies it, forms it, and puts it in the right place must be viewed as teleological, organizing these components to the purpose each part serves in the animal.

It is one thing to regard an object as an end, or goal of nature because of its internal organization; the assertion of its existence as an end of nature is something else. In addition to a theory of possible purpose *in* the thing, the latter assertion requires a knowledge of nature's ultimate purpose. This, in turn, refers to the supersensible realm, far above and beyond man's teleological knowledge of nature, because nature's purpose in existing must always be sought beyond nature. The inner organization of even a blade of grass is evidence enough, from the human point of view, that purpose makes grass possible. Turn, however, to the use other natural beings make of it, from the study of internal organization to external adaptation. The grass feeds the cow, and the cow feeds man. It does not appear from this why man should in fact exist. This would be a difficult question indeed if the men referred to were New Hollanders or Yahgans of Tierra del Fuego! No categorical purpose appears along this route. The reference is always to another condition beyond the horizon, an unconditioned condition outside the physical, teleological view of the world, something like the final purpose of a thing's existence. The final purpose thus conceived is outside of nature's purpose and neither it, nor anything like it, is a natural product.

It is therefore only as matter is organized that it is conceived necessarily as a goal of nature because, having a specific form, it is at the same time nature's product. This leads to the idea that nature, collectively, is a system with a purpose and to this idea nature's mechanisms must all be subordinated as the principles of reasoning require, at least for the study of phenomena. The principles of reasoning are related to nature's system only subjectively, as a personal policy might be: everything in the world is good for something and nothing is good for nothing; the example of nature's organisms justifies and demands the expectation that nature and its laws are on the whole purposive.

Thus, for example, it could be said that the vermin which plague people in clothing, hair, and beds may, by a wise provision of nature, develop a motive for cleanliness, which is important to health. Or there are the mosquitoes and other stinging insects that make the wilderness of America so trying to its wild men. They may goad those primitive inhabitants to drain the swamps, to let light into forests so thick that they shut out the air, and withal, by cultivating the soil, to make their dwellings healthier.

There is also nature's beauty, nature's connection with the free play of mind as it understands and judges phenomena. Beauty can be regarded as a kind of objective purposefulness in nature's system, of which man is a member, if purpose in organisms has justified the notion of a great system of purposes. We may regard it as nature's favor to man that it has covered useful things with so much beauty and charm, and for this we may love it, revering it for its immensity, and feel ennobled withal, as if nature had built and adorned its splendid stage just for our benefit.

These paragraphs have meant that if facilities appear in nature creating things that are intelligible only as final causes, there is a next step. Other creatures which need no principle beyond blind mechanism to explain their possibility may also be judged to belong to the system of purposes, because the idea with which we started has its roots in the supersensual world, a world whose unity is valid not only for certain kinds of nature's creatures but for all creation.

6. *Nature's purposiveness is examined by dialectic*

Reflective judgment has its own policies for dealing with various cases, policies absolutely necessary to the discovery of nature's laws and to getting ideas of nature. There may, however, be conflict in these policies and consequently an antinomy, on which a dialectic is raised. If a pair of these conflicting principles have their roots in mind, the dialectic is said to be natural. This in turn creates unavoidable illusions which, lest they deceive one, must be discovered and resolved in the *Critique*.

The first policy of such a pair is the proposition: The creation of material things and their forms must be judged to be possible by purely mechanical laws.

The second is a counter-proposition: Some material things cannot be judged to be possible by mechanical laws alone. They must be judged by an entirely different law: the law of final causes.

If then these two regulative propositions are made constitutive they would read as follows:

Thesis: All material things may be created by purely mechanical laws.

Antithesis: Some things cannot be created by mechanical laws alone.

Put like this, as objective principles of definitive judgment, they contradict each other, and one of the pair is necessarily false. This creates an antinomy, not in judgment but in the legislation of mind. Neither one of these fundamental propositions can be proved by reasoning because there exists no abstract or prior principle defining the possibility of things by empirical laws.

We have seen that there are questions to which mind can give absolutely no answer if it is restricted to abstract and prior considerations. It is equally certain that nature as a mechanism offers no explanation of the creation of organisms. This, therefore, is a sound principle of reflective judgment: final causes plainly connect things and this connectedness requires a causality apart from mechanism, an intelligent world cause which acts with purposes, however rash and undemonstrable this proposition may be for definitive judgments. For a reflective judgment, it is just a policy and the causality is just an idea for which there is no guaranteed actuality. It is used only as a guide to reflection. All mechanical explanations are still available to it, and it stays strictly within the sense world. For a definitive judgment, however, it would be objective and prescribed by reasoning, to which even definitive judgment is subject. It therefore moves out of the sensed world into transcendent regions and there, perhaps, gets lost.

All appearance of an antinomy between the policies of mechanical and teleological explanation depends on confusing the principles of reflective and definitive judgments. The autonomy of mechanical explanation, which is valid subjectively and only for reasoning about particular empirical laws, is mistaken for the heteronomy of definitive judgments, which is subject to the general and particular laws given by mind.

7. *Teleology subsumes mechanism*

No one has ever doubted that the possibility of certain things in nature, such as organisms, involves judgment implying their relation to final causes. There is in our minds a certain presentiment or hint from nature that with this idea of final cause, it is possible to get out beyond nature and connect it to the last term of the causal series, if we give up research for the time being and simply try to find out where the idea of natural purpose, so alien to natural science, leads.

These undisputed policies of judgment, however, pass over into problems that open up a wide field of difficulties.

If we discuss the philosophic systems which explain nature in terms of final causes, it is remarkable that they all contradict each other dogmatically on the objective principles by which things are possible, on whether there are intentionally operative causes or whether causes operate without intent. Subjective policies by which judgments are made about the causes of purposive creatures, in which disparate principles may well be reconciled, are seldom in dispute. In the systems, however, contradictory laws annul one another and cannot be associated.

There are two kinds of systems dealing with the technique of nature as a purposeful, regulated, creative power, namely, *idealism* and *realism* about natural purposes. Idealism maintains that purpose in nature is unintended; realism, that some purpose, as in organisms, is intended. From realism, it follows hypothetically that the technique of nature is intended to relate all creatures to itself as a whole and that this is nature's purpose. What do these systems intend? They set out to explain teleological judgments of nature, and they go at it by adopting either of two courses. One denies the truth of teleological judgments and explains that they are like art, idealizations of nature. The other course recognizes these judgments as true, and promises to demonstrate the possibility of nature from the idea of final causes.

Theism, also, is incapable of establishing dogmatically that natural purpose is the key to teleology. Even so its principle of explanation is pre-eminent. By attributing intelligence to the *original Being,* it goes about saving nature's purpose from idealism in the best possible way and introduces the notion that creation was caused intentionally. Theism first must satisfy definitive judgment of the impossibility of obtaining unity of purpose in matter by means of mere mechanism if it is to be justified in using a principle not belonging to nature. We can then go no further. Given the nature and limitations of our minds, the chief and inmost principle of nature's mechanism is beyond us, and we are stopped from looking into matter for the principle of definitive purpose. We are left with no other way to judge nature's creatures as being the results of nature's purposes except by the idea of a Supreme Mind as the cause of the world. This, however, is only a principle of reflective rather than definitive judgment and it justifies absolutely no objective assertion.

Certainly the idea of causality through purpose (art) has objective reality, just as the idea of cause in nature's mechanism has. The idea that physical causality follows the rule of purpose, however, and more, that it conforms to the purpose of a Being of which we have no experience, but who is nature's original source, may not be self-contradictory but it is still useless for the purpose of dogmatic definitions. Not experienceable, and unnecessary to the possibility of experience, there is no assurance that this Being actually exists objectively; and even if its existence were assured, how could creatures of divine art be reckoned as nature's, when the appeal to a cause beyond nature is made because nature alone could not create such things?

The right to aim at a strictly mechanical explanation of creation is unabridged, but human power to achieve such an explanation is curtailed by the human characteristics of mind. A principle of judgment adopting mechanism as the sole explanation achieves nothing, and the teleological principle is, accordingly, required; but it is sensible and, indeed, meritorious to try to explain creation by mechanism, as far as this can be done with probable success. If the attempt is abandoned, it is not because it is intrinsically impossible to come to grips with natural purpose along purely mechanical lines; it is because human limitations forbid it. A complete mechanical explanation of creation would require awareness of a realm apart from sense, a definitive knowledge of the intelligible substratum of nature. This is beyond human reach. A naturalist must, therefore, base his judgments of those things to which the idea of natural purpose applies on some original organization, which produces new organisms or new forms using the mechanisms of material nature but adapting them to the purpose implied in the creature.

It is laudable to go over the vast organization of nature with the help of comparative anatomy to see if there is a system in it, a system with a genetic principle. Otherwise, we must be content with the critical principle of judgment. This tells nothing about the processes of creation and would force us to give up all hope of insight in this field. Consider the agreement of so many species of animals in one common schema, an agreement which apparently underlies not only the structure of their bones but also the disposition of their remaining parts. Consider the wonderful simplicity of the original plan by which, in the lengthening of one member and the shortening of another, or the involution of one part and the evolution of another, the immense variety of species has been produced. All this permits a ray of hope, however faint, that mechanism may yet enable an explanation of the course of organic life, since without mechanism there would be no natural science. The analogy of forms, with all their differences, suggests their creation according to an original type, and strengthens the surmise that they are related to each other by descent from a common parent. In the gradual approximation of one kind to another, beginning with man, in whom the principle of purpose seems best authenticated, down to the polyps, then to the mosses and lichens, and on down to nature's lowest observable stage, raw matter, the descent seems unbroken. Here are forces obeying laws like those that govern the formation of crystals, from which the whole technique of nature seems to be developed, a technique so incomprehensible in organisms that another principle of explanation is called for.

In this field the archeologist of nature is free to go back to the surviving traces of nature's earliest revolutions and, using all he knows or can surmise about its mechanisms, to conjecture the genesis of the great family of living creatures. They must be imagined as a family to support the consistent, coherent relationship between them. He can suppose that out of the womb of mother earth, as it emerged from chaos like a great animal, came creatures that at first showed little purpose in their form, and that these gave birth to others better adapted to their environment and to each other. At last mother earth became rigid and ossified, limiting birth to unmodifiable species, so that the varieties remained as they were at the end of that initial formative operation. He must finally ascribe to the universal mother an organization appropriate to her creatures, for otherwise the appropriateness of their forms as members of the animal and vegetable kingdoms would be inconceivable. Even then he has only pushed back the principle of explanation one stage and cannot pretend that the genesis of these two kingdoms is intelligible apart from the condition of final causes.

An hypothesis of this kind may be called a daring adventure in reasoning and there are probably few keen naturalists who have not considered it from time to time. It is not absurd like the notion of the generation of organisms from raw, inorganic matter. It never ceases to be the generation of organic things from organic things, even though it involves differentiation, as when certain water animals are gradually transformed into marsh animals and these, after some generations, are transformed into land animals. There is no abstract or prior contradiction in this and, of course, no example of it within man's experience. On the contrary, all generation known to man follows the rule of *like begets like*. So far as we know, one kind never begets another.

In these paragraphs it has appeared that organisms are inconceivable on the basis of nature's mechanism alone; they must also be attributed to intentional causes, or at least man's mind requires that he conceive it so. Similarly, teleological principles alone are not enough to afford the judgment that an organism is at once the result of purpose and a product of nature. Mechanism has to be associated with the purpose as an instrument of an intentional cause, to an end to which mechanical nature is subordinate. The possibility of uniting two utterly disparate causes like law-abiding nature and an idea that restricts nature to special and alien forms is beyond understanding. It belongs in the supersensible substratum of nature, of which we can say nothing except that it is a thing-itself, of which we know only the corresponding phenomenon. In spite of this, the principle still holds with undiminished force that phenomena and their products are linked to nature by mechanical laws. Apart from this kind of causality, organisms might be nature's ends but they could not be its creatures.

By external appropriateness I mean the way one thing serves the purpose of another. It is entirely different from internal appropriateness, which makes an object possible whether or not its external existence serves any purpose. We may ask about an organism: What is it for? The same question, however, is inappropriate to things in which only nature's mechanism is at work. There is only one case where external appropriateness is intimately bound up with an internal appropriateness of organization. This is the organization of the two sexes in a mutual relation for the propagation of their kind; for here the question can be asked, as of an individual: Why must this pair exist? The answer is: A pair constitutes first of all an organizing whole, though not an organized whole in a single body.

If then one asks why a thing exists, there may be one of two answers. The thing may be said to be derived mechanically from nature and unrelated to any intentional cause; or it may be that it exists contingently, because of some principle by which it was designed. It is difficult to separate the latter thought from the idea of an organism. For since it is internal appropriateness that makes an organism possible, and this depends on a final cause and an underlying idea, we have to think that its external existence also serves a purpose. Here then we may say either that an organism exists for its own sake and that it is not only an end but a final end; or we may say that its final purpose is external to it—in other creatures—and its existence is required because it is a means to an end.

Nature, however, nowhere discloses any being eligible to the distinction of being the final end of all creation. It may be proved abstractly that if something serves as an ultimate end of nature, endowed with whatever properties one might desire of it, it could never be a final end because of its character as a creature of nature.

8. *Physical man is nature's ultimate end*

Look at the vegetable kingdom. It might appear at first, from the fruitfulness with which it is spread all over the earth, that vegetation is a product of nature's mechanisms somewhat like the formations of the mineral kingdom. Closer acquaintance with its incredibly wise organization, however, forbids this view and raises the question: Why do plants exist? If we answer: For the animal kingdom, which is thus fed, so that it too may spread over all the earth in myriad kinds, the next question is: Then why do the herbivora exist? And the answer is: For the carnivora, the predatory animals, who can live only on living creatures. Comes then the final question: What is the good of all these creatures and their predecessors? And the answer: Man's mind has taught him many uses for life's many forms. He is the ultimate end of creation here on earth. He is the only creature able to conceive purposes and, from the aggregate of things with purposes, to work out a system.

There is, then, ample reason to reflect, without definitive judgment, that man is not merely one of nature's ends, as all organisms are, but among beings on this earth he is the ultimate end, to whom all others constitute a system of subordinate ends. What purpose then is served in man by his connection with nature? If the purpose or end is in man himself, it either enables him to be satisfied with nature's beneficence or it furnishes him with the aptitude and skill to use nature externally and internally for all kinds of purposes. The first of these possibilities is *happiness*; the second, human *culture*.

As for happiness, it is not man's nature to rest content with the possession or enjoyment of anything. The other possibility also falls short. External nature has never made man a particular favorite. In its destructive operations, plague, famine, floods, cold, attacks by other animals, great and small, and all such things, it has spared man as little as any other animal. What is more, his own internal discords betray him into evils of his own contriving. He is never more than a link in the chain of nature's purposes. As the only being on earth with a mind for ends of his own choosing, he is certainly the titular lord of nature. Granted that nature is teleological, he is born to be its ultimate end. This is always on the condition, however, that he has the will and intelligence to provide both nature and himself with purposes or ends that are final because they are independent of nature and are self-sufficient. A final end is one that requires no other end as a condition of its possibility; but there is no use in looking for this in nature.

Where or what in man is this ultimate end? To find it, we must look for nature's accomplishments in the preparation of man to do what he has to do to be a final end and to distinguish him from other ends made possible by nature, which sets the conditions. Happiness on earth is an end of the latter kind. This is understood to mean the epitome of all internal or external ends made possible to man by nature. *Happiness* is the material substance of man's earthly purposes, and if he makes it his sole purpose he himself becomes incapable of being a final end or of adjusting his own existence to such an end. Of all nature's ends there remains, therefore, only the formal, subjective condition of man's aptitude for setting his own goals independently of nature and of using nature for his own purposes. This is all that remains of nature's achievement relative to a final end outside itself and other than an ultimate end. *Culture* is the development of man's aptitude for choosing his own ends and so using his freedom. Culture is man's sole basis for the claim that he is nature's ultimate end. Happiness on earth and the claim that man is nature's chief instrument for establishing order and intelligibility in an otherwise irrational nature are ruled out.

Not all culture is suitable to being nature's ultimate end. Certainly skill is the chief subjective condition of aptitude for the achievement of various purposes. It does not, however, effect the definition and choice of the ends of willing, and this is essential to the meaning of aptitude for purposive activity. Choice of ends as a condition of aptitude may be called *culture by discipline* and is negative. It consists of setting willing free from the tyranny of desires. Desires mean attachments to certain natural things and to some degree they make a man incapable of choosing for himself. This occurs when man lets himself become the slave of the drives provided by nature to insure him against neglect or damage to his animal nature, drives he is free to tighten or slacken, lengthen or shorten, as his purpose may require.

Human skill is developed only at the price of inequality among people. Mechanically and without special skill the majority of people can provide the necessities of life required for the comfort and convenience of those who apply themselves to the less necessary elements of culture, such as science and art. The masses are, accordingly, oppressed with hard work and little enjoyment, but in time the culture of the upper classes spreads to them also. Culture thus advances and culminates at a point where luxury appears, and devotion to superfluous things becomes prejudicial to indispensable things, to the misfortune of all. With the lower classes, misfortunes are due to external forces; with the upper classes they are caused by inner discontents. This splendid misery is nevertheless connected with the development of natural tendencies in the human race, and nature achieves its purpose even though, one by one, we do not.

The formal condition by which nature can accomplish its purpose is the existence of a system of government regulating the relations of people to each other. There has to be a civil community, centered in a lawful authority, which opposes the abuse of freedom by individuals who fight each other. The maximum development of human capacities can take place only in a settled community. In addition, if people were only smart enough to see it and be subject to it, there should be *One World*, a world citizenship of states in a system, when otherwise they would be in danger from each other. Failing that, and with the obstacles of ambition, the drive for power, and the greed of those in control, thrown against the possibility of One World, war is inevitable. The result is, sometimes, the fragmentation of states and sometimes their growth in size and power. If, however, war is a thoughtless undertaking and stirred up by unbridled passion, it is nevertheless a deep-seated and perhaps far-seeing effort on the part of the supreme wisdom to prepare states for unity in law-abiding freedom, morally established. In spite of the terrible calamities war visits on mankind, and the hardships of constant preparation for it in times of peace, it may still be the goad that prods man to develop the talents that contribute to culture to the highest possible degree—even when the hope of lasting peace and the happiness for all people is constantly receding.

Turn now to the discipline of desire. Desires are part of man's natural equipment, purposively adapted to the performance of his essential functions as an animal species. They are, however, impediments to the development of humaneness. Yet here again, in respect to the second requirement for culture, nature is trying purposefully to educate man to open doors to ends higher than nature itself affords. There is no denying the preponderance of evil in idealized and extreme refinements of taste, in the scientific luxuries that feed men's vanity, begetting and diffusing endless insatiable desires. Even so, do not ignore nature's intention to make room for humaneness by prevailing more and more over the rudeness and violence of human desires, desires that belong chiefly to man's animal nature and are opposed to his education to higher vocations and enjoyments. Fine arts and the sciences, even if they do not improve the world's morality, do impart a civilizing polish and refinement into society and give pleasure that is universally communicable. They do much to overcome the tyranny of the senses and prepare mankind for the sovereignty to come when reasoning alone brings power. Meanwhile the evils man suffers naturally and because of his own truculent egotism evoke spiritual strength and give him the stamina and courage to resist them. He is thus adapted to higher purposes.

If mechanism alone explains the world, one does not ask what the things of this world are here for. In a system so ideal, only physical possibilities have to be considered and things would be considered ends only by empty sophistry. Whether this state of things would indicate chance or blind necessity is in either case a meaningless question. Suppose, however, that the final connectedness of things is assumed real, and a special, active, and intentional cause is inferred to support it. The final question, then, is not "To what end do things or organisms exist in this or that form?" On the contrary, once mind in man is regarded as causing the possibility of these forms, the forms actually appearing in things, mind must be searched for the objective basis on which it operates to get such results. This basis, when discovered, would be the final end or purpose for which things exist.

9. *Mental man is nature's final end*

I have said above that a final end is not one that nature alone could achieve, given the idea of nature as it is. A final end is unconditioned, and there is nothing in nature or the sensed world whose natural condition is not itself conditioned. This is true not only in the material, external world but in the inner world of thought which I also consider to be natural. When, however, a thing is necessary because of its objective character and is to be the final end of an intelligible cause, it must be independent of every condition other than its own idea or intrinsic meaning.

There is only one kind of being in the world whose causality is teleological or purposeful. It is a being so created that it defines its own purposes by a necessary law, independently of nature. This being is a man, but a man regarded as a *noumenon*. He is the only creature in whom a supersensible element, *freedom*, is discernible. His freedom is both causal and an object; in all the world it is best of all; it is the supreme good.

One may not ask, therefore, why moral man or any other rational being exists. His existence involves the world's supreme purpose, to which he will subdue all nature as he is able. At least he will not think of himself as subject to any natural influence that runs contrary to that purpose. Man is the final end of creation, because the chain of nature's purposes needs man to complete it and because things depend on the supreme cause in man for purpose. Unconditional legislation aimed at a final end, the legislation to which all nature is subordinated, is encountered only in man.

The ancients are not to be blamed for thinking that while their gods were many and diverse in power, purpose, and disposition, they were all limited much as humans are, not excepting the chief of gods. They found ample reason to assume something more than mechanism as nature's cause and to conjecture superhuman purposes behind the world's machinery. They found both good and evil there, purpose and counterpurpose. They did not conceive the idea of one perfect Author of all the world because they could not assume that mysterious, wise, and benevolent purposes, of which they saw no evidence, underlay the apparent antagonisms. Their judgment of the supreme cause of the world could hardly have been otherwise as long as they consistently followed policies of theoretical reasoning.

Others who wanted to be at once physicists and theologians thought that only absolute unity could be satisfactory as a principle of nature. They, therefore, assumed a being in whose substance all natural things were contained as inherent modes. This being did not cause the world because of the mind in it; it was the subject or repository in which all mind in the world would be encountered. Thus, although this being was not moved by any purpose to create anything, it was the medium by which all things would be interconnected, finally and necessarily, not by design but because the encompassing being itself had unity. The idealist doctrine of final causes was thus introduced by converting the unity of a group of things connected by purpose, a unity difficult to deduce from a causal dependence *on* one substance to the unity of inherence *in* one substance. To inherent beings, the system becomes *pantheism;* to the one self-subsisting substance, the original Being, it still later becomes *Spinozism.* It does not resolve the problem of the prime source of purpose in nature; it voids it. Purpose is robbed of all reality and reduced to a misconception of the universal ontological or abstract idea of a thing.

An idea of Godness or deity adequate to a teleological judgment of nature could never be had merely by theoretical reasoning, on which physico-theology relies altogether. It is true that physico-theology urges the provision of a theology, but *it* cannot provide one. It is of no use except as a preparation for theology and then only when it is supplemented by a more reliable principle.

Suppose, however, that the world discloses purposive order and that its conditioned purposes are subordinated, as reasoning requires, to an unconditioned supreme purpose. This does not mean that nature's purpose is subordinated to something that exists because it is included in nature. The unconditioned purpose prescribes nature's actual existence, including its orderly structure. Consequently, the problem is to define the ultimate purpose of creation and thus to explain how and why the supreme intelligence creates the world's beings. The structure of our minds is such that we necessarily refer nature's purposes to an intelligent world cause, and this is a clue to the nature and properties of the First Cause. It is the principle by which the kingdom of ends is defined. This definition was not possible in physico-theology, from which only an indeterminate idea of it could be had, an idea useless in theory and practice alike.

With so clear a principle of the causality of the original Being, it is unnecessary to conceive that Being abstractly, as if it were intelligence legislating for nature. It can be considered as the lawgiving, sovereign head of the moral kingdom of ends. The highest goodness, found in people living under moral laws, is possible only under this sovereignty. The original Being may therefore be conceived as *all-knowing*, so that even man's inmost secrets, which carry the moral worth of human actions, are not hidden from him. He is *all-powerful* and, therefore, able to bend nature to his purpose. He is *just* and *good*: these two properties together constitute *wisdom* and are qualities required by the Supreme Cause of the world if it is to be the source of all goodness under moral laws. Similarly all the other formal attributes such as *eternity*, *omnipresence*, etc., which are presupposed in a final purpose, must be attributed to the original Being, along with *goodness* and *justice*, which are moral attributes. In this way moral teleology makes up for the deficiencies of physical teleology, and so, for the first time, sets up a theology.

Is there any justification, satisfactory to speculative or practical reasoning, for attributing *final* purpose to the supreme and purposive First Cause? Our minds being what they are, a final purpose is simply *a man subject to moral laws* and this may be regarded, abstractly and in advance, as certain. We cannot know, however, what subordinate purposes may lurk in physical nature; it is, moreover, impossible to be sure that nature could not exist without purposes.

Imagine a man at the moment when he is morally receptive. In beautiful, natural surroundings, he is calm and serene in the enjoyment of life; he feels the need to be grateful to someone for all this. At another time, in the same frame of mind but pressed with work that has to be done at a personal sacrifice, he feels the need for the command of a supreme Lord, whom he must obey. Or he may have thoughtlessly transgressed, not so as to be answerable to man; but inwardly, his self-reproach sounds like the voice of a judge to whom he must account for his fault. In a word, he needs a moral Intelligence, a Being who formed both him and the world for a purpose which is also his purpose.

It is a waste of time to peer behind such feelings, looking for motives. They are immediately attached to the purest moral sentiments, *gratitude, obedience, humility,* all conducive to the performance of duty. They are expansions of moral sentiment and to this end one gratuitously imagines an object not of this world, and hopes to establish one's dutifulness before it, if possible. It is, therefore, at least possible to conceive a pure moral need for the actual presence of a Being before whom moral resolve is strengthened or expanded, and there is a basis for this in man's habits of moral thought. In other words, one can assume a moral Legislator outside the world on pure moral grounds, a Legislator not influenced by the objective world, or self-interest, or theoretical proof, and the assumption is made on the recommendation of pure practical reasoning alone.

A mental state like this may be rare or fleeting, without permanent effect, even without a thought bestowed afterwards on that shadowy Object, and without any effort to give it clear definition. It is, nevertheless, based on the moral disposition of man. This disposition will permit neither rest nor contentment with a view of the world which explains purposiveness solely by natural causes. It requires the introduction of an unknown supreme cause which governs nature by moral laws. Moreover, a man feels urged by moral law to reach a universal, supreme goal even though he can never do so. It is only as one tries to reach this goal that he feels that he is in line with the final purpose of the intelligent world cause, *if there is such a Being.*

There is, as we have seen, a physical teleology which provides reason enough for assuming that there is such a Being as an intelligent world cause; being a man and being free imply moral teleology. This deals with the relation of the causality in man to his own purposes and ultimately to the final end or purpose of the whole world. We must therefore ask, Does moral teleology really require that rational, critical judgment in man should reach beyond the world for an intelligent, supreme principle?

If it consisted solely of lifeless beings or in some part, of living but senseless creatures, the world would be worthless because there would be no being in it with any sense of worth. On the other hand, suppose that there were beings who, though intelligent, were able only to evaluate things in terms of their own well-being and who were unable, as free people could do, to assign independent values. There would, in this case, be relative purposes in the world but no absolute purpose; for such beings would themselves be without purpose. The moral law, however, has this distinctive property, that it prescribes an unconditioned purpose to mind, and unconditioned purpose is formally like final purpose. Thus the existence of mind that can be its own supreme law on the level of purposes, or the existence of rational beings subject to moral laws, is conceivable only as it is the final purpose of the world's existence. Given then that happiness is the subjective condition on which man can set himself a final goal and that harmony with the moral law is the objective condition of happiness, a moral world-cause, an author of the world, must be assumed to conjoin these two conditions. In other words, there has to be a God.

This proof, which could easily be given a logically precise form, does not mean that acceptance of the existence of God is as necessary as recognition of the validity of the moral law. A man who is influenced by the weakness of speculative arguments and the irregularities in nature and the moral world, might well assert that there is no God. If, however, he decides that duty's law is imaginary, invalid, not obligatory, and frankly transgresses it, he would be contemptible in his own eyes.

We cite then a righteous man such, perhaps, as Spinoza, who feels convinced that there is no God, and that since there is no object in morality, there is no future life. How does he feel about his own inner purpose, which is derived from the moral law, the law which he, in practice, respects? He expects no personal advantage from moral obedience in this or any other world. He is intent on establishing only the goodness to which the holy law directs his strength, and to that end he will work disinterestedly. His efforts are, however, circumscribed. Now and then, just by chance, he gets a little help towards his purposes from nature, but there is no steady, regular concurrence such as his own personal policies afford him. There is always deceit, violence, and envy around and about him, even though he is honest, peaceable, and kindly. He sees righteous men who deserve happiness fall victims to the evils of want, sickness, and untimely death, as animals do, because nature does not reckon their merits. He knows that this will continue until all go down to one broad grave together, and the just and the unjust alike are thrown back into the maw of the purposeless chaos of matter from which they were derived, in spite of all belief that they were creation's final ends.

This right-minded person may, therefore, feel impelled to give up the impossible purpose which caused him to obey the moral law. This event would, of course, do damage to his moral sentiments. Perhaps, however, he will continue true to his inner calling and will not relinquish moral obedience just because its high and appropriate end is voided. He must therefore assume the existence of a moral author of the world, that is, of God. From the practical point of view this entails no contradiction. We may also say that mind being what it is, a final purpose related to moral law is unintelligible apart from a Creator and Ruler of the world who is also a moral lawgiver. The actuality of a supreme, moral, lawgiving Creator is therefore sufficiently proved for practical purposes, without a theoretical demonstration of his existence.

10. *God's existence is morally demonstrable*

At this point two observations are required to avoid an easy misunderstanding. In the first place, the characteristics of the Supreme Being are conceivable only by analogy: for how otherwise could his nature be investigated, when experience gives us nothing to go on? In the second place, the characteristics of the Supreme Being enable us to *conceive* him but not to *know* him or to justify these characteristics theoretically. They may involve anthropomorphism. Our point in using them is not, however, to define the Supreme Being's inaccessible nature, but to shape our own willing. We do not even wish to distinguish causality in the Supreme Being from causality otherwise discovered in nature. We merely wish to make clear that such a distinction is necessary to mind and valid for reflective judgments, if not for definitive judgments. The regulative judgment, however, becomes definitive when one is concerned only with practical matters or when prudence or wisdom constrain one to pursue certain ends, ends which are conceivable only in a certain way. Regulative or reflective judgments can never be definitive when the possibility of some thing is being considered. This merely means that there may be possibilities other than those prescribed by mind.

This moral proof is new, not in substance but in form. It germinated with mind in primitive man and developed with mental culture. While men were still indifferent to purpose in nature, they took advantage when they could of what appeared to them as nature's usual course. They began to reflect on right and wrong, and then one judgment was inevitable. The difference between honesty and falsehood, gentleness and violence, in human behavior was important even though it appeared that virtue brought no reward and crime no punishment. It was as if a voice within declared to them that morals have consequences. However crudely they conceived the way to adjust wrongs, there was only one way to reconcile nature with the moral law within: there had to be a supreme cause governing the world by moral laws. Furthermore, in all probability it was moral interest that first called attention to beauty in nature.

What about hope for a future life? In obedience to the moral law we are called to fulfill a final purpose. We have a right to take this calling as a clue to the reasonable judgment of individual human destiny, but we have to treat it as being of practical value only. Theoretical judgments about *man the thinker* are generally negative. None of the operations or phenomena of the inner sense can be explained materialistically. No additional and definitive judgment of the special nature of the soul or the duration or non-duration of the person after death is possible in pure theory. These matters are all left to the practical necessities of teleological judgment. The continuance of the soul after death is required absolutely by final purpose as reasoning prescribes it. Here is psychology that is a kind of spiritual anthropology. It is knowledge of the self as alive; it is theoretical knowledge which remains empirical.

All theoretical bases of proof amount to (1) proof by logically rigorous syllogisms, or to (2) inference by analogy, or to (3) probable opinion, or finally to (4) hypothesis. So I say that in general, proofs that aim at conviction within theory do not result in belief in the existence of an original Being, God, as the moral author of the world. Speculative reasoning fails absolutely to show that an original Being, the Godhead, exists, or to give any assurance that the soul is immortal.

There are objects which appear in practical reasoning on behalf of duty, which must be conceived abstractly and in advance either as causes or effects. They transcend theory and are therefore merely matters of faith. One of these is the Supreme Goodness of the world as realized through freedom. No experience demonstrates the objective reality of freedom or its use as theory. At the same time we are told to use the idea of freedom as best we may in pure practical reasoning designed to realize supreme goodness. For this purpose the possibility of freedom must be assumed. This assumption together with the conditions that make its possibility conceivable, namely, the existence of God and the immortality of the soul, are matters of faith.

Faith is a moral disposition of mind, an assurance of the truth of some matter beyond the reach of reasoning. It is a steady disposition and assumes that whatever is required for the possibility of the supreme final end is true because of man's obligation to pursue it, even though we do not understand its possibility or impossibility.

Faith, in its absolute sense, is confidence that when duty requires the attainment of a purpose, that purpose can be attained, even though no one sees how. Faith is therefore moral when it applies to particular objects, provided they are not objects of possible knowledge or opinion. Faith in objects of opinion, particularly in historical matters, becomes credulity. Faith is free assurance of what we assume in the interests of freedom. This does not mean that faith can be adopted as opinions are, on inadequate grounds. It has to be the fruit of practical reasoning and must satisfy the purposes of reasoning. Otherwise, when moral thought collides with pure theory and provides no decisive proof of the possibility of the moral object, it becomes unstable, wavering between practical commands and theoretical doubts.

An unbeliever denies the validity of ideas when theory does not support them. He, therefore, judges dogmatically; but dogmatic unbelief cannot stand against a mind controlled by a moral policy. Reasoning causes no one to pursue a purpose that is merely lucubration. It is different with doubtful faith, where the lack of conviction on theoretical grounds is a hindrance. Here the remedy is to remove the influence of the faith by criticism and to substitute a paramount practical belief.

11. *God, freedom, and immortality*

God, freedom, and the immortality of the soul are the problems to the solution of which all the labors of metaphysics are directed. It used to be believed that the doctrine of freedom was necessary only as a negative condition of practical philosophy, and that the ideas of God and the soul belonged to theoretical philosophy; they had to be demonstrated separately. Religion was achieved subsequently by adding morality to these ideas.

It soon appears, however, that such an attempt must miscarry. It is absolutely impossible to conceive an original Being whose characteristics make him experienceable, and therefore knowable, if one starts with only simple, abstract, ontological ideas. Neither would an idea based on the experience of physical appropriateness in nature adequately demonstrate morality or acquaintance with God. Just as little would knowledge of the soul, acquired from experience in this life, provide an idea of the soul's spiritual, immortal nature, adequate to morality. Neither theology nor spiritualism can be established by empirical data. They deal with matters that transcend human knowledge. Ideas of God and the immortal soul can be defined only by predicates drawn from supersensible sources, predicates whose reality is demonstrated by experience. This is the only way a supersensible Being can be known.

The freedom of man under moral law conjoined with the final end which freedom prescribes by means of the moral law compose the only predicate of this kind. This combination of ideas contains the conditions necessary to the possibility of both God and man. An inference can then be made to the actuality and the nature of God and the soul, both of which would otherwise be entirely hidden from us.

Theoretical proofs of God and immortality fail because natural ideas tell us nothing about supersensible matters. Proofs via morality and freedom do succeed because there is causality in these ideas and their roots are supersensible. The causal law of freedom here establishes its own actuality by the way men behave. It also provides means of knowing other supersensible objects, such as the final moral end and its practicability. The conception of freedom's causality is, of course, based on practical considerations, but that happens to be all religion needs.

It is remarkable that of the three pure, rational ideas—God, freedom, and immortality—whose objects are supersensible, freedom alone proves its objective reality in the world of nature by what it can effect there. Freedom, therefore, makes possible the connection of the other two ideas with nature and of all three with religion. We may thus conceive the supersensible realm within man and around him, so that it becomes practical knowledge. Speculative philosophy, which offers only a negative idea even of freedom itself, can never accomplish anything like this. The idea of freedom, fundamental to unconditioned practical law, reaches beyond the limits within which natural, theoretical ideas remain hopelessly restricted.

INDEX

Set in Electra
Format by Cy Axelrad
Manufactured by The Haddon Craftsmen, Inc.
Published by Harper & Brothers, New York